An A to Z
Practical Guide
to Emotional
and Behavioural
Difficulties

An A to Z Practical Guide to Emotional and Behavioural Difficulties

HARRY AYERS AND CESIA PRYTYS

David Fulton Publishers

London

David Fulton Publishers Ltd
Ormond House, 26–27 Boswell Street, London WC1N 3JZ

www.fultonpublishers.co.uk

First published in Great Britain in 2002 by David Fulton Publishers.

Note: The rights of Harry Ayers and Cesia Prytys to be identified as the authors of this work
have been asserted by them in accordance with the Copyright, Designs and Patents Act 1988.

British Library Cataloguing in Publication Data
A catalogue record for this book is available from the British Library.

ISBN 1 85346 778 2

Typeset by Book Production Services, London
Printed and bound in Great Britain by The Cromwell Press Ltd, Trowbridge, Wilts.

Contents

Preface

This book is intended to be a useful A to Z guide to emotional and behavioural difficulties and associated terms for a wide range of different readers including teachers, mentors, social workers, educational social workers, counsellors, educational psychologists, students, parents, carers, voluntary workers and the general reader. The guide focuses on adults as well as children and adolescents. The A to Z format is intended to make the guide easily accessible and user friendly.

The guide for reasons of space, practicality and intended readership has to be selective in terms of entries. Many of the entries have been selected on the basis of their common or relatively common occurrence and on their practical usefulness to practitioners. But some rarer terms have also been included. Entries have been kept as succinct as possible but at the same time the aim has been to be informative about approaches and interventions where appropriate rather than simply providing definitions of terms.

The focus has not only been on the definition and explanation of terms but where appropriate on different types of perspectives, approaches, treatments, interventions or strategies. An attempt has been made to recognise that controversies and conflicts exist in connection with certain terms while at the same time presenting different viewpoints regarding those controversies.

Every effort has been made to make the guide as up to date and as accurate as our access to recent literature and information allows. The guide also where appropriate provides addresses and phone numbers of supportive organisations. Selected references and bibliography are located underneath the entries but reasons of space have curtailed the provision of references and a bibliography for every single entry.

A

ABC (Behavioural)

The ABC is a means of recording specific, overt and observable behaviour. It forms the basis of a functional analysis of behaviour. It is behavioural in that it focuses on specific, overt and observable behaviours.

A = antecedents, i.e. events that are observed to precede an overt behaviour.
B = the observed behaviour.
C = the observed consequences or events that follow the observed behaviour.

Antecedents	Behaviour	Consequences
Teacher asks student to work	Child out of seat	Child interferes with others

Herbert, M. (1998) *Clinical Social Psychology*, 2nd edn. Chichester, Wiley.
Sturmey, P. (1966) *Functional Analysis in Clinical Psychology*. Chichester, Wiley.

ABC (Cognitive)

The ABC is a way of analysing emotional and behavioural problems devised by A. Ellis in 1977. It is cognitive in that it acknowledges the influence of cognition on emotion and behaviour.

A = an activating event stands for a person's perceptions and inferences regarding events that influence him or her.
B = rational and irrational beliefs about activating events.
C = emotional and behavioural consequences of subscribing to rational and irrational beliefs.

Activating event	Belief	Consequences
Person fails to get a job	Person believes he is worthless	Depression

This model is not simply linear but interactional in that it recognises activating events, beliefs and consequences as influencing each other.

Ellis, A. (1977) 'The basic clinical theory of rational-emotive therapy', in A. Ellis and R. Grieger (eds), Handbook of Rational-Emotive Therapy. New York, Springer.

Abreaction

Abreaction is a psychoanalytic term. It refers to the release of emotional energy that occurs when a repressed memory enters consciousness. It can occur as a part of psychotherapy or spontaneously. Initially abreaction was thought to be therapeutic in that the repressed experience could be relived and thereby controlled.

Absolute thinking

A term used in Rational Emotive Behavioural Therapy (REBT). It refers to thinking about experiences in terms of absolute demands such as 'shoulds', 'musts', 'have to's' and 'ought to's'. Absolute thinking is seen as an aspect of holding irrational beliefs that lead to irrational conclusions such as 'awfulising', 'I-can't-stand-it-itis' and 'damnation'. Absolute thinking can lead to emotional and behavioural problems.

Ellis, A. (1984) 'Foreword: Cognitive, affective, and behavioural aspects of rational-emotive therapy', in W. Dryden, Rational-Emotive Therapy: Fundamentals and Innovations. London, Croom Helm.

Abstinence rule

The rule of abstinence is a psychoanalytic term. Psychoanalysis is arranged so that it does not provide relief or satisfaction of a client's needs that are symptoms external to the therapeutic situation. The analyst presents as it were a blank screen to the patient so that the analyst does not satisfy the patient's unconscious needs thereby enabling the patient's unconscious conflicts to be fully disclosed for analysis.

Acting out

This psychoanalytic term refers to the re-enactment of past events, particularly aggressive and impulsive acts. By extension it refers to individuals who act on impulses without thinking or reflecting either on their feelings, the consequences of their actions or on their behaviour. The individual is unwilling or unable to inhibit their actions or behaviour. Acting out behaviour prevents or impedes the development of self-control. Cognitive-behavioural interventions are used to increase self-reflection in impulsive individuals.

Activating event

An activating event is a component of Ellis's ABC model that is used for describing the development of emotional and behavioural problems. 'A' stands for an activating event.

Activating events are those events that people believe have occurred, are occurring or might occur. These activating events can trigger irrational beliefs that lead to emotional and behavioural problems. Beliefs and their consequences can in turn influence or even produce activating events.

Actor-observer difference or effect

In attribution theory a bias whereby people attribute their behaviour to situational influences but observers perceiving the same behaviour attribute it to those people's personal dispositions. This bias exists due to the salience of the situation for the actor and the salience of the person for the observer but also due to the different types of information available to the actor and the observer. The bias is said to have only a modest effect.

Adaptation

Behavioural adaptation is a process whereby behaviour conforms to or fits a particular environment or context. This process of behavioural adaptation may occur through choice, coercion or persuasion. Coercion might not be effective and as a consequence lead to resistance or indifference. Resistance might take the form of sabotage, protest or rejection. In school terms resistance might manifest itself as disruptive behaviour, vandalism, arson, graffiti and truancy. An inclusive or incorporative ethos and a balance of rewards as well as sanctions assist in the process of behavioural adaptation to school.

Children with emotional and behavioural difficulties may have negative experiences of schools whether mainstream or special and as a result find it difficult to adapt to school routines. They may experience negative relationships with other pupils as well as school staff. Mainstream teachers may have negative attitudes towards EBD pupils who may be perceived as poorly motivated, difficult to teach and disruptive in the classroom. Other pupils in mainstream schools may reject EBD pupils.

Mainstream schools are sometimes reluctant to admit EBD pupils due to fears of adverse effects on league tables, demands on staff time, negative effects on other pupils and negative staff reaction. Such pupils are often at risk of fixed term and permanent exclusion and even other forms of exclusion e.g. internal exclusion, extended study leave, simply being asked to remain at home and encouraging parents/carers to seek admission to another school.

It may take a while before permanently excluded EBD pupils are admitted into a new school during which time they are at risk of falling behind with school work and of delinquency. Children who have been permanently excluded from one mainstream school are sometimes successfully reintegrated into another mainstream school.

Children in special schools can have a higher rate of exclusion than children do in mainstream and it is relatively rare for them to be reintegrated into mainstream schools. It may be the case that EBD children who are educated alongside other children with EBD have their difficulties reinforced through observational learning of negative role models. Other children who *may* have associated emotional and/or behavioural difficulties and who *may* find it difficult to adapt to school life include children in public care ('looked after'), children with disabilities, traveller children and refugee children. This may not be due to any problems they may have but rather on their reception in the receiving school.

Blyth, E. and Milner, J. (1997) Social Work with Children: The Educational Perspective. Harlow, Addison Wesley Longman.

Juvonen, J. and Wentzel, K.R. (eds) (1996) Social Motivation: Understanding Children's School Adjustment. Cambridge, Cambridge University Press.

Sanders, D. and Hendry, L.B. (1997) New Perspectives on Disaffection. London, Cassell.

Addiction (substance abuse)

This term refers to any physical or psychological dependence on a drug. Drugs are taken to enhance mood, i.e. to achieve a state of elation or euphoria. There are various levels of drug use: experimental use, social use, habitual use and abusive use. Experimentation with drugs is common, however only a minority of adolescents move on to substance abuse. Substance abuse in adolescents is correlated with higher rates of suicide, violence, accidental death, arrest, educational failure, unstable relationships, unprotected sex, teenage pregnancy, physical and mental health problems and reduced career prospects.

Generally speaking stimulant and hallucinogenic drugs are associated with increases in heartbeat and changes in blood pressure, in extreme cases disturbances in heart rhythm and heart function may occur. The use of alcohol, sedatives, solvents and opiates can lead to drowsiness and in extreme cases stupor and coma. Withdrawal from stimulants can lead to sleep disturbance and increased appetite and withdrawal from opiates can lead to nausea, vomiting and diarrhoea. Other complications are associated with substance abuse, namely liver and kidney damage, hepatitis and HIV. Accidental death is also possible through overdose and drug impurities. Negative mood states such as anxiety, depression and anger can often be the consequence of substance abuse. Flashbacks and hallucinations can also be the result of taking hallucinogenic drugs and in extreme cases psychotic states may ensue.

Perspectives on substance abuse

The main perspectives are biological, psychogenic, behavioural, systems theory and sociological.

- The biological perspective sees genetic predisposition and physiology as important factors in influencing the development of substance abuse. It also sees a difficult temperament as an important factor in terms of leading individuals to engage in risk-taking activities that are associated with substance abuse. Certain drugs lead to tolerance, dependence and unpleasant withdrawal symptoms. These withdrawal symptoms lead to further substance abuse.

- The psychodynamic perspective sees substance abuse as a means of coping with stress and negative emotional states particularly in relation to loss, separation and bereavement. Psychoanalytic approaches regard insecure attachment as an important factor in leading vulnerable individuals to use drugs to counteract negative moods. Sexual and physical abuse and other traumatic events are also seen as predisposing individuals to substance abuse. Another theory sees the adolescent search for identity and autonomy as leading sometimes to immersion in a drug taking subculture.

- The behavioural perspective sees substance abuse as being maintained by positive reinforcement through drug induced mood enhancement and by negative reinforcement when drugs alleviate withdrawal symptoms. Specific environmental cues are seen as eliciting withdrawal symptoms.

- The systems perspective sees negative parental influence and negative family relationships as contributing to substance abuse. Parental substance abuse is seen as having a modelling effect on their children. The lack of parenting skills is also seen as influential. Some parents fail to lay down and enforce rules about drug use and do not adequately supervise their children. Substance abuse is also seen as being in part the result of family conflicts.

- The sociological perspective sees social deprivation and social alienation as important factors in contributing to substance abuse. Socially deprived neighbourhoods form a context where substance abuse thrives. Substance abuse is seen as socially approved and provides an escape valve from the multiple stresses of the social and economic environment. Adolescents are also seen as alienated from society, this being reflected in a weak attachment to parents, rejection of authority in terms of school and the police and delinquency.

Risk factors

Predisposing risk factors are both personal and situational. Personal factors include pre-existing emotional and behavioural problems, learning difficulties, school failure, risk taking activities and positive attitudes towards drug taking. Other personal factors are low self-esteem and an external locus of control. Situational factors are conflicts with parents, insecure attachment, inadequate parental supervision, parental substance abuse and family disorganisation.

Precipitating factors include drug availability, the wish to experiment, peer pressure, participation in a deviant subculture and the desire to alleviate negative moods. Negative moods may occur through abuse, bullying, loss, separation and bereavement.

Maintaining factors include physical and psychological dependence. Depression and anxiety can encourage continuing substance abuse. Parental modelling and positive parental attitudes towards drug taking also contribute to continuing abuse.

Protective factors

Protective factors contribute to the prevention and treatment of substance abuse. These factors include high ability, high self-esteem, an internal locus of control, high self-efficacy, a positive attributional style and positive relationships with non-deviant peers. Secure attachments with parents alongside parental supervision are also protective factors. The lack of availability of drugs and the presence of social support networks also protect.

Carr, A. (1999) The Handbook of Child and Adolescent Psychology: A Contextual Approach. London, Routledge.
Davison, G.C. and Neale, J.M. (2001) Abnormal Psychology, 8th edn. New York, Wiley.
Heaven, P.C.L. (1996) Adolescent Health: The Role of Individual Differences. London, Routledge.

Contacts

Adfam Helpline 020 7928 8900 (help for families who have a member misusing drugs).
Families Anonymous Helpline 020 7498 4680.
NATIONAL DRUGS Helpline 0800 7276600.

Adolescence and behaviour

Adolescence is a period when young people are at varying degrees of risk of developing various kinds of emotional and behavioural difficulties, psychiatric disorders and health problems. The degree of risk depends on a range of factors including temperament, genetic predisposition, familial, parental, educational and social. The various types of adolescent problems include schizophrenia, depression, suicide and attempted suicide, conduct disorders, eating disorders (anorexia, bulimia, obesity), antisocial behaviour (delinquency), stress (family and parental conflicts, divorce, separation, bereavement and examinations), substance abuse (alcohol, cigarettes, heroin, cannabis, ecstasy), sexual orientation difficulties (hetero- or homosexuality) and sexually transmitted diseases. With regard to schizophrenia, suicide, conduct disorders, delinquency and substance abuse boys are at a greater risk than girls but girls are at a greater risk than boys for eating disorders, depression and attempted suicide.

Heaven, P.C.L. (1996) Adolescent Health: The Role of Individual Differences. London, Routledge.

Aggression

The term aggression is used to cover a wide range of hostile behaviours that include verbal as well as physical attacks on others. There are various forms of aggression including altruistic, anger, anticipatory, displaced, instrumental, fear-induced and territorial aggression.

Although individual differences appear in aggression, aggression is normative in the sense that many children and adolescent at some point engage in aggressive acts. However there are children and adolescents who are highly and persistently aggressive and this aggressiveness is stable over time. Aggression in terms of a pattern of conflict with other children and with adults begins in Years 2 and 3, boys showing higher levels of aggression than girls. In adolescent age groups aggression becomes more organised, taking the form of gangs or groups. With passing time aggression tends to decline, violence rates peaking in adulthood.

Some children show early-onset aggression whereas others show adolescent-onset aggression. Children who experience problems with poor emotional regulation, have inadequate impulse control and manifest legitimacy beliefs with respect to aggression are at risk of developing aggressive tendencies.

Adolescents who display a persistent and pervasive pattern of aggressive behaviour along with theft, vandalism, lighting fires, truancy, lying and absconding are described as having a conduct disorder. Aggressive adolescents are likely to become involved in fighting, temper loss, damage to property, cruelty to children and animals. Within the family they are more likely to be non-compliant, defiant and engage in aversive and coercive incidents. Adolescents who manifest aggressive behaviour are likely to continue that behaviour into adulthood unless treated. Boys are more likely to experience this problem than girls. Girls are more likely to engage in indirect and relational forms of aggression, e.g. excluding others and malicious comments. Highly aggressive adolescents are likely to be hyperactive, have learning difficulties particularly with reading, are often rejected by peers, have inadequate social skills and possess a hostile attributional bias. Perspective taking tends to inhibit aggressive tendencies. Some aggressive adolescents are proactive, i.e. they use aggression to obtain their goals, and others are reactive, i.e. they are easily provoked, perceiving others as having hostile intentions towards them. The parents are likely, particularly the fathers, to have criminal records and suffer from alcoholism. Discipline and supervision is likely to be inconsistent and erratic and alternately harsh and lax.

Risk factors include a difficult temperament (irritability, emotional susceptibility, rumination and poor self-control), neurological problems, problems in school, learning difficulties, parental alcoholism, a high alcohol intake, poor parenting skills, parental conflict, child abuse, witnessing violence, insecure attachment, low self-esteem, larger family size and school failure. High self-esteem can also be a factor contributing to aggressive behaviour especially where there is a perceived threat to high self-esteem in the form of negative responses or provocation.

Protective factors include an easy temperament, higher ability, an higher level of social and problem solving skills, higher self-esteem, peer acceptance and educational success.

Generally adolescents who have conduct disorders have a poor prognosis due to unresponsiveness to interventions.

Perspectives on conduct disorders are biological, cognitive-behavioural, social learning, psychodynamic and systems theories.

- The biological perspective sees hereditary, hormonal and neuropsychological factors as influencing the onset and development of conduct disorders. However there does not appear to be a relationship between levels of testosterone and aggression.
- The cognitive behavioural perspective sees maladaptive, cognitive processing, namely cognitive deficits and distortions as underlying conduct disorders including a hostile attributional bias and social skills and problem solving deficits.
- The social learning perspective sees modelling and parental coercion as crucial in the development of conduct disorders. Aggression is learned through adolescents modelling themselves on others, particularly parents who themselves use or display aggression. Coercive parenting also leads to aggressive behaviour through harsh, inconsistent and ineffective punishment and the predominance of unrewarding over rewarding family interactions.
- The psychodynamic perspective sees deficits in superego functioning and disrupted and insecure attachments as underlying conduct disorders. Indulgent and punitive parenting can both be responsible for superego deficits. The adolescent internalises low standards from indulgent parents and feels guiltless when being aggressive. With the punitive parent the adolescent internalises both good (caring) and bad (punitive) introjects, the adolescent then behaves non-aggressively towards those perceived as good (when they experience a positive transference) and aggressively towards those perceived as bad (when they experience a negative transference). Adolescents who have experienced insecure attachments in the past fail to develop or experience trusting relationships and as a result engage in aggressive behaviour.
- Systems theories include family systems theory, which sees adolescent aggression as resulting from family disorganisation where rules, routines and boundaries are unclear and inadequate. Family communication is also confusing and lacking in empathy. Problem solving skills are poor and depend primarily on coercion. Multiple systems theory sees many mutually interacting systems as generating aggressive adolescent behaviour. Personal factors (e.g. difficult temperament), family factors (e.g. insecure attachment), school factors (e.g. poor achievement) and social factors (e.g. delinquent subculture) are all seen as contributing to the development of aggressive behaviour.

Strategies for preventing aggressive behaviour include:

- Punishment is effective only if the anticipated punishment is experienced as aversive, if there is a high probability of it being implemented, if it is rationally considered, if there are alternatives to the misbehaviour and if it is immediate. It may serve only to suppress or displace aggression elsewhere.
- Parent management training teaches parents to adopt and practice strategies using operant techniques such as positive reinforcement programmes and moderate sanctions such as time out and response cost.
- Anger management aims to enable individuals to control and reduce the anger arousal that frequently leads to aggressive behaviour. Anger management is based on D. H. Meichenbaum's stress-inoculation training. This approach involves identification of triggers, the rehearsal of self-statements and the acquisition of relaxation skills. This type of anger management is only effective if the individuals concerned acknowledge their failure to control their anger and are committed to change. Anger management training should be combined with training that enables the individuals concerned to understand the causes and the circumstances of other people's negative actions.
- Observational learning is the strategy of exposing aggressive individuals to non-aggressive role models combined with appropriate rehearsal, role-play and feedback.

Browne, K. and Herbert, M. (1997) Preventing Family Violence. Chichester, Wiley.

Carr, A. (1999) The Handbook of Child and Adolescent Clinical Psychology: A Contextual Approach. London, Routledge.

Gilligan, J. (2001) Preventing Violence. London, Thames & Hudson.

Herzberger, S.D. (1996) Violence Within the Family: Social Psychological Perspectives. Madison, Brown & Benchmark.

Kazdin, A.E. (1996) Conduct Disorders in Childhood and Adolescence, 2nd edn. Thousand Oaks, CA: SAGE Publications.

Krahe, B. (2001) The Social Psychology of Aggression. Hove, Psychology Press.

Meichenbaum, D.H. (1975) Stress Inoculation Training. New York, Pergamon Press.

Rutter, M., Giller, H. and Hagell, A. (1998) Anti Social Behavior by Young People. Cambridge, Cambridge University Press.

Varma, V. (ed.) (1997) Violence in Children and Adolescents. London, Jessica Kingsley.

Aggression replacement training

Aggression replacement training (ART) is an approach that aims to reduce aggressive behaviour in children and adolescents. It regards all behaviour as primarily learned behaviour and sees aggressive behaviour as due to deficits in social skills, anger control and moral reasoning.

ART aims to address these deficits through combining skillstreaming with anger control training and moral reasoning training. Skillstreaming is the behavioural element and is based on the social learning perspective that aims to equip young people with prosocial skills through modelling, role-play, performance feedback and transfer training. Anger control training is the emotional element and aims to equip young people with self-control techniques that focus on the triggers (external anger stimuli and cognitive appraisals), cues (sensations indicating anger states), reducers (anger-reducing procedures), reminders (positive self-instructional statements) and self-evaluation of the results. Moral reasoning training is the values element and is based on Kohlberg's moral reasoning approach. This approach aims to improve the moral reasoning of young people by providing them with decision making opportunities in relation to specific moral problems. Through this process young people are able to develop their moral reasoning beyond a basic egocentric and pragmatic level.

Goldstein, A.P., Glick, B. and Gibbs, J.C. (1998, revised edn) *Aggression Replacement Training: A Comprehensive Intervention for Aggressive Youth*. Champaign, IL, Research Press.
Kohlberg, L. (1984) *Essays on Moral Development: The psychology of moral development*. San Francisco, Harper & Row.

Agoraphobia

Agoraphobia is a disorder or condition where individuals fear or avoid being alone in a public area, e.g. a supermarket, cinema or open space. There are also fears of crowded and enclosed spaces, e.g. in tube trains. These individuals will frequently experience physical sensations similar to a panic attack, i.e. tensions, feeling unreal and trembling. These feelings can escalate, leading to a full panic attack. Individuals will often feel embarrassed in public if observed having a panic attack. It is found that women are more frequently diagnosed than men are, different reasons being given for this fact, e.g. women are more likely to report symptoms than men. Other conditions are associated with agoraphobia, e.g. depression. It is now thought that it is not fear of public places as such but rather fear of having a panic attack in those places that leads to people avoiding public spaces. Many agoraphobics experience a fear of death, illness, fainting or collapsing, i.e. fears about safety and security.

- From a psychodynamic perspective agoraphobia is seen as an effect of anxious attachment formed in early childhood (see Bowlby 1989 below). Children grow up anxious and dependent and become vulnerable to agoraphobia and panic attacks.
- From a behavioural perspective agoraphobia results from avoidance leaning when a person avoids a conditioned stimulus (CS) and because avoidance relieves anxiety (negative reinforcement), avoidance is maintained. However, at times agoraphobia appears after bereavement or loss, when there is no specific conditioning experience.
- From a cognitive-behavioural perspective agoraphobia is the result of observational learning and cognitive processes. Individuals who have low self-efficacy expectations through past experiences may feel they will be unable to cope in public situations and avoid those situations.

The use of behaviour therapy, in particular *in vivo* exposure to feared places, leads to a reduction in symptoms in many cases. The main focus now is on the panic attacks themselves.

Bowlby, J. (1989) *Secure Attachment*. New York, Basic Books.
Lindsay, S.J.E. and Powell, G.E. (eds) (1994) *The Handbook of Clinical Adult Psychology*, 2nd edn. London, Routledge.
Rachman, S. (1998) *Anxiety*. Hove, Psychology Press.

Aim-inhibition

Aim-inhibition is a psychoanalytic term that refers to behaviours or relationships where there is no conscious awareness of the underlying drive. It is applied to relationships with friends and relatives.

Akathisia

Akathisia is a potential side effect of some anti-psychotic drugs. It is characterised by hyperactivity, agitation, pacing, avoidance of sitting down and a desire to keep moving.

Alcoholism

Alcohol is the most widely used of all drugs, particularly by men; however the rate is rising among women. Adolescents are drinking at a higher rate. Alcohol is considered to be a cognitive and physiological depressant because it dampens the transmission of neuro-chemical impulses. Its main effects are on mood, on judgement and on behaviour. However, negative behaviours are influenced by expectancies of one's self and others as well as by alcohol levels. Reactions to alcohol intake can be inconsistent within the same individual and between individuals. It has been claimed that some people may drink in order to provide an excuse for violence.

Alcoholism has been defined in terms of dependence and as manifesting itself in the following ways:

- a limited drinking repertoire;
- predominance of drinking over other activities;
- increased tolerance for drink;
- withdrawal symptoms and drinking to avoid withdrawal symptoms;
- drinking for relief from problems;
- feeling compelled to drink;
- drinking after a period of abstinence.

Alcohol may be associated with psychological problems and psychiatric disorders. The association may be one of correlation or one where alcohol aggravates a pre-existing problem or may result from a disorder, e.g. anxiety. Alcoholism can be associated with symptoms of depression and result in suicide. It can also lead to auditory and persecutory hallucinations and pathological jealousy.

Physical consequences include euphoria, lack of coordination and stupor, depending on alcohol levels. Intoxication may result in coma and respiratory difficulties leading to death. Withdrawal symptoms include vomiting, diarrhoea, insomnia, sweating and tremor. Severe symptoms include hallucinations and delirium tremens in which there is confusion, visual and auditory hallucinations, paranoid feelings, fear, high blood pressure and a fast heart beat. Nutritional deficiencies may also occur in the form of protein and vitamin deficiencies. Other physical consequences include cirrhosis, pancreatitis, gastritis and peptic ulcer. Alcohol is also a risk factor for high blood pressure and stroke.

High levels of alcohol intake are also linked to accidents, absenteeism from work, health costs in terms of hospital beds occupied, suicides, deaths and criminal offences, e.g. drink-driving, child abuse, physical and sexual assaults. Alcohol can also lead to unprotected sex and its consequences in the form of sexually transmitted diseases.

Perspectives on alcoholism

Successful treatment is now seen as being dependent on a person's motivation to change and also on their level of self-control or self-efficacy. Lapses can occur due to a high emotional state, to peer pressure and to environmental cues. The likelihood of relapses will depend on the alcoholic's assessment of their lapses. It will also depend on the loss of the positive effects of alcohol, the occurrence of stressors, social situations that encourage alcohol abuse and low self-efficacy.

- The biological perspective suggests that there is a genetic predisposition to alcoholism, particularly among men. Endorphins, brain chemicals similar to morphine and the neurotransmitter, dopamine have been suggested as the means through which drugs stimulate parts of the brain thereby producing pleasure and reducing pain.
- The behavioural perspective suggests that positive and negative reinforcement processes contribute to the onset of alcoholism. Negative reinforcement occurs through tension reduction, e.g. the relief from anxiety. Alcohol-related behaviours can also become secondary reinforcers as a consequence of the primary reinforcing effects of alcohol itself. Stimuli connected to the withdrawal symptoms themselves are also seen as acquiring conditioned aversive qualities.
- The cognitive perspective suggests that beliefs, attitudes and expectancies with regard to alcohol use influence levels of alcohol intake. The alcoholic's own perceptions of drinking are important particularly in connection with treatment or interventions. People come to expect alcohol to increase pleasure and performance, to facilitate social

interaction and to reduce tension. Positive expectancies are emphasised by alcoholics in comparison to negative expectancies that are often underplayed. Cognitive interventions focus on the abstinence violation effect, where an alcoholic believes that a lapse signifies a complete loss of control or a relapse. People are trained in coping skills in order to prevent a lapse or lapses turning into a relapse, this being termed relapse prevention.

- The psychodynamic perspective suggests that alcohol be used to manage stressful emotions such as anxiety and depression and also to restore a sense of psychological equilibrium. This is described as 'self-medication'. There appears to be no 'alcoholic personality' type. The aim of psychodynamic treatment is to bring out the painful emotions that alcohol is being used to suppress and to build up ego strength to cope with those emotions without resorting to alcohol.

- The systems perspective sees alcoholism as associated with family relationship problems or with relationship problems between couples. Domestic violence is frequently associated with alcohol abuse, for example, wife-battering.

Alloy, L.B., Jacobson, N.S. and Acocella, J. (1999) Abnormal Psychology: Current Perspectives, 8th edn. New York, McGraw-Hill College.

Lindsay, S.J.E and Powell, G.E. (eds) (1994) The Handbook of Clinical Adult Psychology, 2nd edn. London, Routledge.

McMurran, M. (1994) The Psychology of Addiction. Hove, Psychology Press.

Contacts

Drink line 0800 9178282 (help for drinking problems).

Ambivalence

Ambivalence is a psychoanalytic term that refers to the experience of having opposite thoughts or feelings towards the same person. These opposing feelings are usually love and hate. It also refers to being pulled towards two different and opposite courses of action and is the basis for motivational interviewing.

Amphetamine psychosis

Amphetamine psychosis is a condition similar to schizophrenia that manifests itself in the form of paranoid delusions, tactile (formication) and auditory hallucinations. It is brought on by the excessive consumption of the drug amphetamine. Sufferers are aware that the drug is responsible for their symptoms. They may become suspicious, aggressive and anti-social. Amphetamine psychosis is usually brought on by chronic use although novice users have been known to develop the condition. A full amphetamine psychosis is virtually the same as paranoid schizophrenia. The condition is treated by the drug haloperidol, a dopamine receptor antagonist.

Kaplan, H.I. and Sadock, B.J. (1996) *Concise Textbook of Clinical Psychiatry*. Baltimore, Williams & Wilkins.

McKim, W.A. (2000) *Drugs and Behavior: An Introduction to Behavioral Pharmacology*. London, Prentice-Hall.

Anaclitic

Anaclitic is a Freudian psychoanalytic term that refers to an intense dependency of one person on another, particularly an infant on the mother. It also refers to object choices where individuals choose love-objects similar to their parents. Anaclitic depression refers to depression experienced by infants after sudden separation from a parent after a normal period of development of at least six months. Symptoms include tearfulness, fearfulness and sleep disorders.

Anal

Anal is a Freudian psychoanalytic term that refers to the infantile (ages 2 to 3) anal stage where the anus and defecation are the main sources of physical pleasure. The anal character is characterised by orderliness, obstinacy and miserliness, known as the anal triad.

Anger management training

Anger is a strong feeling or emotion directed at others or oneself. It arises in people when they feel frustrated, when they feel threatened, interfered with or have their property damaged or stolen. It is displayed through a range of physical and verbal expressions. When anger is persistent, pervasive and intense it turns into hatred.

Anger has both physiological and cognitive components. It is influenced by expectations, reactions to events and interpretations of events. Aggression does not necessarily follow anger, however anger is frequently followed by aggression. Aggression can also occur without anger. Anger can also be seen as performing certain functions, e.g. expressing or communicating the content of one's anger and defending one's ego.

- The behavioural perspective sees anger as being reinforced by the termination of aversive events, the attainment of particular goals or rewards or peer and parental approval. This approach to anger management is based on operant techniques such as extinction, positive reinforcement, time out and response cost. The main problem arising with behavioural interventions is a lack of generalisation of their effects across different contexts.
- The cognitive perspective sees cognitive appraisal or cognitive mediation as central to the development and management of anger. Where people or situations are perceived or appraised as threatening then anger is frequently evoked. This may occur even where there are no objective threats or where situations are ambiguous. Where people

are quick to anger there is often a lack of particular anger controlling skills such as self-reflection, problem solving and perspective taking or an absence of motivation. For interventions to be effective a prior ABC analysis is useful in order to identify triggers but also thoughts and feelings about those triggers and their consequences.

The main cognitive interventions with respect to anger control are self-management, self-instructional and stress-inoculation training.

Blum, P. (2001) *A Teacher's Guide to Anger Management. London, Routledge Falmer Education.*

Faupel, A., Herrick, E. and Sharp, P. (1998) *Anger Management: A Practical Guide. London, David Fulton Publishers.*

Feindler, E.L. and Ecton, R.B. (1986) *Adolescent Anger Control: Cognitive-Behavioral Techniques. New York, Pergamon Press.*

Towl, G.J. and Crighton, D.A. (1996) *The Handbook of Psychology for Forensic Practitioners. London, Routledge.*

Anima and animus

Anima and animus are terms used in Jungian analytical psychology to refer to the feminine aspect of the male unconscious and the masculine aspect of the female unconscious. They are manifested in dreams, in the imagination and can be projected on to experience.

Anorexia nervosa

Anorexia nervosa is an eating disorder characterised by:

- refusal to maintain a minimum body weight for weight and height;
- a great fear of becoming overweight or being fat;
- a distorted experience of body weight and shape;
- a disproportionate emphasis on weight and shape and absence of a menstrual cycle for three months or more.

Most anorexics are female, however a small minority are male; roughly a 9:1 ratio of males to females. It is mainly a disorder of adolescence, peak ages of onset being between 14 and 18. There is evidence to suggest that anorexia is appearing in younger children. The families of anorexics often emphasise the values of achievement, attractive appearance and weight control. Anorexics present themselves as compliant children but often feel worthless, powerless and obliged to be perfectionist.

The onset of anorexia is frequently marked by dieting and can continue through fasting and finally end in starvation. Anorexics will attempt to deceive others about their condition and deny they have any problems. In the final stages anorexics will present symptoms of emaciation, physical weakness, growth of body hair, stopping of periods, heartbeat irregularities and electrolyte imbalances in potassium and chloride levels.

Suggested causes of the disorder are genetic vulnerability, biological (e.g. hormonal and neurotransmitter levels), social, cultural and psychological factors. Various links between other disorders have been suggested, e.g. anxiety disorders in particular social phobia and obsessive-compulsive disorder.

A number of factors are thought to contribute towards the development of female anorexia, e.g. personal, biological, cognitive, social, cultural and familial.

- Personal factors include an emphasis on competition, achievement, autonomy and control that may end up being in conflict with certain ideas of female identity, namely subordination to others. Female anorexics may feel inadequate compared to men. They may also feel that thinness enables then to achieve a male body shape and associated male power and influence. Positive reinforcement may occur through the sense of control achieved when dieting leads to an anorexic state. The experiences of loss, separation, illness and bereavement are also personal factors that can contribute to anorexia. Cognitive distortions may also influence the development of anorexia, e.g. illogical thinking or irrational beliefs of the form that unless one is thin one will not be attractive or popular.
- There is probably a genetic predisposition but environmental factors are dominant. Social and cultural factors include the emphasis on the desirability of a slender female body image or shape in certain societies and the influence of fashion and dieting. Until quite recently anorexia was perceived as a western disease. Currently, there appears to have been an increase in the incidence of anorexia in many non-western countries, including Hong Kong, Argentina, Chile, India and Africa. Certain occupations can present greater risk of individuals developing anorexia. These include ballet, modelling, and athletics such as gymnastics and figure skating.
- Family factors include intense parental pressure on daughters to be successful. Some psychodynamic theories of anorexia emphasise the significance of the mother's parenting style towards her daughter, a style that is described as demanding compliance and control. These demands conflict with the daughter's need for independence and autonomy and leads to the daughter attempting to wrest control through refusing to eat. Anorexia is seen as an attempt to control this conflict. Other psychodynamic theories emphasise regression as a means by which the anorexic avoids the demands of puberty and adult sexuality. Sexual abuse can also play a part in the development of anorexia, for instance in inducing the sufferer to acquire a body shape that avoids or prevents further abuse. However it is not thought to be a major factor in the development of anorexia.
- With regard to male anorexia, factors include participation in particular sports, namely athletics, horse racing and wrestling, obesity during childhood and adolescence and conflicts over masculinity and sexual orientation.

The treatment of anorexia has been mainly through psychodynamic therapy, cognitive-behavioural, biological and family interventions.

- Classical psychodynamic therapy involves interpreting defences and understanding the transference.
- Behavioural techniques used include the use of operant techniques such as positive reinforcement of appropriate eating behaviour.
- Cognitive-behavioural techniques used with anorexics include cognitive restructuring that involves addressing irrational ideas or faulty thinking about body image (weight and shape).
- Biological treatment has focused on the use of antidepressants and anxiolytics to reduce the depression and anxiety that may be associated with anorexia. Hospital in-patient treatment is indicated where there are physical symptoms such as slow heart beat, low temperature, low blood pressure and changes in electrolyte balances.
- Family systems approaches focus on the interactions and relationships between family members that influence the development of anorexia.

Blau, G.M. and Gullotta, T.P. (eds) (1996) Adolescent Dysfunctional Behavior: Causes, Interventions and Prevention. Thousand Oaks, CA: SAGE Publications.
Gilbert, S. (2000) Counselling for Eating Disorders. London, SAGE Publications.
Gordon, R.A. (2000) Eating Disorders: Anatomy of a Social Epidemic, 2nd edn. Oxford, Blackwell.
Thompson, S.B.N. (1993) Eating Disorders: A guide for health professionals. London, Chapman & Hall.
Williamson, D.A. (1990) Assessment of Eating Disorders: Obesity, Anorexia and Bulimia Nervosa. New York, Pergamon Press.

Contact

Eating Disorders Association, 44 Magdalen Street, Norwich NR3 1JE. Tel. 01603 621414 (9.30 a.m. to 6.30 p.m., Monday–Friday).

Antisocial behaviour

Antisocial behaviour in adolescents is associated with hyperactivity, poor verbal and planning skills, temperamental characteristics such as impulsivity, sensation seeking and risk-taking behaviours, poor self-control and a hostile attribution bias. Psychosocial factors include family conflict, coercive or punitive parenting, inadequate parental supervision, and participation in an antisocial peer group and unemployment. Persistent antisocial behaviour begins in early childhood and in view of this early multimodal intervention is indicated. The aim should be to increase positive behaviour as well as decrease disruptive behaviour. In the predelinquency stage interventions have been based on pre-school education programmes such as the US Head Start programmes, parent skills training, parent and teacher behavioural management training, life-skills training and anti-bullying programmes. In the post-delinquency stage interventions have been based on increasing after-school programmes and leisure opportunities, diversionary measures such as cautioning, curfews, electronic monitoring, befriending, compensation, reparation schemes and finally incarceration. With regard to psychological interventions these have been based on cognitive-behavioural approaches, parent management training and problem solving skills training. The effectiveness of interventions depend on a number of factors including whether an intervention is active-directive in its approach, whether community based, whether multimodal or whether social skills and cognitive-behaviourally based.

McGuire, J. (ed.) (1995) What Works: Reducing Reoffending. Chichester, Wiley.
Muncie, J. (1999) Youth and Crime: A Critical Introduction. London, SAGE Publications.
Rutter, M., Giller, H. and Hagell, A. (1998) Antisocial Behavior by Young People. Cambridge, Cambridge University Press.

Antisocial personality disorder

Antisocial personality disorder is characterised by illegal or deviant activity commencing prior to age 15 and continuing into the adult years. The types of activity include truancy, delinquency, vandalism, substance abuse, running away from home and disruptive behaviour in school. Other characteristics include irresponsibility in their personal (walking out on their children or partners) and occupational lives (walking out of jobs), mendacity, irritability, aggressiveness, recklessness and impulsivity. Severe antisocial behaviour in childhood often predicts adult antisocial personality disorder. Rates are higher among younger working class men than among women. It is associated with substance abuse.

Perspectives on antisocial personalities include the biological, behavioural and the cognitive.

- The biological perspective focuses on impaired prefrontal lobe functioning leading to an incapacity to respond to fear-inducing stimuli or alternatively to stimulus seeking behaviour as a reaction to underarousal.
- The behavioural perspective focuses on harsh and inconsistent parental discipline, domestic violence and media influences that model and reinforce aggression.
- The cognitive perspective focuses on information processing such as an hostile attribution bias where ambiguous cues are interpreted as signs of hostile intent.

It is very difficult to treat antisocial personality disorder although group psychotherapy has been used in penal institutions. The effects of the disorder appear to decrease after the age of forty.

Carr, A. (2001) Abnormal Psychology. Hove, East Sussex. Psychology Press.
Rutter, M., Giller, H. and Hagell, A. (1998) Antisocial Behavior by Young People. Cambridge, Cambridge University Press.

Anxiety

Anxiety is a prevalent and pervasive emotion and anxiety disorders are relatively common. It is of particular interest to those coming from a cognitive perspective.

Anxiety is often defined as a negative emotion, a fear of unpleasant consequences or events. Fear can be rational or irrational and is directly related to and focused on specific things or happenings. It tends to be of temporary duration and has distinct antecedents. Anxiety tends to be pervasive, persistent, diffuse and unpleasant and does not have a distinct onset or end. It tends to linger in the background and there is a feeling of being on edge or being threatened. There are different types of anxiety including generalised anxiety, separation anxiety, social, free floating and unconscious anxiety.

Fear is seen as having three components, cognitive, physiological and behavioural. The three components are interconnected but are, to a certain extent, independent. Therefore the assessment of fear depends on looking at all the components. The more common fears tend to be of snakes, heights, of public places, public transport, injury, illness and separation.

Anxiety disorders include panic attacks, agoraphobia, social phobia, specific phobia, generalised anxiety, obsessive-compulsive disorder and post-traumatic stress disorder. Animal phobias and separation anxiety are more common in childhood whereas social phobia, generalised anxiety disorder and agoraphobia tend to originate during adolescence. There is also state and trait anxiety. State anxiety refers to a transient and limited anxiety state whereas trait anxiety refers to a persistent tendency to react with anxiety to threatening situations. People who experience a high degree of anxiety are characterised as being hypervigilant or as being extremely aware of threatening situations and as vulnerable, i.e. as being in a constant anticipatory state with respect to anxiety provoking events. They are also said to be characterised by a high level of self-monitoring, i.e. they experience a preoccupation with internal sensations. Although anxiety is generally seen as having negative effects on behaviour, in certain circumstances moderate anxiety can serve to increase performance on tasks. People who engage in successful emotional processing are able to cope with anxiety without experiencing undue stress. This is facilitated through gradual exposure to threatening situations, relaxation exercises and cognitive restructuring of misinterpreted threats. It is now thought likely that some emotional processing can be at the non-conscious level.

Perspectives on anxiety

- Biological: This approach sees particular disorders, e.g. panic attacks and obsessive-compulsive disorders as being the result of biological processes. The genetic theory sees an anxiety disorder as being the result of an inherited predisposition that is triggered by environmental cues. In order to explain why some stimuli rather than others evoke anxiety a specific evolutionary based preparedness is posited, e.g. as in the case of fear of snakes. There are a variety of biological hypotheses to account for the different anxiety disorders. In the case of phobias and generalised anxiety a dysfunction with respect to gamma aminobutyric acid (GABA) is thought to be operative. Treatment by benzodiazepines, e.g. Valium or Librium, reduces anxiety by binding to GABA neuroreceptors. However anxiety reduction ceases when the drug is no longer taken and in the long term dependence can arise. Panic attacks are thought to be due to dysregulation of the adrenergic and noradrenergic systems. Treatment is by prescribing tricyclic antidepressants, e.g. imipramine. In the case of obsessional compulsive disorder (OCD) a dysregulation in the basal ganglia or a dysregulation of the serotonergic system are thought to be a cause of the disorder. A specific serotonin reuptake inhibitor (SSRI), e.g. clomipramine, is prescribed to address the dysregulation of the serotonergic system.

- Behavioural: Direct conditioning of fear responses occurs when a person experiences a traumatic event and becomes fearful. Future occurrences of the event lead to further fearful responses. This approach sees fear and anxiety as being the result of learning or conditioning. Fears lead to escape or avoidance behaviours. Escape or avoidance is reinforcing because it leads to a reduction in anxiety and fear. However it is not always the case that fears are the product of conditioning, particularly common fears. Treatment requires rapid or gradual exposure to the phobic object *in vivo* or in the imagination.

- Cognitive: This approach recognises the influence of conditioning experiences but focuses on the contribution of maladaptive thinking and reasoning processes to anxiety and fear. Cognitive schemas and cognitive distortions that are threat-orientated are activated, resulting in fears and anxiety. For instance panic attacks are seen as catastrophic misinterpretations of particular bodily sensations. Cognition and behaviour are seen as having reciprocal influences on each other. Treatment is through challenging people's irrational beliefs and cognitive distortions with respect to threat and danger. Challenges to irrational beliefs and faulty thinking are made on empirical, logical and pragmatic grounds. OCD is treated through exposure to cues that elicit the sufferer's obsessional thoughts and compulsive behaviour and response prevention where the sufferer is stopped from performing their anxiety-reducing rituals.

- Social learning: This approach sees fears as being acquired through observational learning or modelling. People exposed to the fearful responses of others may in turn imitate those responses. Treatment is through sufferers observing others being exposed to or even handling phobic objects without those people experiencing fear or anxiety.

- Psychodynamic: This approach regards anxiety as being the product of unconscious and morally unacceptable aggressive or sexual impulses that have been repressed. Unacceptable aggressive and sexual impulses find expression in the form of anxiety disorders. Fears and anxieties are displaced from the original forbidden object on to a more socially acceptable object. The aim of treatment is to interpret the patient's defence mechanisms in order to enable the patient to develop insight into the nature of the repressed aggressive and sexual impulses.

- Systems theory: Within the family parents or carers may suffer from fears or anxiety who then model, elicit and reinforce fear or anxiety for other members of the family. Family crises, transitional difficulties and parental reaction to those crises and difficulties may activate and reinforce fears and anxieties. Parental reaction may manifest itself in the form of the encouragement of avoidance strategies rather than the provision of coping skills.

Carr, A. (2001) Abnormal Psychology. Hove, Psychology Press.
Craig, K.D. and Dobson, K.S. (eds) (1995) Anxiety and Depression in Adults and Children. Thousand Oaks, CA, SAGE Publications.
Rachman, S. (1998) Anxiety. Hove, Psychology Press.

Contacts

National Phobics Society 0870 7700 456.
No Panic Helpline 01952 590545.

Archetype

Archetype is a Jungian term that refers to the basic and universal elements of the collective unconscious. Although universal to everybody they are expressed in people in a way that is particular to the individual. They are predispositions to react and behave in certain ways. These elements therefore have the ability to initiate and control experiences and behaviour. They elicit particular thoughts, images, myths and feelings. The personal unconscious is composed of complexes that reflect the archetypes existing in the collective unconscious. Archetypes strive to actualise themselves within the personality structure of the individual. They include the persona (a mask or front, our expected role), the shadow (the unpleasant, unacceptable dark side of our personality, our weaknesses and failings-demons, devils), anima (a man's feminine aspect) and animus (a woman's masculine aspect). A variety of specific archetypes have appeared in history including the child-god (elves, dwarfs), old wise man (king, hero) and the great mother (Virgin Mary, the Church, and fertility goddess).

Fordham, F. (1959) An Introduction to Jung's Psychology. Harmondsworth, Penguin Books.
Monte, C.F. (1999) Beneath the Mask: An Introduction to Theories of Personality, 6th edn. Orlando, FL, Harcourt Brace College Publishers.
Stevens, A. (2001) Jung: A Very Short Introduction. Oxford, Oxford University Press.

Arson or fire raising

Arson is a legal term that refers to the offence of deliberately setting property on fire.

Arson with respect to adolescents is likely to occur because of attention-seeking or status-seeking behaviour on the part of an individual. In other cases there are a variety of motives including revenge, anger, a cry for help, a desire to have a sense of power and to relieve tension or depression. The cost of arson is seen in terms of the rising number of burnt out cars and in the increasing damage to schools. Arson affecting schools is mainly due to adolescent boys in the inner cities whose actions are linked to other antisocial activities. Arson involving schools mainly occurs at night when the buildings are empty. In these cases revenge may be a motive. Arsonists in the main are young adult males who are not able to maintain relationships and who often have histories of a difficult childhood or of psychological problems.

Prins, H. (1995) Offenders, Deviants or Patients?, 2nd edn. London, Routledge.

Asperger's or Asperger syndrome

Asperger's syndrome was not a familiar diagnosis until 1981 and only in 1994 was it added to the DSM and ICD diagnostic manuals. There are similarities with autism, e.g. a predominance of males, social isolation, impaired verbal and non-verbal communication skills, lack of empathy and creative play, repetitive and stereotyped behaviours, unusual reactions to stimuli, clumsiness, disruptive behaviours and special skills. The main difference with autism is that Asperger cases have normal or above average intelligence and no significant cognitive delays.

There is currently general agreement that Asperger's syndrome falls on the autistic continuum and growing awareness of the range of manifestations of the socialisation, communication and imagination impairments in autism led Lorna Wing (1981) to introduce the term Asperger's syndrome for the higher functioning child and adult with autism. Both versions of the two major diagnostic manuals, ICD-10 (WHO 1994) and DSM-IV (APA 1994) now include Asperger's syndrome as a diagnostic category. In both cases, Asperger's syndrome is diagnosed on the basis of social impairments and restricted patterns of behaviour, as for autism, but is differentiated from autism by a lack of cognitive delay.

Prevalence

On the basis of a diagnostic census, prevalence rates have been recorded of around 4 per 1,000 in a total population study of 1,519 children aged 7–16 years in the mainstream schools of one borough in Sweden. Boys and men are affected three to four times more often than girls and women although among those with severe or profound disabilities this ratio is not so pronounced. Currently, there is an impression that the incidence of autism is increasing. This may be due to wider diagnostic criteria, greater awareness or an actual change in incidence but, as yet, studies providing answers are not available.

Cause

There is a significant genetic contribution to the disorder. Similar characteristics are found in parents and close relatives.

Interventions and practical strategies

These can be divided into the home context, whole-school, and classroom context.
From the perspective of home/school partnership the following are very important:

- obtaining information from parents of a child with Asperger's syndrome to ensure a high level of joint understanding of the child's strengths and difficulties at home and at school;
- agreement on the priorities, strategies and methods of intervention;
- regular reviews to monitor interventions.

From the perspective of the whole-school context the following interventions and strategies are considered good practice:

- both non-teaching as well as teaching staff to acquire knowledge and understanding of the needs of children with Asperger's syndrome;
- school routines such as assemblies, breaktimes should be visually explicit;
- the child with Asperger's syndrome should be provided with a 'place of safety';
- changes in routine, both expected and unexpected, should be explained with the support of a visual communication system;
- consideration should be given to providing the child with Asperger's syndrome peer support, e.g. 'Circle of Friends';
- opportunities for structured activities during lunchtime and breaktimes.

From the perspective of the classroom context the following strategies and interventions are considered good practice:

- access to a distraction-free work space with minimal sensory distractions and clearly labelled resources;
- a written or visual timetable with learning tasks broken down in the form of diagrams and key words;
- support during lesson changes.

Cumine, V., Leach, J. and Stevenson, G. (1998) *Asperger Syndrome: A Practical Guide for Teachers.* London, David Fulton Publishers.
Frith, U. (ed.) (1991) *Autism and Asperger Syndrome.* Cambridge, Cambridge University Press.

Howlin, P. (1998) Children with Autism and Asperger Syndrome. Chichester, Wiley.

Jordan, R. et al. (1998) Educational Interventions for Children with Autism: A Literature Review of Recent and Current Research. Nottingham, DfEE Publications.

Rutter, M., Taylor, E. and Hersov, L. (eds) (1994) Child and Adolescent Psychiatry: Modern Approaches, 3rd edn. Oxford, Blackwell Scientific Publication.

Wing, L. (1981) 'Asperger's syndrome: a clinical account', Psychological Medicine, 11, 115–29.

Assertive discipline

Assertive discipline is an approach to whole-school behaviour and classroom management devised by L. Canter. It is based on the idea that teachers and pupils have rights and responsibilities. Given that pupils respond to limits and boundaries teachers should ensure that these limits are established. In order to establish these limits teachers need support from school management and parents. Teachers need to instruct pupils in positive behaviour and to discuss with disruptive pupils the problems they present in school.

A positive classroom ethos is established through meeting pupils' needs, planning and implementing classroom rules, teaching pupils how to behave correctly, providing positive attention and engaging in positive dialogue and positive interactions with pupils. Teachers are described as assertive if they effectively communicate the behaviour required of their pupils and the actions through which they intend this behaviour. Positive actions must follow words otherwise responses are non-assertive and ineffective. Teachers should respond positively to pupils displaying appropriate behaviour, recognising pupils' efforts to meet teachers' goals and expectations. Pupils failing to meet teachers' expectations must learn that negative consequences will ensue but these should not be physically or psychologically damaging.

The assertive disciple approach comprises the following elements:

- Classroom discipline plans: Plans should be based on a limited number of observable rules that are appropriate for all contexts and activities. The rules need to be clear, unambiguous, realistic, and enforceable. Rules and consequences should be explained, discussed and understood by pupils. Positive recognition and rewards should be given to pupils, classes and groups who meet teachers' expectations. Teachers should plan consequences for pupils who do not observe classroom rules. These consequences should be presented as choices for pupils to make if they infringe rules. Consequences should be proportionate, experienced as unwelcome but not physically or psychologically damaging. Consequences should be hierarchically organised in accordance with the severity of the offence.
- Teaching responsible behaviour through positive recognition: There should be consistent praise that is personal, specific and descriptive. Teachers should scan the class seeking out opportunities to praise pupils. They should also circulate around the classroom complimenting pupils for on task behaviour, and work of good quality and quantity. Pupils who are off task should receive non-verbal communication to prompt on

task behaviour. Consequences should be delivered in a calm, firm manner. Pupils should be reminded of past, present and future consequences. Conflicts should be defused through offering pupils opportunities to communicate their accounts of incidents in writing or in private. Difficult pupils should attend teacher-pupil problem-solving conferences and be shown an interest in through teachers asking about the pupil's leisure time activities and by contacting the pupil's home with positive messages. Individualised plans can be developed analogous to classroom behaviour plans.

Canter, L. and Canter, M. (1992) Assertive Discipline: Positive Behavior Management for Today's Classroom, 2nd edn. Santa Monica, CA, Canter Associates.

Assertiveness and assertiveness training

Assertiveness is a learned or acquired skill that relates or is appropriate to specific contexts or situations. Assertive behaviour is behaviour that respects other people's rights while at the same time standing up for one's own rights in a non-aggressive manner. The expression of rights is central to assertion along with admission that this expression of rights will impact on the other person and that this impact is understood.

Effective assertion depends on behavioural factors such as voice volume, intonation, fluency, response timing, latency and duration, eye contact, facial expression, gestures and body language. It also depends on cognitive factors such as positive self-statements, self-monitoring, perceived self-efficacy, rational ideas, empathy, perspective-taking and problem solving. Effective assertion also depends on the personal, occupational and cultural context with respect to social reactions to assertive behaviour.

Assertiveness training is based on a cognitive-behavioural approach. A functional analysis is undertaken before training occurs. The main elements are behaviour rehearsal, modelling or observational learning, coaching, shaping, cognitive restructuring, self-instruction, self-monitoring, problem solving, feedback and practice. Assertiveness training is best conducted with a homogeneous and motivated group.

Rakos, R.F. (1991) Assertive Behavior: Theory, Research and Training. London, Routledge.

Assessment

There are various forms of assessment as well as a range of perspectives relating to assessment. There are child, adolescent, adult, group and family forms of assessment.

Assessment of behaviour depends on the chosen perspective or theoretical basis, e.g. the behavioural approach uses structured observational schedules or instruments whereas the psychodynamic approach uses projective tests.

Assessment refers to signs and symptoms that appear connected to particular problems or difficulties. Causes are usually inferred from signs and symptoms rather than being directly observable. Accurate and reliable assessment is important for the treatment of behavioural and emotional problems. Often standardised assessment instruments are used in assessment such as self-report inventories, parent rating scales, teacher rating scales and structured diagnostic interviews. These may vary in their validity and reliability. Common forms of assessment include behavioural, cognitive, psychiatric and holistic. Behavioural assessment is based on the formal observation of a sample of overt, specific behaviours using assessment instruments including behavioural checklists, rating scales and observation schedules. It also uses behavioural type interviews that attempt to identify the antecedents and consequences of problem behaviours.

Cognitive assessment uses cognitive-type interviews that attempt to identify the cognitive processes that are associated with problem behaviours and also questionnaires that collect information on cognitions including attitudes, beliefs, expectations and attributions. Psychodynamic assessment is based on interpretations of the following unconscious processes namely defence mechanisms, resistances, dreams, transference and counter-transference. It also uses projective techniques such as the Rorshach Test and the Thematic Apperception Test that are believed to reveal unconscious conflicts. Psychiatric assessment or diagnosis is based on the use of diagnostic manuals, mainly DSM IV (1994) and ICD-10 (1992), to classify mental disorders according to specific criteria. These manuals are regularly updated and include new categories as well as modifications to existing categories.

Holistic forms of assessment focus on seeing people as a whole or in their entirety, i.e. in terms of their strengths as well as their weaknesses and in terms of their family and social networks. Changes seen in one aspect of the person are seen as having repercussions for other aspects. Focus is therefore on interactions between different systems.

Psychological assessment and the psychiatric diagnosis of emotional and behavioural problems is not an exact or accurate science in the sense of the physical sciences. Assessments can also have unintended consequences such as labelling and stigmatisation. Various factors can negatively affect assessments including the resistance and reluctance of clients to communicate, the personal characteristics of the assessor, reactivity to being under observation, variability of behaviour across settings and the lack of validity and reliability of some types of assessment instruments.

Ayers, H., Clarke, D. and Ross, A. (1996) Assessing Individual Needs, 2nd edn. London, David Fulton Publishers.

Barnett, D.W. (1990) The Personal and Social Assessment of Children. Needham Heights, MA, Allyn and Bacon.

Goodman, R. and Scott, S. (1997) Child Psychiatry. Oxford, Blackwell Science.

Kamphaus, R.W. and Frick, P.J. (1996) Clinical Assessment of Child and Adolescent Personality and Behavior. Needham Heights, MA, Allyn and Bacon.

Kline, P. (1998) The New Psychometrics: Science, Psychology and Measurement. London, Routledge.

Palmer, S. and McMahon, G. (eds) (1997) Client Assessment. London, SAGE Publications.

Wilkinson, I. (1998) Child and Family Assessment, 2nd edn. London, Routledge.

Attachment and attachment theory

Attachment theory was originally associated with J. Bowlby. His approach is both psycho-dynamic and ethological. Attachment refers to the quality of an individual's attachment to others and is believed to have a genetic and an evolutionary basis. Attachment is regarded as having social, emotional, behavioural and cognitive aspects. Children develop working models of attachment, conceptions of themselves and others that can influence their interpersonal relationships in later life. These working models are formed through inter-actions with primary care-givers. There are secure and insecure attachments. Secure attachment is where an infant feels safe and secure with the main carer usually the mother whereas insecure attachment refers to a feeling of dependency on the carer but at the same time feeling insecure with that carer. The insecure infant fears rejection. Attachment behaviour is where an infant manages to stay near to a preferred carer, keeping the carer visually or physically close. This behaviour is elicited particularly when there is separation or a threat of separation.

Attachment is based on seeking out a preferred carer, particularly the mother. The preferred carer serves as a secure base from which to explore the surrounding environ-ment. If a secure base is absent then the child resorts to defensive and negative responses. Insecure attachment can assume two forms, anxious-avoidance and anxious-ambivalent. Anxious-avoidance occurs when carers avoid comforting the child. This results in the child avoiding other people. Anxious-ambivalent relationships develop when carers are inconsistent in providing comfort to the child. Such children cling to others but are also prone to anger. Dependent attachment is characterised by dependency and the lack of a sense of personal identity. Disorganised attachment combines resistance and avoidant behaviours characterised by the child being uncertain about whether to approach or avoid the carer. The different patterns of attachment appear to exist in diverse cultural contexts.

The quality of attachment is seen as influential in the development of adult relation-ships with other people. Children displaying insecure attachments are more likely to become clinical referrals than children with other types of attachment. However, insecure attachments can become secure in later life due to the development of close emotional relationships with carers, friends and partners. On the other hand secure attachments can become insecure due to parental divorce, parental separation and loss of a sibling. There-fore attachment patterns, although frequently stable over time, are also changeable.

Holmes, J. (1993) *John Bowlby and Attachment Theory*. London, Routledge.

Shaffer, D.R. (1996) *Developmental Psychology: Childhood and Adolescence*, 4th edn. Pacific Grove, CA, Brooks/Cole Publishing.

Slater, A. and Muir, D. (eds) (1999) *The Blackwell Reader in Developmental Psychology*. Oxford, Blackwell Publishers.

Attention deficit hyperactivity disorder (ADHD)

ADHD is defined using DSM IV or ICD-10 criteria. The presenting symptoms are inattention, poor concentration, impulsive behaviour and restlessness. Diagnosis refers to three types: inattentive, hyperactive-impulsive and combined. Inattention in the school context includes failure to follow instructions, lack of organisation, reluctance to work, loss of equipment, forgetfulness and distractibility. Impulsivity includes difficulty in waiting one's turn, interrupting and intruding on peer activities. Hyperactivity includes fidgeting, leaving one's seat or place, running about, being excessively noisy and talkative. Symptoms must be extreme relative to age, persist for six months, be present in two settings (home and school) and have their onset before the age of seven. A diagnosis of ADHD is made only after ruling out medical, emotional or environmental causes that produce similar symptoms to ADHD. Symptoms of ADHD occur early in life but can continue into adulthood.

The estimates of the prevalence of ADHD depend on the strictness of the diagnostic criteria, in particular the location of cut-off points. Under- or over-diagnosis is possible. Estimates range from 1 to 20 per cent, but are usually from between 1 to 7 per cent. There is a preponderance of boys over girls, a ratio of 8:1 or 10:1. ADHD is frequently associated with other conditions such as conduct disorders, anxiety disorders and oppositional defiant disorders. Therefore, aggressiveness and antisocial behaviours are often found combined with ADHD. Children with ADHD are at risk in terms of underachievement, peer rejection, delinquency, substance abuse and truancy. Peer rejection is brought about by interruptions, aggression and temper loss. Parents with children with ADHD are likely to experience high levels of stress, feelings of parental incompetence and negative parent-child interactions.

Perspectives

There are a number of perspectives on the causes of ADHD. There are also specific risk factors.

- Biological: Genetic factors may contribute to ADHD but environmental factors are still significant. Temperamental factors with regard to activity and arousal levels may also contribute to the development of ADHD. Neuropsychological deficits have been suggested in terms of inadequate response inhibition. Neurotransmitter malfunctions have also been suggested. Diet, e.g. the presence of allergies and food additives, have been suggested but the evidence is controversial. Generally speaking biological factors are seen as predisposing children towards ADHD.
- Behavioural: The effects of operant conditioning are seen as shaping the behaviour of children with ADHD. Specific environmental contingencies are thought to trigger and maintain the symptoms of ADHD.

- Cognitive: ADHD is seen as being characterised by poor self-regulation. This refers to a child's inability to control or regulate arousal and behaviour in relation to changes in settings or contexts.
- Interpersonal: Children with ADHD have substantial difficulties in relating to their peers, teachers and parents. In particular they experience peer rejection through attempts at dominance and control over their peers.

Assessment

There is no single assessment procedure that conclusively establishes a diagnosis of ADHD. Information should be collected from a range of different sources and a case history carefully undertaken to rule out other conditions. ADHD may not manifest itself during a clinical interview. Behaviour should be sampled across both time and settings, e.g. home and school. Ratings from several teachers and other observers should be collected.

Assessment instruments used include rating scales, structured diagnostic interviews, systematic behavioural observation, intelligence tests and sociometric assessment. Areas of strengths as well as weaknesses should also be assessed. Multidimensional assessment is therefore required.

Interventions: Multimodal interventions are suggested with regard to treating ADHD. However, biological treatment is the predominant intervention but it is combined with other types of intervention.

Biological: The main treatment of ADHD is through the prescription of psychostimulant medication, particularly methylphenidate (MPH), known as Ritalin. With medication most pupils (60 to 90 per cent) manage to sustain greater levels of attention, are less impulsive, less aggressive and comply more readily with instructions. However some children do not respond to medication and even those that do may relapse at times. The positive effects of medication will wear off if medication is stopped. While short-term gains are achieved, fundamental long-term improvement is not achieved through medication. Stimulants may also have various side effects such as suppression of appetite, sleep disturbance, headaches, stomach aches, motor and vocal tics. However, medication is generally safe and effective, at least in the short term.

Behavioural: Operant techniques have been applied to children with ADHD. The aim is to change or alter the contingencies that are observed to trigger and maintain specific behaviours such as aggressiveness and impulsivity. Parents and teachers are encouraged to change the antecedents and consequences of inappropriate behaviour. They should positively reinforce on task and compliant behaviours through the use of immediate, non-material and material reinforcers. In addition, teachers and parents should use mild punishments such as response cost and time-out techniques at appropriate times. Home-school report cards and home-school linked reward/punishment systems are also advised.

Children are more likely to respond to direct, unambiguous instructions in a context where distractions are absent. Reprimands should be delivered privately. One-to-one supervision is advised. Parent training in behavioural methods is also recommended.

Cognitive-behavioural: Anger management training and problem solving training are seen as useful interventions with children with ADHD. They should be combined with reinforcement programmes to increase their efficacy. Self-monitoring, self-evaluating and self-reinforcing programmes are also useful. Self-instructional training is not effective unless it is combined with other interventions.

Summary

There is controversy over the nature and treatment of ADHD. The controversy is over whether ADHD is a biologically based disorder and whether the treatment of ADHD by methylphenidate (Ritalin) is ethically justifiable. However ADHD is probably best thought of as a disorder that indicates a poor 'fit' between a genetic predisposition and environmental demands and constraints.

Although thought to be a biologically based disorder, ADHD can also be treated adjunctively through the application of behavioural methods. Therefore multimodal approaches are advised. ADHD can be treated first using behavioural methods; however if they are not effective medication should be prescribed.

Advice for teachers and parents who have children with ADHD

* Structure: Structured approaches are necessary in dealing with children with ADHD: providing a structure such that the child knows what to do, when to do it and how to do it in simple, clear and definite terms.
* Boundaries: Sharp boundaries and limits should be established from the outset such that the child is aware of what is or what is not permissible.
* Instructions: Simple instructions should be presented in small steps, be predictable and there should be prompts and reminders about instructions.
* Seating arrangements: Children should be seated nearby or be easily visible.
* Contact: Regular eye contact with and scanning of the child should take place and escape routes should be made available enabling the child to avoid explosive confrontations.
* Opportunities: The child should be provided with opportunities to self-monitor, self-report and self-regulate.
* Tasks: The child should be provided with small tasks or errands and large tasks should be broken down into smaller step by step tasks. If the child is likely to be placed in unstructured situations then preparations should be made to deal with these situations. Distractions and distracting environments should be avoided.

American Psychiatric Association (1994) *Diagnostic and Statistical Manual of Mental Disorders, 4th edn. (DSM IV). Washington, DC.*

Cooper, P. and Ideus, K. (1996) *Attention Deficit/Hyperactivity Disorder: A Practical Guide for Teachers.* London, David Fulton Publishers.

DuPaul, G.J. and Stoner, G. (1994) *ADHD in Schools: Assessment and Intervention Strategies.* New York, The Guilford Press.

Hinshaw, S.P. (1994) *Attention Deficits and Hyperactivity in Children.* Thousand Oaks, CA, SAGE Publications.

International Classification of Diseases (ICD-10), (1992) World Health Organisation.

Kendall, P.C. and Braswell, L. (1993) *Cognitive-Behavioral Therapy for Impulsive Children, 2nd edn.* New York. The Guilford Press.

Peterson, C. (1996) *The Psychology of Abnormality.* New York, Harcourt Brace College Publishers.

Rutter, M., Taylor, E. and Hersov, L. (eds) (1994) *Child and Adolescent Psychiatry: Modern Approaches, 3rd edn.* Oxford, Blackwell Science Publications.

Contacts

ADD Information Services, PO Box 340, Edgware, Middlesex HA8 9HL. Tel. 020 8906 9068.

ADHD National Alliance, Contact a Family, 209–211 City Road, London EC1. Tel. 020 7608 8760.

Child Psychotherapy Trust, Star House, 104–108 Grafton Road, London NW5 4BD. Helpline 020 7485 5510 (Monday–Thursday, 9 a.m. to 5 p.m.).

Hyperactive Children's Support Group, 71 Whyke Lane, Chichester PO19 2LD. Tel. 01903 725182.

Attribution theory

Attribution theory comprises a variety of approaches describing and analysing the ways in which people use information to arrive at causal explanations for people's behaviour. It investigates the kinds of information collected and the way this information is combined to make causal attributions. Research into causal attributions has thrown up a number of biases in the attribution process including the fundamental attribution error, the actor-observer effect, the false consensus effect.

- The fundamental attribution bias is where people attribute other people's behaviour to their disposition or trait rather than their situation.
- The actor-observer effect is where people attribute their own behaviour to circumstances and other people's to their disposition.
- The false consensus effect is where people regard their own behaviour as normal or typical and that others in a similar situation would behave in the same way. Therefore others should behave as they do.
- The hostile attributional bias is where people tend to interpret ambiguous behaviours as implying hostile attitudes or intent.

There are individual differences with respect to making attributions including locus of control and attributional style.

- Locus of control refers to internal and external locus of control. Those who have an internal locus of control believe they have control over reinforcing events whereas those who have an external locus of control believe that reinforcing events are under the control of external factors such as luck, chance or other people.
- Attributional style refers to the tendency to make certain kinds of causal attributions rather than others. For example a pessimistic attributional style perceives negative events as being caused by internal, stable and global factors. This attributional style is likely to be associated with depression.

Reattribution training is a therapeutic approach that attempts to train people in making more productive causal attributions regarding their feelings and behaviours. Emotional and behavioural difficulties are seen as being the consequence of making negative or unproductive causal attributions with regard to the performance of behaviours.

Fiske, S.T. and Taylor, S.E. (1991) Social Cognition, 2nd edn. New York, McGraw-Hill.

Autism

Autism is a disorder first described by L. Kanner in 1943. By the end of the 1970s autism was included in the two principal diagnostic systems used to classify mental disorders (DSM IV, American Psychiatric Association) and (ICD-10, World Health Organisation). The main characteristics of autism are:

- impaired development before the age of 3 in verbal communication, in social attachment and in social interaction;
- repetitive and unimaginative play;
- restricted and stereotyped behaviour;
- limited interests and activities;
- preoccupations with special interests;
- compulsive adherence to routines and rituals and resistance to change;
- lack of understanding of spoken language and repetitive and echolalic speech;
- limited social communication with others;
- attachments to objects and collections of facts and objects.

There are four types described by Wing and Gould:

- aloof (avoiding social contact and remaining isolated);
- passive (do not avoid social contact but do not initiate it);
- active but odd (more cognitively developed but engage in inappropriate social interactions);
- over-formal and stilted (have above average ability but treat parents and other family members as strangers).

Children with other conditions or developmental disorders may manifest some of the symptoms of autism, e.g. developmental language disorders, elective mutism, neurological disorders (Rett's syndrome, Landau-Kleffner syndrome), genetic disorders (tuberous sclerosis, Fragile X) and in some cases of severe neglect. Although autism has a high correlation with learning disability most children with mental retardation do not have autism. However the incidence of autism increases with those children with a severe or profound learning disability. Many children with autism experience hearing and visual impairment.

Prevalence

Depending on the definition of typical autism rates ranging from 3.3 to 21.0 per 10,000 have been cited.

L. Kanner's original description of autism has been modified over time with the recognition that the same disorder may be manifest in a number of different ways.

Perspectives on autism

- Biological: A number of studies provide evidence for a genetic cause in many cases of typical autism. Pre-natal and birth complications have been shown to be associated with autism. Brain lesions and other abnormalities have not been identified with autism. Immunisation against whooping cough and, more recently, the triple vaccine for mumps, measles and rubella have been suggested as causes but there is no consistent scientific evidence either for or against this. There is no evidence that autism is a childhood form of schizophrenia. The results from twin and family studies indicate that a genetic predisposition exists for autism and a heritability figure of 91 to 93 per cent is cited. The genetic factors are unknown and there are no diagnostic tests available.
- Psychodynamic: Early theories that autism was due to being reared by cold and distant parents have been refuted. It has been pointed out that an autistic child's behaviour may well affect parents' reactions to the presence of autism.
- 'Theory of mind/mind blindness': Current psychological theories of autism have tried to explain autism as a syndrome in which impairments in socialisation, communication and imagination cohere and it is suggested that one single cognitive deficit underlies these three features of autism: a deficit in 'theory of mind'. In other words, the child with autism cannot imagine the thoughts or anticipate the behaviour of others.

Treatment

There is no current curative treatment for autism. However, numerous therapies and approaches have been developed but scientific evidence for their efficacy is not definitive. Nevertheless, there is a general consensus that education rather than therapy is the treatment of choice. In a recent review commissioned by the DfEE the interventions were grouped under the following headings: Interactive Approaches, Approaches to Communication, Integration Approaches, Division TEACCH, Daily Life Therapy as practised at the Boston Higashi School, and Behavioural Approaches. The study concluded that there is no real evidence to suggest that one approach to a child with autism is better than any other approach. However there was general agreement that early intensive education which involves parents and includes direct teaching of essential skills with opportunities for planned integration can produce significant changes for the child.

Approaches

There is no treatment available that provides a cure for autism. Many therapies and approaches have been developed but evidence for their effectiveness varies. A number of the most common approaches are listed below.

- Interactive approaches emphasise the importance of developing relationships with carers and teachers through fostering communication skills. They include Musical Interaction therapy, Music therapy, and Kaufman's Option approach. Musical Interaction therapy aims to develop the communication skills of the child with autism through using a musician playing an instrument who supports the establishment of a relationship between the child and the key worker. Music Therapy aims to develop the relationship and communication between the child with autism and the music therapist. The Option approach involves intensive individual intervention to engage with the child with autism on their own terms in an attempt to engage them in interacting socially.
- Communication approaches emphasise language and communication teaching through specific communication programmes. They include the Picture Exchange Communication System, Augmentative Communication, and Facilitated Communication. The Picture Exchange Communication System (PECS) aims to teach functional communication skills in particular to initiate communication in a social exchange through using pictures. Augmentative Communication uses sign, pictures, symbols or written words in order to help the individual to understand and to express their needs. Facilitated Communication uses physical prompts to facilitate the individual with autism in communicating their ideas and thoughts.
- Behavioural approaches use various behavioural techniques and strategies such as time out, extinction, positive and negative reinforcement, differential reinforcement in order to increase appropriate behaviour and reduce unwanted behaviours. Skills analysis and shaping procedures are also utilised in order to teach new skills. Although behavioural techniques are also used in other approaches the work of Lovaas is the most well-known of the behavioural approaches. His programme is called applied behaviour analysis and it is based on the principles of Skinnerian operant conditioning, i.e. all

behaviour is learned and can be changed through shaping and rewarding desired behaviours.

- Division TEACCH is a very well known and well regarded approach. It was started in America in 1972 and its aim was to provide a community based service for children and young people with autism. The main principles of this approach are its emphasis on structured teaching, the use of visual channels of learning and on providing a safe and predictable environment which is effective in reducing anxiety and building on the strengths of the individual with autism.

- SPELL is the acronym for the approach adopted by the National Autistic Society in their organisation of schools that they have set up. It stands for Structure, Positive, Empathy, Low arousal and Links. This approach recognises the importance of reducing anxiety and increasing security through structure at all levels; the need for positive approaches and expectations to ensure that the child with autism has confidence and a positive self-esteem; empathy is recognised as ensuring that the assessment of the individual needs of children with autism are a priority; low arousal settings are important to provide the child with autism with the best environmental conditions for learning and links with parents, carers and the child's environment are a key element in their approach.

- The Earlybird Project was established in 1997, also by the National Autistic Society, in recognition of the importance of close partnership with parents as early as possible after a diagnosis of autistic spectrum disorder. It is a three-month programme aimed to provide information, practical advice and support to parents and families of pre-school children. The programme follows the SPELL approach. It aims to enable parents to be in control through understanding their child's autism and through developing their skills in interacting and communicating with their child.

- Daily Life Therapy (Higashi) is a holistic approach first developed in Japan in the 1970s. It offers a 24-hour programme focusing on daily living skills, physical education, music and craft. The teaching approach used is based on the importance of the group in promoting the child's development.

- Auditory Integration Training is a technique, which was first introduced by Dr Berard, an ear, nose and throat specialist. The treatment involves the child in listening to electronically filtered music through headphones. The theory behind this intervention is that distortions in hearing can be removed and that the resulting decrease in sound sensitivity will have a positive effect and eliminate the behavioural difficulties which children with autism frequently have.

It is generally accepted that early intensive education that involves parents and includes direct teaching of essential skills with opportunities for planned integration can produce significant changes for the child. A combination of intervention approaches based on full discussions with parents and assessment of the child's strengths as well as their difficulties can be effective.

Cumine, V., Leach, J. and Stevenson, G. (2000) Autism in the Early Years. London, David Fulton Publishers.

Frith, U. (ed.) (1991) Autism and Asperger Syndrome. Cambridge, Cambridge University Press.

Howlin, P. (1999) Children with Autism and Asperger Syndrome: A Guide for Practitioners and Carers. Chichester, Wiley.

Jordan, R. (1999) Autistic Spectrum Disorders: An Introductory Handbook for Practitioners. London, David Fulton Publishers.

Jordan, R. et al. (1998) Educational Interventions for Children with Autism: A Literature Review of Recent and Current Research. Nottingham, DfEE Publications.

Rutter, M., Taylor, E. and Hersov, L. (eds) (1994) Child and Adolescent Psychiatry: Modern Approaches, 3rd edn. Oxford, Blackwell Science.

Contacts

The National Autistic Society (NAS), 393 City Road, London EC1V 1NE. Tel. 020 7903 3555 (helpline for parents and people with autism/Asperger syndrome).

Parents for the Early Intervention of Autism in Children (PEACH), PO Box 10836, London SW13 9ZN. Tel. 020 8891 0121. A parent's run organisation providing parent to parent helplines, newsletters about the latest research, programmes and therapy advice.

The Light and Sound Therapy Centre, 99 Queen Elizabeth's Walk, London N16 5PQ. Tel. 020 8880 1269.

Aversion therapy

Aversion therapy is a controversial behavioural technique used to terminate unwanted habits such as excessive drinking by pairing a noxious stimulus such as electric shock, a nauseous inducing drug or social criticism with the unwanted habit. In theory the unwanted habit is then inhibited and undergoes extinction. It has been used for alcoholism (taking Antabuse), paraphilias (sexual disorders) and compulsive behaviours. It is controversial because there are doubts concerning its effectiveness and because it produces uncomfortable feelings.

Cramer, D. (1992) Personality and Psychotherapy. Buckingham, Open University Press.

Avoidance conditioning or learning

In operant conditioning, avoidance conditioning is a form of negative reinforcement whereby a person avoids an aversive stimulus by performing some response. Active avoidance is where the person avoids the aversive stimulus by having to perform the response whereas passive avoidance occurs when the person has to refrain from performing the response in order to avoid the aversive stimulus.

Cramer, D. (1992) Personality and Psychotherapy. Buckingham, Open University Press.

Avoidant personality disorder

Avoidant personality disorder is a type of personality disorder characterised by the avoidance of social and interpersonal situations where criticism or rejection might be experienced. In social situations those with the disorder feel anxious, inhibited and restrained and are reluctant to engage in social interactions. They feel inferior and incompetent. This disorder originates in childhood and adolescence.

Carr, A. (2001) Abnormal Psychology. Hove, Psychology Press.

B

Baseline

The term 'baseline' is used in behavioural assessment and refers to information collected with respect to an overt, target behaviour. A baseline provides a means of comparison for information collected at a later date, that is, after the termination of an intervention. This provides evidence as to whether there has been an increase or decrease in the target behaviour. The information collected should be a representative sample of the target behaviour and be categorised according to its frequency, duration and intensity. It may take one or two weeks to establish a representative baseline.

Herbert, M. (1987) Behavioural Treatment of Children with Problems: A Practice Manual, 2nd edn. London, Harcourt, Brace Jovanovich College Publishers.

Basic rule or fundamental rule

A psychoanalytic term used with regard to clients or patients. This rule requires patients to agree to divulge all the thoughts that enter their minds without hesitation or restraint. Therefore there should be no attempt by patients to edit their thoughts. However, the patient's resistances and defences may interfere with this process. The analyst will interpret resistances and defences in order to reveal the patient's underlying unconscious conflicts.

Behaviour

Behaviour is a general term describing physical actions and responses in relation to the environment. The use of the term tends to reflect a chosen perspective. For example, the behaviourist perspective defines behaviour as overt, observable and measurable actions without referring to cognitive and unconscious processes. The cognitive-behavioural perspective sees behaviour as associated with particular cognitive processes, that is, internal states in the form of thinking, reasoning, inferring, believing and imagining. However behaviourists would not deny the existence of internal cognitions and feelings but would see them as being expressed in overt and observable behaviour. The psychodynamic perspective sees behaviour as the observable manifestation of underlying and unconscious, dynamic conflicts. The way in which behaviour is conceptualised will determine the treatment of emotional and behavioural problems.

Behaviour rating

Behaviour ratings are scales used to assess overt, objective and observable behaviours. They are a brief and efficient method of collecting information. They require training and practise in their use. The observer rates the given behaviour of a person or referral on a scale. The aim is to record specific behaviours, the presence or absence of behaviours and their intensity, frequency and duration. There are different types of rating scales, some broad and some narrow. Broad ones focus on general problems whereas narrow ones focus on specific problems. Sometimes rating scales are used for screening and sometimes for choosing target behaviours. They depend on accurate and reliable observation and clearly defined terms. In particular rating scales depend on interrater reliability, i.e. the extent to which two observers agree on their ratings or observations. Behaviour rating scales are also susceptible to response sets. Various rating scales exist for teachers and parents. Teachers' ratings are particularly useful across a range of settings, for externalising behaviours and for a comprehensive view of behavioural problems.

Kamphaus, R.W. and Frick, P.J. (1996) Clinical Assessment of Child and Adolescent Personality and Behavior. Boston, MA, Allyn and Bacon.

Behaviour therapy (or behaviour modification)

Behaviour therapy is the application of learning theory, in particular classical and operant conditioning techniques, to emotional and behavioural problems. Maladaptive cognitions are also modified cognitively and behaviourally.

Main assumptions

- Current behaviours or symptoms constitute current problems, therefore there is no need to consider traits nor underlying causes.
- Heredity sets limits on how much of behaviour can be learned.
- Traits are seen as convenient shorthand descriptions but suffer from drawbacks in that traits are non-observable, frequently imprecise and are circular in definition, therefore traits need to be translated into specific behaviours.
- Maladaptive or inadequate learning leads to and is associated with problem behaviours.
- Current problem behaviours are triggered and maintained by current, empirical contingencies.
- Observation enables contingencies to be identified, in particular the antecedents and consequences of specific, problem behaviours, and allows those contingencies to be manipulated.
- Specific problem behaviours can be measured in terms of intensity, duration and frequency and can then be placed along a continuum.
- Covert behaviours (thinking, feeling and physiological processes) are inferred from overt behaviours (observable actions and events).

Procedure

- At the beginning a precise and objective assessment and formulation of specific emotional and behavioural problems is undertaken.
- Target behaviours are specified.
- A pre-intervention baseline enables behavioural change to be evaluated.
- Specific interventions to achieve the target behaviours are identified, these being based on the assessment and formulation stages.
- The interventions are implemented and evaluated.
- Interventions can be evaluated using reversal and multiple baseline designs.
- Effectiveness of an intervention is judged according to the criteria of acceptability, generalisation, clinical significance and durability.

Main interventions

- Positive reinforcement.
- Negative reinforcement.
- Differential reinforcement.
- Time out from positive reinforcement.
- Response cost.
- Overcorrection.
- Punishment.
- Token economy.
- Contingency contracting.
- Systematic desensitisation and graduated exposure.
- Rapid exposure or flooding.
- Modelling.
- Social skills training.
- Cognitive restructuring.
- Self-instructional training.
- Problem solving training.

Emerson, E. (1995) *Challenging Behaviour: Analysis and Intervention in People with Learning Difficulties.* Cambridge, Cambridge University Press.

Herbert, M. (1998) *Clinical Child Psychology: Social Learning, Development and Behaviour,* 2nd edn. Chichester, Wiley.

Spiegler, M.D. and Guivrement, D.C. (1998) *Contemporary Behavior Therapy,* 3rd edn. Pacific Grove, CA, Brooks/Cole.

Behavioural assessment

Behavioural assessment is a form of assessment based on the behavioural perspective. This type of assessment focuses on current, overt, observable and measurable behaviours of an individual person, child or adult. The assessment focuses on the individual's behaviours in and across particular settings or contexts. Behaviour is seen as being stable or variable through time and across contexts. The main focus however is on behaviour in the current situation and its controlling variables. The causes of behaviour are seen as being identifiable triggers and maintaining factors that are operating in the current context. It requires a functional analysis using the ABC model, i.e. antecedents, behaviour and consequences.

A variety of observational methods are used to acquire information for the assessment such as time sampling, internal recording, event sampling and behavioural frequency counts, along with behaviourally based and structured interview techniques. The behaviour is described in terms of its latency, frequency, duration and intensity. This information is used to establish a pre-intervention baseline for the purpose of evaluating the effectiveness of an intervention. It is also used to construct a formulation, i.e. a statement describing what triggers and maintains the observed behaviour. Observers need to agree over definitions of behaviour and they also need to check that they are recording the same behaviours. A variety of errors and problems can arise in the course of assessment, namely reactivity, unreliability and bias in observation.

Marsh, E.J. and Terdal, L.G. (eds) (1988) Behavioral Assessment of Childhood Disorders, 2nd edn. New York, The Guilford Press.

Behavioural or contingency contract

A behavioural contract is a type of behavioural intervention used with individuals who have emotional and/or behavioural problems. Contracts can be useful in minimising disputes about the conditions of an intervention. They encourage active participation in the intervention. They can facilitate the practice of negotiation and cooperation.

The contract takes the form of a written agreement between the individual who is the target of the intervention and other participants involved in the intervention. The aim of the contract is to specify SMART targets along with roles and responsibilities of the participants. It must be clear as to the contingencies between target behaviours and consequences. Appropriate rewards and sanctions are linked to achievement or non-achievement of the targets. Success criteria need to be established in order to determine the effectiveness of the contract. The contract is monitored and reviewed at appropriate intervals and evaluated according to whether there has been an increase in desired behaviour or a decrease in undesired behaviour.

The contract terms should be clear, unambiguous, realistic and achievable. It should where possible be couched in positive terms and avoid punitive sanctions. The participants should consent to the contract terms and not feel coerced. All the participants should benefit from the contract. Changes to the contract should be negotiated and agreed. Reasons for the success or failure of contracts should be recorded and evaluated.

Herbert, M. (1981) *Behavioural Treatment of Childrens' Problems: A Practice Manual*, 2nd edn. London, Harcourt Brace Jovanovitch College Publishers.

Spiegler, M.D. and Guivrement, D.C. (1998) *Contemporary Behavior Therapy*, 3rd edn. Pacific Grove,CA, Brooks/Cole.

Behavioural genetics

Behavioural genetics is a scientific approach to the determination of the relative contributions of heredity and the environment to emotional and behavioural disorders. It does not subscribe to predetermination but to probabilities, in other words it does not believe in genetic determinism or fatalism. It focuses on individual differences and in particular on the concepts of heritability, shared and non-shared environments. Environmental effects are seen as having as great an influence as heredity. Heritability refers to the variation in scores of a particular trait that can be attributed to genetic differences within a given population. Heritability is seldom greater than 50 per cent; therefore environment accounts for another 50 per cent, this being mainly of the non-shared type. Heritability also changes with development, this means that planned changes in the environment might decrease genetic risks. Shared environment refers to environmental influences that family members share in common and non-shared environment refers to influences that are not shared by family members.

The ultimate aim of behavioural genetics is to identify genes that predispose individuals to specific disorders. This aim is to be achieved through molecular genetics, which it is hoped will lead to the identification of genes that act together to contribute to a particular quantitative trait. Currently, however, its methodology is based on twin and adoption research. This research leads to estimations regarding the relative contribution of heredity and the environment to specific behaviours. For example genetic influence is regarded as apparent in autism, ADHD and schizophrenia. Currently no specific genes have been identified with particular mental disorders; in fact single genes contribute very rarely if ever to human behaviour. Behaviour is more likely to be caused by the interaction of many genes interacting with each other and with the existing environment. However, a single defective gene can adversely affect human behaviour as in the case of Huntington's disease. Environment and environmental change contributes substantially to human behaviour, e.g. as in the case of increasing obesity due to changing diets and a reduction in physical exercise.

With regard to environmental factors, non-shared environmental influences are seen as predominant. Non-shared environments refer to influences that are not shared by family members, for example siblings brought up in the same family are often different. This could be due to different friendships or different schooling but even where siblings share the same physical environment they may well interpret it differently. This approach sees the quality of adolescent friendships as particularly important in influencing behaviour.

Clark, W.R. and Grunstein, M. (2000) *Are We Hardwired? The Role of Genes in Human Behaviour.* Oxford, Oxford University Press.

Faraone, S.V., Tsuang, M.T. and Tsuang, D.W. (1999) *Genetics of Mental Disorders: A Guide for Students, Clinicians, and Researchers.* New York, The Guilford Press.

Kaplan, J.M. (2000) *The Limits and Lies of Human Genetic Research: Dangers for Social Policy.* London, Routledge.

Plomin, R., DeFries, J.C., McClearn, G.E. and Rutter, M. (1997) *Behavioral Genetics,* 3rd edn. New York, W.H. Freeman.

Behaviourism

Behaviourism is a psychological perspective that aims to study behaviour scientifically and objectively. The main contributors were I. Pavlov (classical conditioning), J. B. Watson (classical conditioning of an emotional response) and B. F. Skinner (operant conditioning).

Behaviourism is based on scientific methodology and modern behaviourism is methodological behaviourism. The elements of this methodology include objectivity, hypothesis testing, observation, experiment and measurement. It originated as a reaction against introspectionist psychology. Self-report is seen as subjective and therefore unreliable. Cognitive and unconscious processes are seen as irrelevant in the explanation of behaviour. Behaviour is explicable through learning or conditioning after taking genetic influences into account. There is, therefore, no need to posit underlying causes for behaviour.

The main elements of behaviourism are:

- a focus on individual responses to internal and external stimuli, i.e. their learning histories;
- that stimuli and responses are objective events that can be observed and measured;
- to predict and control behaviour through experimentation;
- to look for the causes of behaviour outside rather than within individuals.

The two basic learning processes are classical (respondent) and operant (instrumental) conditioning. In classical conditioning the individual responds passively to environmental stimuli whereas with operant conditioning the individual operates, as it were, on the environment.

Behaviourism explains the origin and development of psychological problems in terms of classical and operant conditioning. There is no need to postulate underlying causes of symptoms. Symptoms are simply the observable behaviours. Once the presenting symptoms (observable behaviours) of an emotional or behavioural problem have been extinguished then the problems have been treated. This approach would therefore deny that any underlying cause remains or that symptom substitution occurs.

Pavlov, I.P. (1927) Conditioned Reflexes. London, Oxford University Press.

Skinner, B.F. (1953) Science and Human Behavior. New York, Macmillan.

Spiegler, M.D. and Guivrement, D.C. (1998) Contemporary Behavior Therapy, 3rd edn. Pacific Grove, CA, Brooks/Cole.

Watson, J.B. (1913) 'Psychology as the behaviorist views it', Psychological Review, 20.

Bereavement

Bereavement refers to the state of having suffered a loss through death and the process of grief and mourning that is the result. Bereavement is the normal process of reacting to a loss. Intense, confusing and conflicting emotions can be experienced following the loss or death of a significant person in one's life. Some frameworks for understanding the bereavement process suggests that people need to go through stages or phases in the process of coming to terms with the loss.

- The first phase is shock and numbness, family members may find it difficult to believe the death and the reality of the loss may be denied. Children may believe the dead person is still alive and ask relatives to contact the deceased person. Some children may have hallucinations of the dead person and attempt to converse with them.
- The second phase is characterised by yearning and searching where the survivors experience separation anxiety and cannot accept the reality of the loss; feelings of anger and wishing to blame someone are also common at this stage as are feelings of guilt. Children may actually search for the dead person. Adolescents and children may become angry and as a consequence have temper tantrums, engage in delinquency and resort to substance abuse. Children may also think that they will die or that they are seriously ill.
- The third phase consists of despair, helplessness and disorganisation, family members experience feelings of depression and have difficulties concentrating and planning for the future. Children may lose their appetite and concentration, have sleep disturbances and become withdrawn. They may also regress in their behaviour, e.g. wetting the bed and sucking their thumb.
- The final phase is one of reorganisation and involves the realisation and acceptance of the loss. The survivor adjusts to life without the person who has died and becomes able to engage emotionally in new relationships. Children may engage in rituals and keep symbolic reminders of the dead person. These various stages will often overlap and show themselves in different ways in different people and it would be unusual for children as well as adults to go through the stages in a prescribed way.

However, although these stages are observed to occur, they do not necessarily occur in any particular order and the sequence can change. Furthermore, not everybody experiences all these stages. For example depression does not always occur after bereavement. After bereavement some people use distraction, avoidance, confrontation and working through techniques to deal with their grief. Some people grieve for many years, particularly if they unexpectedly lose a child or a loved one in an accident. People during bereavement also become prone to infections and illnesses due to deficiencies in their immune systems.

Children and bereavement

A recent study found that 15,000 children are bereaved annually, a figure that translates into 40 children each day. It is important to recognise that children, like adults, respond to bereavement and loss in their own way and that there is no right or wrong response. Young children and adolescents may manifest temper tantrums, delinquency, substance abuse and refuse to go to school. There is evidence that unresolved childhood bereavement can affect adult life and that the loss of a mother during childhood is associated with depressive disorders in adult life. An understanding of how children experience bereavement is important in order to ensure a child's emotional well being both at the time of the loss and in the longer term. Bowlby has described the behaviour of young children aged from 12 months to 3 years when the children were removed from their mother and placed with strangers. Initially, the baby protested and exhibited behaviours aimed at restoring the lost person. Bowlby suggested that this type of behaviour lasted for about a week and was followed by despairing behaviour where the child became withdrawn and miserable. After this phase the child begins to form new relationships. Even very young children can be affected by the loss of a significant person. It has been reported that when infants are separated from their care-giver or when they are bereaved they may become restless and irritable and they respond to the emotions of the surviving family members. Although at this age children do not understand the concept of death it is generally accepted that even from infancy children grieve and feel great distress. From the age of 3 onwards children's understanding of death develops and even children as young as 3 are able to conceive death as irreversible and due to natural causes. However, the extent of their understanding is highly dependent on the information they are given and their exposure to death. It is important to provide children with true information as well as the necessary emotional support necessary to deal with the loss. Children as young as 5 or perhaps even younger can have quite a developed understanding of the concept of death, including the fact that it is permanent, irreversible, universal, has a cause, and that dead people are different from living people. Children do not appear to feel the same intensity of feelings of grief as adults nor do they appear to grieve for the length of time that adults do. However, their adjustment to bereavement depends on their level of cognitive and emotional development. It also depends on parental and family problems and parental coping skills. Children feel the greatest loss when they lose a parent, particularly if it is an unexpected death. If a child does lose a parent in early life they are at risk of depression in adult life. In order to deal with bereavement of a parent children can benefit from leave-taking rituals such as attending the parent's funeral, visiting the grave and bidding farewell to the parent.

Interventions

Bereavement interventions are aimed at acknowledging and validating the feelings that the individual is experiencing. It is especially important that the individual accepts that grief is a normal process, that there are a variety of ways in which it can be expressed and that the feelings experienced are valid and natural. Two critical components to enable a bereaved child to develop coping strategies include the presence of supportive and responsive care-givers and the kind of information provided. Often the surviving parent may not be able to recognise and provide as much support as necessary as they are grieving themselves and may be preoccupied by the loss. Adults tend to underestimate the amount of information that children require and may try to protect the child, albeit with the best of intentions. This can be counter-productive and result in a confused and frightened child. For example, telling a child that the person has 'passed away' or 'gone away' rather than that the person has died and is not coming back, may make the child more distressed and fearful and may affect their grieving. Research has shown that children require information that is truthful and not ambiguous. It also has to be appropriate to the child's cognitive development in order to ensure that the child can use it to make sense of the death. The importance of this can be further illustrated by a recent survey that found that 60 per cent of children excluded from school had suffered a significant bereavement.

Black, D. (1983) 'Bereaved children – family intervention', Bereavement Care, 2(2), Summer.
Bowlby, J. (1963, 1973, 1980, 3 vols) Attachment and Loss. Harmondsworth, Penguin.
Brown, G. and Harris, T. (1978) Social Origins of Depression. London, Tavistock Publications.
Corr, C. and Balk, D. (1996) Handbook of Adolescent Death and Bereavement. New York, Springer.
Duffy, W. (1991) The Bereaved Child. Ongar, The National Society.
Kubler-Ross, E. (1986) On Children and Death. New York, Macmillan.
Smith, S. and Pennell, M. (1996) Interventions with Bereaved Children. London, Jessica Kingsley.
Wagner, P. (1999) Issues No. 1: Endings. Kensington and Chelsea Education Psychology Consultation Service.

Contacts

National Association of Bereavement Services, 20 Norton Folgate, London E1 6DB. (This is a nationwide network of organisations and individuals offering services to bereaved people.)
The Compassionate Friends, 53 North Street, Bristol BS3 1EN. Helpline 01272 539639. (A network of parents who help parents whose child has died from any cause at any age.)
Cruse Bereavement Care, Cruse House, 126 Sheen Road, Richmond, Surrey. Helpline 020 8332 7227. (A national organisation that provides bereavement counselling on a wide scale.)
The Samaritans offers 24 hour telephone support. Helpline 0345 909090.

Big Five

The Big Five or the five-factor model of personality refers to the factors derived from factor analysis that make up the basic dimensions of personality. They are openness to experience, conscientiousness, extraversion, agreeableness and neuroticism (OCEAN).

Illustrative examples of the dimensions are openness to experience (curious-narrow minded), conscientiousness (reliable-unreliable), extraversion (sociable-reserved), agreeableness (helpful-uncooperative) and neuroticism (nervous-calm). It is claimed that these traits have a significant hereditary component and also evolutionary significance in terms of adaptation and survival.

Goldberg, L.R. (1993) 'The structure of phenotypic personality traits', American Psychologist, 48.
Pervin, L.A. (1996) The Science of Personality. Chichester, Wiley.

Biofeedback

In the past it was considered impossible to consciously control physiological processes like heart rate, blood pressure and the constriction of blood vessels because such autonomic functions do not depend on conscious control. However in the late 1960s through the use of an electrical monitor people were able to receive biofeedback about the status of particular autonomic functions. People are able to increase and decrease heart rate and blood pressure. People are also able to control alpha waves in their brains using electroencephalography (EEG). Through electromyography (EMG) muscle activity can also be recorded and assessed.

Evidence indicates that stress and pain relief, e.g. for migraine, can be achieved through biofeedback; however this effect needs to be separated from a placebo effect that may be associated with biofeedback.

Biological perspective

The biological perspective focuses on the influence of physical processes on behaviour, in particular it concentrates on the influence of genetic, physiological, neurological factors on abnormal behaviour. This approach is also referred to as the medical or disease model. Behaviour is described as abnormal and diagnosis is based on symptoms and is treated through biologically based drug therapy. Classification of abnormal behaviour is through the use of diagnostic manuals, either DSM IV or ICD-10. It is already known that physical illnesses can have psychological consequences and psychological problems may also have physical consequences. Brain damage can produce psychological symptoms that are then misdiagnosed as psychological problems, e.g. in the case of brain tumours. Alternatively psychological problems may be misdiagnosed as an organic disorder, e.g. in the case of dementia in elderly people.

The main components of the perspective are:

- Behavioural genetics is research into genetic influences on behaviour through the means of the family method, twin and adoption studies. Molecular genetics attempts to identify the genes that influence behaviour.

- Neurological studies investigate the influence brain structure and neurotransmitters have on behaviour. Specific neurotransmitters are studied such as dopamine, serotonin, and norepinephrine. The methods used to study brain processes are electroencephalography (EEG), positron emission topography (PET), computerised tomography (CT) and magnetic resonance imaging (MRI) and functional MRI (fMRI). These techniques reveal brain structure and with fMRI the function of brain processes.
- Endocrinology studies the influence of hormones on behaviour, in particular the influences of hormonal imbalances on abnormal behaviour.
- There are a number of biological treatments used to treat abnormal behaviour. Drug therapy is the treatment of psychological and psychiatric disorders through the prescription of psychoactive drugs, e.g. minor tranquillisers and anti-psychotics. Psychosurgery is the use of surgical techniques to treat severe mental disorders. Electroconvulsive therapy is used to treat severe depression through applying an electric shock to the brain.

The effectiveness of drug therapy can be adversely affected by a number of factors. Some people do not respond to specific drugs, others may experience side effects and others stop taking the drug. As with other types of therapies people may also experience spontaneous remission; they would have improved anyway. Furthermore, the fact that a drug used to treat mental disorders affects abnormal brain biochemistry does not necessarily mean that the abnormal biochemistry is the cause of the disorder. The abnormal biochemistry may in fact be the consequence of the disorder. The cause of a disorder can be social, for example depression caused by unemployment or loss of a close relationship, but it can still be treated by drugs that affect brain biochemistry.

Alloy, L.B., Jacobson, N.S. and Acocella, J. (1999) Abnormal Psychology: Current Perspectives, 8th edn. New York, McGraw-Hill College.
Kalat, J.W. (2001) Biological Psychology, 7th edn. Belmont, CA, Wadsworth/Thomson Learning.

Biological treatment

Biological treatment is mainly drug therapy or the drug treatment of psychiatric disorders but also includes electroconvulsive therapy for depression, phototherapy for Seasonal Affective Disorder (SAD) and brain or psychosurgery. Drug treatments are not cures but serve to reduce or eliminate psychiatric symptoms while the drug is being taken. Drugs are not effective with all patients; some do not respond to treatment. Many drugs have unwanted side effects, some serious, particularly in the case of patients who have physical illnesses as well as a mental disorder. Some drugs interact adversely with certain foods, alcohol, nicotine, caffeine and other medically prescribed drugs. Compliance can be a problem with people forgetting or refusing to take a prescribed drug. Relapses are possible and so are rebound effects.

- Anxiety disorders are treated with minor tranquillisers, the most heavily used being the benzodiazepines, these being CNS depressants, e.g. Valium, Xanax and Tranxene. They are also used for patients who are experiencing severe anxiety over a physical illness. These drugs can have adverse side effects, e.g. drowsiness, impaired memory and motor function. There can also be withdrawal and rebound side effects.
- Depression is treated with antidepressants. Antidepressants are also used to treat anxiety disorders, panic disorder and obsessive-compulsive disorder. Monoamine oxidase inhibitors (MAO), e.g. Nardil and Parnate are used to treat depression. These too can have adverse side effects on the brain and liver and can interact very adversely with particular foods, e.g. certain kinds of cheese, wine and beer. Tricyclics, like monoamine oxidase inhibitors, can also have adverse side effects and as a consequence are being replaced by selective serotonin reuptake inhibitors (SSRIs), e.g. Prozac. However SSRIs too can have side effects. Recent antidepressant drugs include Effexor and Serzone. Other disorders such as borderline and avoidant personality disorders can respond to antidepressants.
- Bipolar disorder is treated with lithium carbonate. Potential problems with taking lithium include the possibility of an accidental overdose and possible rebound after cessation of the drug.
- Schizophrenia is treated with anti-psychotic drugs (neuroleptics), mainly phenothiazines, e.g. Thorazine. They reduce the positive symptoms of schizophrenia but are less effective at reducing negative symptoms. Anti-psychotic drugs are not effective for all people and can have adverse side effects, e.g. tardive dyskinesia. Recent drugs include Clozaril and Risperdal, which have an effect on the negative symptoms of schizophrenia.

Aldridge, S. (2000) *Seeing Red and Seeing Blue: The New Understanding of Mood and Emotion*. London, Arrow Books.

Alloy, B., Jacobson, N.S. and Acocella, J. (1999) *Abnormal Psychology: Current Perspectives*, 8th edn. New York, McGraw-Hill College.

Kalat, J.W. (2001) *Biological Psychology*, 7th edn. Belmont, CA, Wadsworth/Thomson Learning.

Lader, M. and Herrington, R. (1990) *Biological Treatments in Psychiatry*. Oxford, Oxford University Press.

Biorhythms

Biorhythms are inborn, periodic cycles discovered in biological processes. There are physical and psychological cycles that are repeated over certain time intervals. They are grouped according to frequency and duration.

Circadian rhythms have a cycle of 24 hours, e.g. the sleep-wake cycle, metabolic rate and the body-core temperature. The sleep-wake cycle is believed to be inborn and appears to function independently of environmental stimuli called zeitgebers.

Ultradian rhythms have cycles of less than 24 hours, e.g. sleep stages of alternating rapid eye movement (REM) sleep and non-REM sleep (NREM). REM sleep is associated with a higher frequency of dreaming than NREM sleep.

Infradian rhythms have cycles that spread over 24 hours, e.g. the female menstrual cycle is approximately monthly (28 days). However the cycle varies between 20 and 60 days. The menstrual cycle is inborn and is regulated by hormones that are produced by the endocrine system. At times the menstrual cycles of women or girls who live or work together become synchronised, this may occur through the release of pheromones or chemical messengers.

Circannual rhythms are yearly cycles that are infradian. Seasonal affective disorder (SAD) is an example. People with SAD become depressed during the winter months of darkness and feel better in the spring. SAD is believed to be due to neurotransmitters that display seasonal changes. Melatonin, a hormone and neurotransmitter, varies with light and low levels are thought to be a possible cause of depression in the winter months.

Biorhythms are produced and regulated by a number of mechanisms. Internal clocks are inborn biological processes that set and maintain cycles. Environmental stimuli (zeitgebers) can also influence the setting and resetting of internal clocks.

Bentley, E. (2000) Awareness: Biorhythms, sleep and dreaming. London, Routledge.

Bipolar disorder

Bipolar disorder is a severe mood disorder in which both manic and depressive conditions occur and alternate. Mania is characterised by intense but unfounded euphoria along with hyperactivity, flights of ideas and impractical grand plans. It is now divided into two types, bipolar I and II disorders. In bipolar I disorder people have at least one manic or mixed episode usually followed by a depressive episode. In bipolar II disorder people have a depressive episode and a hypomanic (mild manic) episode but do not have a manic or mixed episode. This disorder first occurs during late adolescence and in the 20s and 30s, rarely beyond 50. The average duration is two to three months but it can last for weeks or even years, over 50 per cent start with mania. The incidence of the disorder is much less frequent than depression, however women are at greater risk than are men but not as much as with depression. However it is more frequently diagnosed in middle class people and in people who experience hyperactivity. Depression is more likely to take the form of an excess of sleep. The risk of suicide is high.

The main type of treatment is drug therapy. Lithium carbonate is prescribed but can have side effects, e.g. frequent urination and problems with memory and concentration. There may be drug non-compliance due to the sufferer feeling they have improved sufficiently or because they miss the excitement of the manic episode.

Hammen, C. (1997) Depression. Hove, Psychology Press.

Body dysmorphic disorder

Body dysmorphic disorder (BDD) is a condition where people suffer such severe anguish over their imagined or real appearance that they cannot function socially. Most sufferers complain of facial imperfections but other bodily imperfections are also the focus of suffering. Considerable periods of time are spent in attempting to correct the imperfections, some through camouflage, others through cosmetic surgery, some through constantly seeking reassurance and others through avoidance of other people. It is associated with social withdrawal, depression and in some cases with an obsessive-compulsive disorder. The onset is gradual during adolescence and may be triggered by teasing, by having physical blemishes or by being neglected as a child.

The psychodynamic perspective sees BDD as a defence against unconscious anxiety that has arisen from unacceptable desires. Alternatively BDD is seen as a means of resolving conflicts that have arisen through unconscious hostility.

The cognitive perspective sees BDD sufferers as possessing a cognitive schema that leads them to exaggerate minor physical blemishes and so fear rejection.

Alloy, B., Jacobson, N.S. and Acocella, J. (1999) Abnormal Psychology: Current Perspectives. Boston MA, McGraw-Hill College.

Borderline personality disorder

Personality disorders refer to people who manifest enduring ways of thinking, feeling and behaving that are personally and socially maladaptive in the given culture. There is debate over the validity and reliability of diagnostic categories of personality disorders. Personality disorders are rare in the general population. Many people with personality disorders do not seek and are resistant to treatment.

Borderline personality disorder has been described from the psychodynamic perspective by O.F. Kernberg and was incorporated into the DSM as a diagnostic category in 1980. It is one of the most frequently diagnosed categories of personality disorders and is difficult to treat successfully. Its prevalence rate is one to two per cent and usually begins in adolescence. In children the disorder fluctuates between psychotic-like and neurotic symptoms. The psychotic-like symptoms appear as fears of body dissolution and a loss of contact with reality. These children are characterised by low self-esteem, impulsivity, losing self-control and self-destructiveness. By adolescence these children are likely to suffer from ADHD, conduct disorder, separation anxiety or mood disorders. They become self-centred, requiring continual attention, attempting to coerce others to do what they want and exploding in rage when met with rejection or indifference. Perspectives on this disorder in children and adolescents include psychodynamic (separation-individuation and splitting), biological (predisposition to mood disorders and separation anxiety) and family systems (parental loss or separation and physical and sexual abuse).

In adulthood more women than men are diagnosed. It tends to run in families. The core symptoms are difficulties in establishing and maintaining a self-identity; difficulties in maintaining stable relationships; impulsive, unpredictable, distrustful and self-destructive behaviour, and difficulties in controlling feelings, particularly anger and chronic depression, suicidal and self-mutilating tendencies. People with borderline personality disorders tend to end up in clinics suffering from substance abuse or eating disorders.

The psychodynamic perspective regards borderline disorder patients as having weak egos and as manifesting the defence of splitting in their relationships with others. Borderline disorder is seen as arising from problems of separation-individuation within the parent-child relationship.

The behavioural perspective sees borderline disorder as resulting from the failure to acquire appropriate skills to cope with emotional distress. Dialectical behaviour therapy aims to improve the patient's problem solving skills and social skills but also provides strategies for coping with emotions,

The cognitive perspective sees borderline disorder as being the consequence of a faulty schema that is characterised by dichotomous thinking. The aim of cognitive therapy is to modify, reinterpret or 'camouflage' the faulty schema.

The biological perspective sees borderline disorder as running in families and as therefore influenced by genetic factors. Antidepressants are prescribed for those suffering from a borderline disorder.

Kernberg, O.F. (1985) Borderline Conditions and Pathological Narcissism. New York, Aronson.
Linehan, M.M. (1993) Cognitive-behavioral Treatment of Borderline Personality. New York, Guilford Press.
Lubbe, T. (ed.) (2000) The Borderline Psychotic Child: A Selective Integration. London, Routledge.

Brief therapy (also known as solution focused brief therapy)

Brief therapy is a counselling/therapy approach that focuses on the development of solutions rather than the exploration of problems. The therapist engages in solution talk, i.e. asking questions in a way that helps the individual to identify the successful strategies they are using and encouraging them to work towards further successes. It is characterised by being a pragmatic and practical description of a way of talking with a client that focuses on problem-free and solution-oriented communication, thinking and describing; in contrast to problem-dominated talk, thinking and description. The approach has no theory of the problem, either of what causes or what maintains the problem. Rather it makes the assumption that in relation to every problem there are exceptions. Exceptions can be thought of as times when the problem does not happen, happens less or affects the client less. These exceptions need to be identified as they hold the solution to the problem. The task of the therapist in solution focused brief therapy is to guide the session by using particular questions in such a way so as to enable the client to reach a position of belief that they are able to change. Brief therapy techniques can be applied in working with children with emotional and behavioural difficulties in the school context.

Specific interventions and techniques used include:

- Reframing: This refers to changing how the problem is perceived in the belief that the new view may lead to different behaviours. Examples of reframing are a student's uncooperative behaviour being viewed by the teacher as unconfident behaviour; an uninvolved parent seen as a parent who trusts the expertise of the school; and a critical teacher seen as someone who has extremely high expectations of the student.
- Miracle questions: This involves asking the individual to imagine that a miracle has happened and that the problem has disappeared. The therapist then asks the individual to say how other people would know that this has occurred and what would be happening that was different.
- Scaling questions: These are used to identify goals and to find out how confident an individual may be of changing and trying to do something different. The person is asked to say on a scale of 1 to 10 (where, for example, 1 is the worst that things have been in your life and 10 is the best) where would you place yourself today? If the response is higher than 1, then the individual can be asked to say what they are doing that means they are not at 1. Scaling questions are very helpful in identifying the first small steps to change. The therapist can ask the question, 'I see you have put yourself on 4, how will you know when you have reached 5? How will things be different? What would need to happen?'
- Observational tasks: This involves identifying those times when things are going well, when the individual does something in a different way or when the individual is succeeding; feeding this back can then provide a basis for further success.
- Practising success: This refers to continuing doing more of what works.
- Pretend tasks: These are tasks where the individual agrees to pretend that the problem is solved and to behave as if it is in the belief that different behaviour will follow.

Durrant, M. (1993) Creative Strategies for School Problems. Eastwood Family Therapy Centre, Epping, NSW, Australia.

George, E., Iveson, C. and Ratner, H. (1990) Solution Brief Therapy with Individuals and Families. London, BT Press.

Selekman, M.D. (1997) Solution-Focused Therapy with Children. New York, Guilford Press.

Contact

Brief Therapy Practice, 4D Shirland Mews, London W9 3DY. Tel. 020 8968 0070.

Bulimia nervosa

Bulimia nervosa is an eating disorder that was not identified until the 1960s and the term bulimia was not used until 1980. It is characterised by an onset in late adolescence or early adulthood and by:

- episodes of consuming quantities of high calorie food or 'forbidden food' in a short time (often referred to as binge eating) twice a week for minimum of three weeks;
- feeling out of control while doing so;
- self-induced purging (self-induced vomiting, rumination, laxative abuse that may result in dehydration and depletion of electrolytes, particularly potassium, enema and diuretic abuse); fasting or excessive exercise is used to prevent the weight gain associated with the binge eating;
- these behaviours being usually carried out in secret, the eating is not being perceived as giving pleasure but rather as something shameful;
- preoccupied with body shape and weight gain;
- depression, anxiety, personality and interpersonal problems are associated with severe bulimia;
- however, unlike anorexia, bulimia is not characterised by low body weight and amenorrhea (lack of periods).

The age and sex distribution is similar to that of anorexia nervosa but the age of presentation tends to be slightly later. However bulimia is far more common than anorexia and affects one to three per cent of adolescent girls and young women. Bulimia may begin after an episode of anorexia or it may start out as a deliberate method of weight control. Bulimia can have serious physical consequences including major disturbance of the blood chemistry and dehydration. Repeated vomiting and abuse of laxatives result in changes of the body chemistry. Occasionally, although quite rare, excessive vomiting can lead to rupture of the stomach or oesophagus. Acid from the stomach can erode the enamel that will cause lasting damage to teeth. There is also an association with ovarian cysts that may reduce fertility. The psychological consequences of bulimia include depression and social isolation.

The causes of bulimia remain unknown. Suggested causes of the disorder are similar to that of anorexia and include genetic vulnerability, biological, social, cultural and psychological factors.

The treatment of bulimia is mainly through cognitive-behavioural therapy (cognitive restructuring), behaviour therapy (exposure with response prevention) and group therapy often in conjunction with antidepressant medication. Bulimics who are extremely underweight overlap with the diagnosis of anorexia nervosa and may require hospitalisation. Some bulimics require hospital care due to having multiple disorders (abusing drugs, alcohol or self-harm).

Clark, D.M. and Fairburn, C.G. (eds) (1997) Science and Practice of Cognitive Behaviour Therapy. Oxford, Oxford University Press.
Gilbert, S. (2000) Counselling for Eating Disorders. London, SAGE Publications.
Gordon, R.A. (2000) Eating Disorders: Anatomy of a Social Epidemic, 2nd edn. Oxford, Blackwell Publishers.

Contact

The Eating Disorders Association (see under Anorexia).

Bullying

Bullying refers to deliberate and persistent verbal, psychological or physical intimidation which occurs over a period of time and which is directed at victims who are not in a position to protect themselves from attack.

The incidence of bullying is now known to be high; the Sheffield Bullying Project 1991 found that ten per cent of children in primary schools and five per cent of children in secondary schools were bullied at least once a week. In addition, 27 per cent of primary school children and ten per cent of secondary schoolchildren reported that they had been bullied at some time during that term. The researchers found that there was a steady decrease in the numbers of children being bullied as they got older but the number of children who continued to bully remained the same. These results are broadly in line with other findings and there is now official recognition that bullying in schools is a serious and widespread problem. Between 1998 and 1999, 22,332 calls from children complaining of bullying were received by the national charity Childline. It has been reported that between ten and 14 cases of childhood suicide take place every year as a direct result of bullying. The severity and high incidence of bullying was first recognised and referred to in The Elton Report 'Discipline in Schools' 1989. Staff and teachers were instructed to be alert to signs of bullying and racial harassment, to deal firmly with such behaviours and to take appropriate action to protect and support victims of bullying. Since September 1999, schools are required by law to draw up an anti-bullying policy. In the framework for the inspection of schools that are carried out by OFSTED, inspection teams are expected to collect evidence on the views of parents, teachers and pupils on the incidence of bullying. The inspection report should include a statement on bullying and the school's policy and practice to counter it.

Both boys and girls bully others; however the most common perpetrators of bullying are individual boys or groups of boys, although that this has been found to be so is likely to be because it is more socially acceptable for boys to admit to bullying. Boys are more likely to be involved in physical bullying whereas girls are more likely to be involved in relational bullying. Bullies are often characterised as being antisocial, physically robust and coming from families that are coercive and cold. Victims of bullying are often characterised as timid and anxious and frequently over-protected within the family context. Children with special educational needs appear to be at a greater risk of being bullied. Peers may encourage the bully by being spectators, by commenting, by taunting and by fearing or respecting the bully. The long-term effects of bullying have been investigated and it has been established that young bullies have a one in four chance of having a criminal record by the age of 30 while other children have a one in twenty chance. There is evidence that factors related to a child's upbringing affected their chances of becoming bullies. Three significant factors have been established:

- lack of parental warmth and concern in the early years;
- parents who use or tolerate aggressive behaviour;
- parents who use physical punishment as a matter of routine.

Interventions to tackle bullying in schools

These can be divided into (a) preventative work and (b) responding effectively to a bullying incident. Preventative work includes assertiveness training for bullied pupils that is aimed at developing a child's self-esteem and increasing their confidence through learning a series of techniques which facilitate effective communication. Another intervention is anger management training whereby young people are taught how to identify situations that result in aggressive responses in order to learn more appropriate strategies for managing their feelings and behaviour. There are a number of different approaches to responding effectively to bullying. Peer Mediation schemes involve training students in the formal skills of peer mediation. The 'No Blame' approach is a counselling method that stresses a non-punitive response to bullying. It acknowledges that many bullies have problems themselves and tries to effect change through facilitating the bullies to think about how the bullied child feels and to seek a solution to the situation. Conciliation is another intervention which involves older students volunteering to act as counsellors. The students are trained in counselling and supervised by an experienced adult. Circle Time is a method which involves the whole class talking about any worries or problems they might have and this can result in discussion of bullying that individuals are experiencing.

Besag, V.E. (1989) Bullies and Victims in Schools. Oxford, Oxford University Press.
Smith, P.K. and Sharp. S. (eds) (1994) School Bullying: Insights and Perspectives. London, Routledge.
Tattum, D. and Herber. G. (1993) Countering Bullying Initiatives by Schools and Local Authorities. Stoke on Trent, Trentham Books.

Contacts

General Advice on Bullying: Kidscape, 152 Buckingham Palace Road, London SW1W 9TR. Helpline for parents Tel. 020 7730 3300 (Monday to Friday, 10 a.m.–4 p.m.). Provides free leaflets and booklets for parents, children and teenagers about bullying.

The Samaritans, PO Box 90 90, Slough SL1 1UU. Tel. 0345 909090. Provides confidential emotional support for anyone in crisis. Specially trained volunteers will listen to callers without judging them or telling them what to do. They can be contacted by telephone, face to face visit, letter or e-mail.

Childline, Freepost 1111, London N1 0BR. Freephone 0800 1111. A 24 hour helpline for children and young people in danger or distress or with any problem.

British Association of Counselling, 1 Regent Place, Rugby, Warwickshire CV21 2PJ. Tel. 01788 578328. Members of the BAC have experience of a wide range of counselling.

Bullying at School:

Advisory Centre for Education (ACE), 1B Aberdeen Studios, 22 Highbury Grove, London N5 2EA.
Advice line for parents, teachers and governors: Tel. 020 7354 8321 (2 p.m.–5 p.m. Monday to Friday).

Children's Legal Centre. Tel. 01206 873820 (10 a.m.–noon, 2 p.m.–5 p.m. Monday–Friday). Free legal advice on the bullying of children.

National Child Protection Helpline (NSPCC). Freephone 0800 800500.

A 24 hour helpline for anyone concerned about a child at risk of abuse (including bullying), including children themselves.

Bullying in the workplace:

National Workplace Bullying Advice Line, Dept C5, PO Box 67, Didcot, Oxon OX11 0YH. Advice Line 01235 834 548.

C

Capgras syndrome

This syndrome is a delusion that impostors or 'look-a-likes' have replaced people whom one knows, particularly one's friends or family members.

Case study

A case study is an intensive study of an individual or group. A single subject case study is a study of the treatment of an individual's emotional or behavioural problems and the results of that treatment over time. A single case cannot be deemed representative of other people and does not provide a definitive explanation of that individual's change in relation to behavioural or emotional problems. Other concurrent factors may bring about change. Case studies may suffer from researcher or subject bias. Therefore case studies have low reliability. Confidentiality issues may arise over the use of case studies. However case studies can be useful in studying rare conditions and for generating and testing hypotheses.

Case studies can be structured according to the RAFIE five stage model: referral, assessment, formulation, intervention and evaluation. The assessment, formulation, intervention and evaluation stages will reflect a chosen perspective. The evaluation of an intervention or treatment applied to a case can be through single subject, reversal and multiple baseline studies.

Castration complex

A Freudian psychoanalytic term. Men and boys are said to suffer from castration anxiety over real or imagined castration threats, loss of the ability to perform sexual functions and diminution in terms of masculinity. Women and girls are said to experience a castration complex whereby they experience a lack of a penis and seek symbolic substitutes or experience anxiety over an organ or activity that is a penis substitute.

Catalepsy

Catalepsy is a condition where a person maintains a rigid bodily position over a long period of time. This can occur when people suffer from catatonia, in certain cases of brain damage and under hypnosis.

Catatonic behaviour/catatonia

Catatonia is a combination of extreme negative symptoms found in schizophrenia. These symptoms take the form of negativism or non-compliance with reasonable requests, mutism, a refusal to communicate, stupor, not responding to external events as if in a stupor. Patients if in a state of waxy flexibility or catalepsy can as it were be posed through the manipulation of the position of their limbs. Alternatively patients may assume unusual postures for extended periods of time, called posturing.

Catecholamine hypothesis

The catecholamine hypothesis asserts that there is a biochemical basis for schizophrenia and for mood disorders such as mania and depression. Catecholamines that function as neurotransmitters include norepinephrine, serotonin and dopamine. Excessive levels of norepinephrine are believed to elicit mania and reduced levels are thought to produce depression. Mood disorders are thought to involve serotonin. Schizophrenia is seen as resulting from excessive levels of catecholamines, especially dopamine in synaptic clefts in the brain.

Catharsis

Catharsis is a Freudian psychoanalytic term that refers to the feelings of release from tension, fear and anxiety that are the consequence of the discharge of repressed desires, wishes and memories into consciousness. There are doubts about the alleged cathartic effect of watching or engaging in sporting activities. Engaging in or watching sporting activities is likely to increase or maintain aggression rather than diminish or extinguish it.

Cathexis

Cathexis is a Freudian sychoanalytic term that refers to the emotional energy or charge connected to a drive. It also refers to the process of investing emotional energy into a part-object or an external object or person.

Causation

The development of behaviour and in particular the development of emotional and behavioural problems is influenced by many factors, therefore the focus is on multiple or plural causation. Causal factors cited will depend on the chosen perspective(s), e.g. biological, behavioural, cognitive or systems perspectives. However, generally speaking, reference is frequently made to the following factors: risk, protective, contextual, predisposing, precipitating and perpetuating factors.

Protective factors include physical healthiness, easy temperament, high intelligence, high self-esteem, high self-efficacy, optimism, coping skills, secure attachment, mature defence mechanisms and a social support network.

Contextual factors include those that are operative in the family and school contexts.

Predisposing factors include genetic abnormalities, pre-natal and perinatal complications, injuries and diseases, low intelligence, temperamental difficulties and low self-esteem. Other predisposing factors include family disorganisation and stress, insecure parent-child attachment, parental mental illness, marital conflict, authoritarian, permissive and neglecting parental style, child abuse, separation and bereavement.

Precipitating factors or triggers include stressors such as traumas, illnesses, injuries, physical, sexual and emotional abuse, bullying, separation and bereavements. Other precipitating factors include lifespan transitions such as adolescence, change of schools and loss of friendships. Family precipitating factors include divorce and separation, financial difficulties and moving to a new home or neighbourhood.

Perpetuating factors include maladaptive beliefs, irrational beliefs, cognitive distortions, low self-efficacy, learned helplessness, hostile attributional bias, immature defence mechanisms, inadequate coping strategies, neurotransmitter and hormonal dysfunctions.

Child abuse

Child abuse includes physical, emotional and sexual abuse. Where abuse is suspected multidisciplinary assessment and multisystemic interventions are advised.

Physical abuse

Physical abuse often occurs along with neglect but also may occur along with emotional and sexual abuse. It usually occurs within families. It takes the form of intentional injury. The prevalence of physical abuse depends on one's definition. Physical abuse often results in low self-esteem, low self-efficacy, attachment difficulties, relationship problems and emotional and behavioural problems such as anxiety, depression, self-injury and aggression. These problems are frequently manifested in adolescence and adulthood. There may also be short-term cognitive and language difficulties. Many children who run away from home have been abused. Physical abuse is manifested in a variety of ways but there are no definitive criteria or guidelines. However, certain types of injuries raise suspicion, e.g. patterns of bruises, burns, bites, head injuries, scalding, rib fractures and black eyes. Parental responses also raise suspicion, e.g. incompatible, contradictory accounts of the injuries, blaming others including the child, delay in seeking help, defensiveness and refusals to cooperate.

Physical abuse is usually triggered by the child's behaviour in the form of crying, wetting or disobedience, particularly if the parents are already in an emotionally aroused state. Parents who abuse are unable to cope without resorting to corporal punishment as the main coping strategy. These parents attribute negative intentions to the child in order to justify their actions and fail to empathise with their child's situation. Parents may abuse their children in ways that they were abused as children themselves.

Children who are abused are often young, below five years and of both sexes. There are various possible risk factors, e.g. premature birth, developmental delays, illness, difficult temperament and aggressive behaviour.

Parents who are young and who frequently resort to corporal punishment are more likely to abuse their children. Those parents who experience depression, personality disorders and who are substance abusers are also more likely to abuse their children. They are also more likely to have experienced attachment difficulties with their parents in their childhoods, to have developed negative attributions about their children and to be experiencing marital conflict. This conflict takes the form of rigid demands, winner-loser negotiating styles and blaming each other for their problems that often ends in cycles of violence.

Social factors also play a part, e.g. the parents' social isolation, poverty, overcrowded housing, single parenthood and a poor level of educational achievement.

Interventions with the parents are based on parent training and family therapy approaches practised in the parents' home. Interventions are more likely to be effective where parents accept responsibility, are concerned to meet their children's needs and are willing and able to pursue their own psychological health. Parents are trained in problem solving, communication skills, anger management, cognitive-behavioural and family therapy techniques (reframing) in order to achieve specific targets. Social support may be available through for example a home help, a parent support group, a mother and toddler group, relief foster care and housing transfer.

Physical abuse has been predicted on the basis of checklists that screen for child abuse potential; these are, however, associated with a significant number of false positives.

Emotional abuse

Emotional abuse can take active or passive forms. It is difficult to reach a consensus on the definitions of emotional abuse and neglect. Many cases are undetected and therefore untreated. Neglect can take the form of not meeting the child's physical, safety, social and emotional needs. This neglect is often unintentional and due to the parent's lack of awareness and knowledge and lack of appropriate coping skills. Abuse is the intentional and frequent use of punishment, negative criticism, rejection, denigration of friends, family members and other people. Such abuse is often based on negative attributions, inappropriate developmental expectations, inadequate or negative socialisation and using the child to meet parental emotional needs.

Where emotional abuse or neglect has occurred, children can manifest a failure to thrive, e.g. in terms of low weight, short stature, cognitive, social and motor developmental delays, insecure attachment, passivity, tearfulness, sadness and social withdrawal. They can also suffer from psychosocial dwarfism, i.e. be very short for their age, display unusual eating habits, attachment problems and behavioural difficulties.

Interventions take the form of parent training.

Sexual abuse

Sexual abuse is defined as using a child for sexual pleasure and varies in terms of frequency and degrees of intrusion. Abuse may occur from within or from outside the home. The prevalence of sexual abuse depends on definitions and criteria. More females are abused than males and most abusers are men. It occurs at all ages but peaks with girls at ages six to seven and at the onset of adolescence. Within the family, abuse tends to be committed by fathers, stepfathers and siblings, and outside the family abuse is due to babysitters, club leaders, friends, neighbours and teachers. Abusers often seek to justify their actions and deny the negative effects of their abuse. They use coercion and rewards to beak down the child's resistance, to gain the child's compliance and to enforce secrecy. Abused children may develop negative self-beliefs, e.g. blame themselves and feel as though they are 'damaged goods'. These beliefs may then result in self-destructive behaviours, e.g. self-injury, substance abuse and suicide. Abused children may also develop behavioural and educational problems. Other family members may blame the child for the abuse. Abused children may also develop feelings of powerlessness and may later in life when the opportunity arises use coercion to control others who are vulnerable.

Risk factors associated with the abused child include learning difficulties, physical disabilities, total deference to the wishes of others, incomprehension, lack of support and lack of positive relationships, low self-esteem and low self-efficacy.

There are various perspectives on child abuse.

- the attachment perspective regards child abuse as being due to poor or inadequate adult-child relationships;
- the psychodynamic as due to a punitive superego directing aggression towards children;
- the learning as due to inadequate parenting skills;
- the cognitive as due to parents seeing children as simply being an extension of themselves;
- the social interactionist perspective sees child abuse as the consequence of an interaction between inadequate parenting skills and the responses of children that highlight those inadequacies;
- the family systems perspective sees child abuse within the family as a consequence of scapegoating, as a means of attacking the other parent or partner or as a means of keeping the family together;
- the ecological perspective sees child abuse as a function of social and economic deprivation, social stress and social isolation;
- the sociocultural perspective sees child abuse as deriving from socially sanctioned forms of corporal punishment;
- the feminist perspective regards child abuse as a consequence of the exercise of patriarchal authority.

Corby, B. (2000) Child Abuse, 2nd edn. Buckingham, Open University Press.

Deblimger, A. and Heflinger, A. (1996) Treating Sexually Abused Children and their Non-offending Parents: A Cognitive Behavioural Approach. Thousand Oaks, CA, SAGE Publications.

Drauker, C.B. (2000) Counselling Survivors of Childhood Sexual Abuse, 2nd edn. London, SAGE Publications.

Iwaniec, D. (1995) The Emotionally Abused and Neglected Child: Identification, Assessment and Intervention. Chichester, Wiley.

Pearce, J. and Pezzot-Pearce, T. (1997) Psychotherapy of Abused and Neglected Children. New York, Guilford Press.

Contacts

Child Line 24 hour helpline 0800 1111.
NSPCC 24 hour helpline 0800 800500.

Childhood disorders

There are a variety of perspectives on childhood disorders: biological, behavioural, cognitive, cognitive-behavioural, psychodynamic and systems approaches. Childhood disorders are seen in relation to normal psychological development. The assessment of childhood disorders is based on observations and ratings by parents, carers and teachers and also through the self-reports of children. Childhood disorders are often assessed or rated through the use of standardised rating scales, e.g. the Child Behavior Checklist, (Achenbach 1991). The DSM IV (APA 1994) is a widely used classification system for diagnosing childhood disorders.

Childhood disorders are often seen as belonging under two categories, externalising and internalising disorders. Internalising disorders include anxiety, depression, withdrawal, isolation and eating disorders. Externalising disorders include aggression, violence and hyperactivity. Boys are more frequently referred for externalising disorders and girls for internalising disorders.

The main childhood disorders are conduct disorders, ADHD, anxiety disorders (generalised anxiety disorder, obsessive-compulsive disorders and school phobia), depression, eating disorders (anorexia nervosa, bulimia nervosa and obesity), pervasive developmental disorders (autism, Asperger's syndrome) and tics and elimination disorders (enuresis and encopresis).

Carr, A. (1999) The Handbook of Child and Adolescent Clinical Psychology. London, Routledge.
Carr, A. (2001) Abnormal Psychology. Hove, Psychology Press.
Kendall, P.C. (2000) Childhood Disorders. Hove, Psychology Press.

Circle of Friends

Circle of Friends originated in Canada as a specific method for supporting children and young people with disabilities in mainstream schools. It has also been used as a way of supporting young people with severe emotional and behavioural difficulties by providing the child with a friendship group. Circle of Friends is based on an approach, which attempts to mobilise peers to provide support and to engage in joint problem solving with the target or focus child. It attempts to change the negative cycle of isolation or rejection which the child is experiencing by mobilising the peer group to help the target child feel supported and to reduce negative behaviour. The method involves an educational psychologist whose role initially is to talk with a whole class, without the target child present, but with the agreement of the child and parents. The aim of the discussion is to enlist a small group of children who then form a circle, which meets regularly with the target child. A teacher or counsellor acts as a facilitator for the group and supports the group in identifying problems and strategies. The progress made in these sessions can be reviewed at the next meeting. The key characteristics of Circle of Friends includes forming a friendship group, promoting a positive ethos, encouraging problem solving, developing active listening, maintaining confidentiality, openness and empathy. Circle of Friends is a tool for inclusion as it aims to build relationships around individuals who are vulnerable to exclusion.

Newton, C. and Wilson, D. (1999) Circle of Friends. Folens Ltd.

Circle Time

Circle Time is a peer group intervention, which has been introduced in schools to support all children, including those with emotional and behavioural difficulties. It involves a group work approach focusing on sharing perceptions and working through problems as a group.

The aim of Circle Time is to support children's emotional well being and learning by developing self-esteem and confidence in a safe and containing setting – the Circle. In Circle Time, the children sit in a circle and take part in a programme of activities that takes account of their age. These activities are aimed to both motivate and challenge children and to develop their active listening skills, social skills, problem solving skills, increase their awareness of their own feelings as well as feelings of others with the overall objective being to promote positive behaviour. Activities may include cooperative games, rounds, talking and listening exercises, brainstorming and conferencing. The essential prerequisites for Circle Time to be a successful includes:

- sitting in a circle so as to promote equality and inclusion;
- establishing ground rules in particular confidentiality;
- valuing all contributions, i.e. when one person speaks we all listen, allowing children to 'pass' if they do not wish to contribute to an activity;
- positive comments are made throughout the sessions as well as ending the circle

session on a positive note.

Circle Time sessions are flexible but they typically start with a 'warm-up' activity: for example, a game, the aim of which is to encourage the group to work together cooperatively; following this 'a round' can be introduced to enable everyone to contribute to the work of the circle. In a round children usually complete a phrase, for example, 'A friend is someone who …'. This is followed by the main activity, which will be dependent on the age of the children who take part and the focus of the circle, for example, bullying and friendships. The Circle Time usually concludes with a game in order to bring the group back together in an enjoyable way.

Since Circle Time was first introduced it has been used with small groups of children, classes and whole schools. The age range of children and young people that take part is from five to eighteen. The sessions are usually held at least once a week and the length of the session varies according to the age of the children, usually half an hour for primary age children and up to an hour for secondary age students.

There have only been a few studies that have tried to evaluate the effectiveness of Circle Time in promoting positive behaviour and enhancing the self-esteem of the participants. Most proponents of Circle Time tend to rely on impressionistic reports by the adults involved. The few studies that have been undertaken have reported some discrepancies between the adults and the children who participated, as well as identifying practical difficulties.

Curry, M. and Bromfield, C. (1995) Circle Time. Stoke-on-Trent, Nasen.
Mosely, J. (1996) Quality Circle Time. Cambridge, LDA.
Mosely, J. and Tew, M. (1999) Quality Circle Time in the Secondary School: A Handbook of Good Practice. London, David Fulton Publishers.

Classical conditioning

Classical conditioning is a form of learning whereby a neutral stimulus produces an involuntary response. It involves conditioned and unconditioned stimuli and responses. A neutral stimulus that is frequently paired with a perilous situation becomes a conditioned stimulus and leads to an unconditioned response, namely fear. When the neutral stimulus itself leads to fear, the fear becomes a conditioned response. Phobias or specific fears (a fear of animals) have been explained as due to classical conditioning.

Classical psychoanalysis

Classical psychoanalysis refers to basic Freudian analysis and analytic techniques. It includes the following concepts: the unconscious, id, ego and superego, sexual and aggressive drives or instincts, the death instinct, the pleasure and reality principles, psychosexual stages, fixation, regression, repression, the Oedipus complex, the fundamental or basic rule, free association, interpretation, defence mechanisms, resistance, transference and counter-transference. Classical psychoanalysis focused on neuroses, in particular actual, infantile, narcissistic and psychosomatic neuroses, and psychoneuroses such as anxiety, phobia, obsessional, conversion and transference neuroses. The aims of psychoanalysts were to resolve unconscious and dynamic conflicts through bringing them into their patients' conscious awareness. The patients thereby gained insight into their problems and were now in a better position to resolve their problems. There were various schisms from classical psychoanalysis (Freudian) including Jung's analytical psychology, and Adler's individual psychology. Later other post-Freudian approaches developed, including those of Klein, Winnicott, Erikson, Bion, Bowlby, Kohut, Lacan, Object Relations and the Neo-Freudians such as Fromm and Horney. There are disagreements over theory and practice between the different schools of psychoanalysis; and there are controversies over the evaluation of psychodynamic approaches to emotional and behavioural problems, for example whether scientific methodology is the appropriate means of evaluating psychodynamic approaches.

Bateman, A. and Holmes, J. (1995) Introduction to Psychoanalysis: Contemporary Theory and Practice. London, Routledge.

Claustrophobia

Claustrophobia is one of a group of phobic disorders known as specific phobias. It is characterised by an intense fear of closed and confined spaces such as lifts, small rooms, etc. The incidence of specific phobias is relatively high and can affect up to 11 per cent of the general population, with women being twice as likely to suffer as men.

See under Anxiety

Client-centred therapy (person-centred therapy)

Client-centred therapy (also known as person-centred or Rogerian therapy) is a holistic or humanistic therapy developed by Carl Rogers. The focus of client-centred therapy is the individual client or person as a whole rather than any theoretical system or rules for understanding behaviour. Consequently, the therapist does not provide goals for clients but encourages clients to decide on their own goals and assists clients in exploring and developing their own inner resources. The principle underlying client-centred therapy is the belief that human beings are intrinsically trustworthy and motivated to actualise their potential for growth, 'the actualising tendency'. People are perceived as basically constructive, social and as motivated to seek self-fulfilment and as needing self-regard. The client-centred therapist offers the client empathy, congruence or genuineness and unconditional positive regard. This is done by creating a warm and accepting atmosphere, by mirroring whatever feelings the client expresses and by trying to see the world through the eyes of the client. This results in the client accepting his or her experience of reality as a source of value. The examination of self and experience in a non-threatening and supportive setting encourages the client to become aware of previously denied feelings. This in turn affects their self-perception and as a result their behaviour. A client's self-concept is not fixed but can change over time. If a significant discrepancy arises between the perceived self and actual experience then incongruence occurs. This occurs where experience is distorted or denied. This incongruence is perceived as a threat to the self and leads to psychological problems that generate anxiety and confusion. If for example parents impose conditions of self-worth on their child, then experiences that undermine the child's conception of self-worth will be seen as threatening and will be rejected.

Rogers, C.R. (1951) Client Centred Therapy, Boston, Houghton Mifflin.
Nelson-Jones, R. (2001) Theory and Practice of Counselling and Therapy, 3rd edn. London, Continuum.
Thorne, B. (1992) Carl Rogers. London, SAGE Publications.

Cognitive appraisal

Cognitive appraisal is a theory of the emotions that refers to a process whereby experiences are mediated through an individual's belief system. The emotion felt will depend on the application of the individual's belief system to the experience. People who experience panic attacks are seen as misinterpreting anxiety sensations in a catastrophic fashion, for example seeing them as symptoms of an impending heart attack.

Cognitive appraisal is also a factor in problem-solving approaches. It can be divided into three components: primary appraisal, deciding whether a difficulty exists; secondary appraisal, deciding whether one can cope with the problem, and finally tertiary appraisal, beliefs about one's control over the problem. Cognitive appraisal will therefore be influential in determining whether stress occurs.

Cognitive-behavioural perspective

The cognitive-behavioural approach regards all behaviour normal and abnormal, as being associated with or influenced by cognitions (attitudes and assumptions) or cognitive appraisal, i.e. thinking and reasoning processes. The main aims of this approach are to monitor cognitions and to identify the connections between thoughts, feelings and behaviour and to substitute positive cognitions for negative ones. The approach is psychoeducational and aims to enlist the active involvement of the client.

The two main cognitive-behavioural treatment approaches are Rational-Emotive Behavioural Therapy (REBT) (A. Ellis) and Cognitive Therapy (CT) (A. T. Beck). Other approaches include Self-Instructional Training (D. Meichenbaum), Problem-Solving Therapy (T. J. D'Zurilla), Stress-Inoculation Training (D. Meichenbaum) and Attribution Retraining (A. Bandura and M. L. Weiner).

The main concepts of REBT are rational and irrational beliefs. The main concepts of

CT are the cognitive triad; cognitive schemas, in particular the depressogenic schema; automatic thoughts, cognitive deficits and distortions. Irrational thinking and reasoning is characterised by absolutistic thoughts and unwarranted inferences. Modification or rectification of irrational thinking or reasoning promotes adaptive behaviour.

Cognitive-behavioural approaches have been used to address anger, depression and anxiety. Anger has been addressed through self-monitoring and increasing self-awareness and self-understanding of anger reactions. Interventions include planned avoidance of provocation, distancing oneself in space and time from provocative situations and disrupting anger through introducing new anger-incompatible stimuli. Other interventions include relaxation, restructuring cognitive distortions (examples of distortions are overestimating negative events, arriving at negative attributions and conclusions, making rigid absolutistic demands, assuming catastrophic consequences, inflammatory and either-or thinking and over-generalisation).

Clark, D.M. and Fairburn, C.G. (1997) Science and Practice of Cognitive Behaviour Therapy. Oxford, Oxford University Press.

Craighead, L.W., Craighead, W.E., Kazdin, A.E. and Mahoney, M.J. (eds) (1994) Cognitive and Behavioral Interventions. Boston, MA, Allyn and Bacon.

Graham, P. (ed.) (1998) Cognitive-Behaviour Therapy for Children and Families. Cambridge, Cambridge University Press.

Ronen, T. (1997) Cognitive Developmental Therapy with Children. Chichester, Wiley.

Sheldon, B. (1995) Cognitive-Behavioural Therapy: Research, Practice and Philosophy. London, Routledge.

Tarrier, N., Wells, A. and Haddock, G. (eds) (1998) Treating Complex Cases. The Cognitive Behavioural Therapy Approach. Chichester, Wiley.

Cognitive dissonance

Cognitive dissonance refers to a perceived discrepancy or inconsistency between two cognitions such as attitude or beliefs that leads to a state of psychological tension. This is referred to as dissonance. This dissonance is experienced as a tension that leads to attempts to reduce the dissonance by changing one's attitude or belief, by diminishing the perceived importance of one's attitudes or beliefs and by adopting further justifying attitudes or beliefs. In other words, attempts are made to change or modifying one's beliefs in order to make the beliefs consistent.

Cognitive restructuring

Cognitive restructuring is a cognitive technique that aims to restructure or change distorted or negative thinking and reasoning patterns into ones that are positive. For example, in the case of eating disorders there are examples of distorted thinking in terms of weight-related and shape-related cognitions. Cognitive-restructuring can be facilitated by a cognitive functional analysis and through the use of a cognitive restructuring diary that asks people to record their positive and negative thoughts and their evidence for and against those thoughts.

Graham, P. (ed.) (1998) Cognitive-Behaviour Therapy for Children and Families, Cambridge, Cambridge University Press.

Winston LeCroy, C. (ed.) (1994) Handbook of Child and Adolescent Treatment Manuals. New York, Lexington Books.

Cognitive therapy

Cognitive therapy originated in the work of Aaron T. Beck. His approach is based on a phenomenological and information-processing model. The emphasis is on conscious, cognitive processes, namely perceiving, thinking and reasoning. The focus is on how cognitive processes affect feelings and behaviour. People are seen as constructing their own experiences and beliefs, i.e. people perceive and assign meanings to happenings in their lives. Feelings and behaviour are influenced by cognitive appraisal, the ways in which we think or reason about our feelings and behaviour. Beliefs are accessible through direct questioning, i.e. self-reports. Voluntary thoughts are the most accessible; automatic thoughts arise apparently spontaneously, are difficult to control and likely to cause emotional distress. Out of awareness lie schemas, deeper cognitive processes that determine one's views of one's world, self and one's relationships with others. Schemas are formed through early learning experiences and contain one's core beliefs. Schemas when activated are maintained and reinforced by cognitive distortions. Cognitive distortions bias the selection of information and serve to maintain a given schema. Cognitive distortions include over-generalisation, dichotomous thinking, abstraction, minimisation, maximisation, arbitrary inference and personalisation. Cognitive deficits, e.g. in memory, inference and perception also help to maintain schemas. An example of a cognitive deficit is a failure to foresee the consequences of one's actions. As a result thinking and reasoning become rigid and inflexible and judgments become absolute.

Psychological problems are seen as lying along a continuum and are conceived of as exaggerations of normal responses, this is called the continuity hypothesis. Such problems are addressed through encouraging and supporting people in logical and empirical reappraisal of their beliefs. People are encouraged to look for alternative explanations and interpretations of events, different courses of actions and ways of behaving.

Beck developed a theory of depression that is based on the idea of a latent, negative depressogenic schema, a cognitive vulnerability, triggered by events like loss, separation and failure. There is a bias towards selecting negative events while screening out positive events. The activation of the schema leads to hopelessness, sadness and apathy. People as a result become inactive, passive, pessimistic and socially isolated. The cognitive triad is triggered in depression, a negative view of one's self, one's world and one's future. Depression is not caused by the activation of negative schemas but rather affects its development. The causes of depression may be due to the interaction of a number of factors.

Beck also developed a theory of anxiety. The cognitions identified are unrealistic ideas of danger, catastrophic feelings of loss of control and perceived negative changes in relationships. The cognitive distortions maintaining anxiety are seen as overestimating the likelihood and severity of feared events and underestimating one's coping skills, resources and external support. Panic reactions are seen as being triggered by a person's catastrophic misinterpretation of physiological responses as symptoms of an impending medical emergency, e.g. a heart attack.

Beck's therapeutic approach is based on his cognitive model of emotional disorders. Cognitive therapy is brief and depends on accessing the client's conscious thinking and reasoning processes. There must be an understanding of clients' thinking and reasoning processes and their underlying schemas in relation to their emotional problems. The therapist actively questions the client through a Socratic dialogue about their relevant beliefs but the client also assists the therapist to identify and test those beliefs, this process is called collaborative empiricism. Clients are seen as co-investigators and are further involved through generating hypotheses, finding solutions, setting goals, planning and practising homework and providing feedback. Through guided discovery clients are able to identify illogical beliefs and their connection to experiences. Clients are required to understand the cognitive approach, for example the relevance of their images, thoughts and beliefs to their problems and to identify their maladaptive beliefs. They are also taught to monitor thoughts associated with their emotions, i.e. automatic thoughts and core beliefs about themselves and about the future. Clients are asked to recall salient emotions and to record the thoughts accompanying them. Behavioural techniques such as exposure and respiratory control are used to facilitate positive changes in thoughts and beliefs.

Beck, A.T., Rush, A.J., Shaw, B.F. and Emery, G. (1979) Cognitive Theory of Depression. New York, Wiley. Nelson-Jones, R. (2001) Theory and Practice of Counselling and Therapy, 3rd edn. London, Contiuum. Weishaar, M.E. (1993) Aaron T. Beck. London, SAGE Publications.

Collective unconscious

The collective unconscious is a Jungian term that refers to that part of the unconscious that contains the archetypes, memories and experiences that all people share. These unconscious elements are inherited and are reflected in archetypes finding expression in dreams, myths, fairy tales and religious imagery. It is additional to the personal unconscious.

Compliance

Compliance refers to people conforming to certain procedures or protocols. People are compliant for example if they take prescription drugs as directed or conform to the requirements of therapeutic interventions. The effectiveness of biological treatments and psychotherapy are dependent on patients and clients being compliant. Non-compliance can be a serious problem affecting the recovery of patients from psychiatric disorders particularly if drugs are prescribed in the community rather than in the hospital context. Lack of compliance is due to a number of factors including negative drug side effects, lack of insight and knowledge of the disorder and treatment, dislike of medication and the need to go through complicated treatment procedures.

Compulsion

Compulsion refers to compulsive behaviour such as tidying and checking and compulsive mental processes such as counting and reciting. People feel compelled to perform compulsive behaviours or to think certain thoughts in order to avoid anxiety or some dire outcome. Compulsive rituals are seen by sufferers themselves as excessive and as not being likely to achieve the desired outcome, namely to reduce anxiety or avoid the feared outcome. However they do usually bring some relief, albeit temporary. Compulsions are a significant component of obsessive-compulsive disorder. The techniques of thought-stopping, distraction and setting time aside for rumination are used to treat compulsive thinking.

Concordance

Concordance is a term in genetics that refers to the proportion of monozygotic twins (identical twins) or genetically related relatives who share the same characteristics or phenotype. For example if both twins of a pair are schizophrenic they are described as concordant but if only one is schizophrenic they are described as discordant. The proportion of concordant pairs out of a total number of pairs in which one is schizophrenic is the concordance rate. The concordance rate for schizophrenia is about 53 per cent for identical twins and 15 per cent for fraternal twins. This indicates that there is a hereditary component to schizophrenia but that there is also an environmental component.

Faraone, S.V., Tsuang, M.T. and Tsuang, D.W. (1999) Genetics of Mental Disorders. New York, Guilford Press.

Conditioning

Conditioning is a generic term that covers various types of associative learning. Approaches based on conditioning assume that behaviour is learned except where it is influenced by genetic factors. Usually conditioning is divided into two main types, classical (respondent, Pavlovian) and operant (instrumental, Skinnerian).

In classical conditioning a neutral stimulus **(NS)** (bell) is paired with an unconditioned stimulus **(UCS)** (food) that produces an unconditioned response **(UCR)** (salivation). After a number of pairings the previously neutral stimulus becomes a conditioned stimulus **(CS)** (bell) that will of its own accord elicit the **(CR)** (salivation). If the **(CS)** (bell) is rung without the **(UCS)** (food) the **(CR)** (salivation) will eventually cease or extinguish.

Similar stimuli to the **CS** (bell) will also elicit the **(CR)** (salivation): this is called stimulus generalisation.

Classical conditioning has been put forward as an explanation for the acquisition of fears and phobias. Behaviour therapy is based on classical conditioning, for example in the treatment of enuresis (bell-and-pad procedure).

Operant conditioning occurs where an operant response (i.e. a behaviour having an effect on the environment) comes under stimulus control. The occurrence of a response depends on its subsequent reinforcement. Where this is the case then operant conditioning is in evidence. Responses are affected by subsequent events. If the events are positively reinforced then the responses are likely to increase or are strengthened. If the events are not reinforced then the responses are likely to decrease or be weakened. In a particular situation where an **SD**, a discriminative stimulus (teacher explains topic) is present, **R**, an operant response occurs (student attention) resulting in an **SR** reinforcing stimulus (teacher praise). Positive reinforcement occurs where the reinforcing stimulus (praise) increases the likelihood that the operant response (pupil attention) will recur. Negative reinforcement is where an operant response is increased or strengthened through the avoidance or withdrawal of a negative reinforcing stimulus (an unpleasant event). For example, a pupil pays attention, the teacher stops criticising and the student works harder. This is also called escape or avoidance learning. Punishment is different from negative reinforcement in that with punishment an unpleasant event (detention) is administered after an operant response (pupil shouts at teacher) and as a consequence the student stops shouting. Reinforcement can be continuous or intermittent, the various types of intermittent reinforcement are known as schedules, either interval or ratio in combination with fixed and variable, four in total.

Cramer, D. (1992) *Personality and Psychotherapy*. Milton Keynes, Open University Press.
Domjan, M. (1998) *The Principles of Learning and Behavior* (4th edn). Pacific Grove, CA, Brooks/Cole.

Conduct disorder

Conduct disorders are defined using DSM IV or ICD-10 criteria. The presenting symptoms are extreme antisocial behaviours, including fighting, stealing, vandalism, truancy, running away from home and substance abuse. Diagnosis refers to four categories: aggression against people or animals; destruction of property; theft, and other serious violation of rules such as truancy, running away from home. A diagnosis of a conduct disorder is made if an individual under 18 has committed any three behaviours in either of the categories within the period of a year and also presents with severe adjustment problems at home or at school. Conduct disorders are characterised by a need to assert one's self without feeling constrained, to be disobedient, to be negative, rude and argumentative and to sulk, bully others and to be selfish and impatient. There is also a lack of concern about the consequences of one's actions for the future. Disruptive children are less likely to understand or appreciate the feelings of victims.

Estimates of prevalence depend on the strictness of the diagnostic criteria. Estimates range from 4 to 16 per cent in the under-18 population. There is a preponderance of boys over girls by a ratio of between 4:1 to 12:1. Boys are seen as assertive, competitive and aggressive in relationships whereas girls are seen as more cooperative and conciliatory. Girls when aggressive are seen as more involved in relational forms of aggression.

Age of onset is considered to be significant enough to warrant a distinction between the childhood-onset type and the adolescent-onset type of conduct disorder. DSM IV requires the diagnostician to distinguish between those individuals who present with at least one symptom before the age of ten (a childhood-onset conduct disorder) and no symptoms before the age of ten (an adolescent-onset conduct disorder). Temper tantrums are common among pre-school children but disappear by the age of eight or nine. Childhood conduct disorders are frequently associated with anxiety and depression. Early onset is associated with adult antisocial behaviour and with alcohol and drug use. Adult antisocial behaviour can be ameliorated through marital and occupational stability and a move to a different geographical environment.

Risk factors include a difficult temperament, neurological problems, poor verbal skills, impulsivity, sensation-seeking behaviours, hostile attribution tendencies, problems at school and a family history of antisocial or aggressive behaviour. In the home risk factors include harsh and inconsistent disciplinary practices, lack of parental supervision and monitoring, parental conflict, parental psychiatric disorders, criminality and alcoholism, domestic violence and parental divorce. Other risk factors include large family size, over-crowding, inadequate accommodation and poor education. Disruptive and aggressive children are more likely to associate with deviant peer groups, to truant, to leave school with few qualifications and to commence sexual relationships and become parents at an early age.

Protective factors include an easy temperament, sociability, academic success, positive relationships with parents, higher self-esteem and internal locus of control, external support in the form of friendships and a significant adult.

Perspectives on conduct disorders are biological, behavioural, cognitive-behavioural, social learning, psychodynamic and systems theories.

- The biological perspective sees hereditary, hormonal, temperamental and neuropsychological factors as influencing the onset and development of conduct disorders.
- The behavioural perspective sees positive reinforcement of negative behaviours due to association with deviant and antisocial peers and modelling of negative behaviours by punitive parents as contributing to conduct disorders.
- The cognitive behavioural perspective sees maladaptive cognitive processing, namely cognitive deficits and distortions as underlying conduct disorders including a hostile attributional bias, social skills and problem solving deficits.
- The social learning perspective sees modelling and parental coercion as crucial in the

development of conduct disorders. Aggression is learned through adolescents modelling themselves on others, particularly parents who themselves use or display aggression. Coercive parenting also leads to aggressive behaviour through harsh, inconsistent
and ineffective punishment and the predominance of unrewarding-over-rewarding
family interactions.

- The psychodynamic perspective sees deficits in superego functioning and disrupted
and insecure attachments as underlying conduct disorders. Indulgent and punitive
parenting can both be responsible for superego deficits. The adolescent internalises
low standards from indulgent parents and feels guiltless when being aggressive. With
the punitive parent the adolescent internalises both good (caring) and bad (punitive)
introjects, the adolescent then behaves non-aggressively towards those perceived as
good (when they experience a positive transference) and aggressively towards those
perceived as bad (when they experience a negative transference). Adolescents who have
experienced insecure attachments in the past fail to develop or experience trusting relationships and as a result engage in aggressive behaviour.

- Systems theories include family systems theory, which sees adolescent aggression as
resulting from family disorganisation where rules, routines and boundaries are unclear
and inadequate. Family communication is also confusing and lacking in empathy.
Problem solving skills are poor and depend primarily on coercion. Multiple systems
theory sees many mutually interacting systems as generating aggressive adolescent
behaviour. Personal factors (e.g. difficult temperament), family factors (e.g. insecure
attachment), school factors (e.g. poor achievement) and social factors (e.g. delinquent
subculture) are all seen as contributing to the development of aggressive behaviour.

Many different types of interventions are used in the treatment of conduct disorder,
including psychotherapy, medication, home, school and community-based programmes as
well as residential and hospital treatment. Kazdin (1996) has identified over 200 different
therapy techniques the most promising of which in his view are cognitive problem solving
skills training, parent management training, functional family therapy and multi-systemic
therapy. Cognitive problem solving skills training focuses on cognitive processes that
underlie social behaviour. This approach aims to generate alternative solutions to conflict
situations. It appears more effective with adolescents than young children. Parent management training (PMT) is aimed at changing aversive parent-child interactions and enabling
parents to manage their child's behaviour more effectively. PMT includes operant techniques such as positive reinforcement along with mild sanctions. This demanding
approach depends on parental compliance and commitment and is more successful with
children than adolescents. Functional family therapy uses systems theory and behaviour
modification to bring about changes in the interactions, communication and problem
solving behaviour of the family members. Multi-systemic therapy addresses individual,
family and school systems and their interrelationships to promote appropriate social
behaviour. Family therapeutic techniques include reframing, paradoxical interventions

and allocating specific tasks. Conduct disorders generally have a poor long-term prognosis. Early-onset disorders in particular have a poor prognosis but adolescent-onset disorders have a better prognosis. Drop out rates from and terminations of treatments and interventions are high. Preventive interventions such as early childhood cognitive-behavioural interventions can be effective as can parent training and child social skills training.

Advice for teachers and parents who have children with conduct disorders

- Structure: Structured approaches are necessary such that the child knows what to do, when to do it and how to do it.
- Boundaries: The child should know and be aware of limits and boundaries and the consequences for overstepping those boundaries. The consequences should be immediate, definite and proportionate.
- Commands: The child should be given soft, clear, firm and definite commands.
- Seating arrangements: the child should sit nearby or be easily visible.
- Contact: The child should be closely supervised and monitored through discrete eye contact and scanning. The child should be offered escape routes in order to avoid explosive confrontations. Children should be supervised and monitored where possible outside the home as well as in the home. They should be discouraged or dissuaded from associating with deviant or antisocial peers.
- Opportunities: Children should be offered opportunities to self-regulate and to self-report.
- Tasks: Tasks should be structured, programmatic and at the child's level of competence. Feedback should be provided.
- Targets: Both learning and behavioural targets should be specific and achievable.
- Positive reinforcement (material and/or non-material) should be given for achieving specific target behaviours, minor rule infringements should be ignored and when punishment is appropriate it should be immediate, proportionate and effective.
- Where parents feel they lack adequate parenting skills they might benefit from acquiring parent management training skills.
- Where teachers feel they lack training in managing behaviour they may benefit from acquiring behaviour management skills or counselling skills.

Hill, J. and Maughan, B. (eds) (2001) Conduct Disorders in Childhood and Adolescence. Cambridge, Cambridge University Press.
Kazdin, A.E. (1996) Conduct Disorders in Childhood and Adolescence. London, Sage Publications.
Peterson, C. (1996) The Psychology of Abnormality. New York, Harcourt Brace College Publishers.

Confirmation bias

This term refers to the tendency for individuals to seek out evidence that confirms or validates beliefs and attitudes and to ignore evidence that might contradict those beliefs and attitudes. This tendency helps to explain prejudice and stereotyping.

Conflict resolution

Conflict resolution originated within business management and business-labour negotiations and is now applied to the field of education. Conflict resolution refers to negotiation strategies designed to reduce or eliminate conflicts. These can occur within a person, between two people, or between groups of people. Conflicts can be manifested in physical form (violence and vandalism) or symbolic form (abuse and threats). Avoidance, denial, diffusion and confrontation are some of the strategies used to resolve conflicts. Conflict resolution involves negotiation strategies. The distributive strategy is where people see themselves as adversaries trying to gain as much as possible for themselves (win-lose) but who reach agreement through a series of concessions. The integrative approach is where people try to find mutually beneficial solutions (win-win) and the people involved make concessions as well as look for mutually beneficial alternatives. It looks at problems in depth, particularly at underlying motives, needs and fears. The interactive problem solving approach begins with an analysis of the motives, needs, values and fears of the parties involved and of the factors that impede resolution of the conflict. The aim of this approach is to persuade the adversaries to approach the conflict as a problem to be jointly solved.

The success or failure of conflict resolution depends on the attitudes and skills of the people in conflict and on the skills of the mediator or arbitrator. These skills include awareness of the self in relation to others, awareness of others, awareness of and ability to articulate thoughts and feelings, listening skills and a readiness to respond to the thoughts and feelings of others. Resolution of conflict may proceed through several phases or stages: withdrawing completely, requesting or demanding concessions, providing reasons for concessions, providing alternative solutions and perspective taking. Conflict resolution can be integrated into the school curriculum, in workshops for negotiation and mediation skills and in mediation programmes. Peer mediation is an approach where students or pupils attempt to resolve disputes themselves. The aim is to prevent escalation of minor conflicts rather than to address physical conflicts. The process involves identifying problems, describing those problems, looking at underlying feelings, generating alternative solutions and finally coming to a mutually agreed solution expressed in a contract.

Conflict resolution is more likely to succeed where optimistic expectations are created, where perspective taking occurs and where perceptions of compatibility between the disputants' positions and needs are encouraged.

Advice to parents and teachers with regard to children and violent conflicts:

- Avoid modelling violent or threatening behaviour as a means of solving disputes or conflict.
- Describe the physical, psychological and legal consequences of violent conflicts and why they are best avoided.
- Advocate the following strategies for dealing with violent conflicts:
    - think before acting;
    - debate the opponent's point of view;
    - do not attack the opponent's personality, ethnicity, culture, religion, gender or sexual orientation;
    - do not show disrespect or try to humiliate opponents;
    - do not attempt to coerce others;
    - be prepared to lose an argument;
    - use humour to defuse conflict;
    - walk away from conflicts;
    - avoid associating with people who get into trouble;
    - avoid conflict situations;
    - compromise if possible;
    - try to see the other's point of view;
    - propose solutions that are win-win.

Girard, K. and Koch, S. (1998) Conflict Resolution in the Schools: A Manual for Educators. San Francisco, CA: Jossey-Bass.

Context effect

This term refers to any effect or influence of the environment or specific setting on an individual's response to a specific stimulus.

Contingency management

Contingency management is a behavioural approach that uses operant techniques such as positive and negative reinforcement and punishment programmes to manage individualised (unique target behaviours) standardised (token economy) and group (peer related) contingencies. This approach aims to manipulate the consequences of people's responses in order to change the frequency of those responses.

Conversion disorder (formerly known as 'hysteria')

The term conversion disorder refers to a condition in which the individual presents with a physical symptom which has no organic cause but is actually an expression of a psychological conflict or need. Some of the most common symptoms include blindness, hearing loss, paralysis and anaesthesia (loss of sensation) although less severe symptoms also occur such as nausea or constipation. The term conversion refers to the fact that the underlying psychological conflicts are unconsciously converted into physical symptoms. The condition is involuntary and it is generally agreed that conversion disorders provide relief for some internal conflict. Conversion disorders are at least twice as common in women than in men. DSM-IV criteria include the symptoms that are characteristic of Conversion Disorder and additionally require the diagnostician to provide evidence as to the psychological factors involved in the onset and exacerbation of the physical symptoms displayed.

Peterson, C. (1996) The Psychology of Abnormality. New York, Harcourt Brace College Publishers.

Counselling

Counselling is a generic term that is often used to refer to person-centred (client-centred or Rogerian) approaches to counselling. Sometimes the term counselling is used as a synonym for therapy. However there are many different types of counselling besides person-centred counselling. Some of the prevalent ones are behavioural, rational emotive behavioural, cognitive-behavioural, psychodynamic, gestalt, personal construct and transactional analysis. Other forms of counselling refer to particular types of client as well as to specific approaches, for example adolescent, transcultural, marital, feminist and gay counselling or they focus on specific problems such as anxiety, depression, post-traumatic stress and substance abuse.

Some counsellors are eclectic in that they use different approaches depending on the problem. Others integrate or combine different approaches. Counselling can be of couples, families, groups as well as individuals.

Counselling generally means a process whereby a counsellor forms a therapeutic alliance or relationship with clients who present particular emotional problems that they are experiencing. The counsellor in collaboration with the client helps the client to address the problem. The type of help and relationship depends on the nature of the counselling approach. Generally speaking an effective counsellor is required to possess the core qualities of genuineness, acceptance and empathy. Many different types of counselling have not been scientifically evaluated. Although counselling approaches differ, all depend to a significant extent on the personal qualities of the counsellor and the quality of the counselling relationship. Counselling has been found to be more effective than no counselling at all.

Bergin, A.E. and Garfield, S.L. (1994) Handbook of Psychotherapy and Behavior Change, 4th edn. New York, Wiley.

Feltham, C. and Horton, I. (eds) (2000) Handbook of Counselling and Psychotherapy. London, SAGE Publications.

McCleod, J. (1998) An Introduction to Counselling, 2nd edn. Buckingham, Open University Press.

McLaughlin, C., Clark, P. and Chisholm, M. (1996) Counselling and Guidance in Schools: Developing Policy and Practice. London, David Fulton Publishers.

Nelson-Jones, R. (2001) Theory and Practice of Counselling and Therapy, 3rd edn. London, Continuum.

Contacts

Counselling helplines:

Childline 24 hour helpline 0800 1111 (counselling for children).

Nafsiyat 020 7263 4130 (counselling for ethnic minority families and children from 12 years of age).

Samaritans helpline 0345 909090.

Counter-conditioning

Counter-conditioning occurs where an incompatible response is conditioned to an already conditioned stimulus. In behaviour therapy for example, counter-conditioning occurs where new responses to stimuli become incompatible with old responses. For instance, in systematic desensitisation relaxation is conditioned to a stimuli that originally produced a response of anxiety or fear.

Counter-transference

Counter-transference occurs where a counsellor or therapist experiences a positive or negative emotional response towards the client. The counter-transference responses are those evoked by the client. Counter-transference can be positive or negative. The counsellor can feel positively or negatively towards the client. The existence of counter-transference is now viewed as beneficial in that it enables counsellors or therapists to help further understand their clients through examining their own positive and negative feelings evoked by their clients.

Culture bound syndromes

Culture bound syndromes are behaviours that appear to relate to particular cultural or ethnic groups. Most psychiatric disorders are universally recognised, e.g. schizophrenia and depression. However certain disorders are related to particular cultures, e.g. amok (some countries in Asia), windigo (Algonquin Canadian Indians), latah (Malaysia) and koro (Southeast Asia). It is argued that culture influences the experience of disorders and the expression and presentation of symptoms.

Matsumoto, D. (2000) Culture and Psychology, 2nd edn. London, Wadsworth Thomson Learning.

D

Defence mechanisms

Defence mechanisms is a Freudian concept referring to the unconscious mechanisms that protect the ego from anxiety, unacceptable thoughts and desires. In psychoanalytic theory, anxiety is viewed as the product of unconscious, aggressive or sexual impulses that have been repressed. Defence mechanisms are mostly adaptive as they protect us from unpleasant feelings of anxiety, conflict and shame. A number of defence mechanisms have been hypothesised by Sigmund Freud and other psychoanalytic theorists such as Anna Freud and Melanie Klein. The main ones are repression, projection, displacement, rationalisation, regression, sublimation, reaction formation and denial. Repression is the most fundamental and universal of the defence mechanisms as it is the basis of all the other defence mechanisms. Generally it refers to the process whereby thoughts, memories and impulses that are unacceptable to the ego are pushed into the unconscious. Primal repression is where unacceptable impulses stemming from the id are prevented from reaching consciousness. Primary repression is where anxiety-inducing material in consciousness is excluded and prevented from returning. Secondary repression is where anything in consciousness that reminds one of repressed impulses is also excluded from consciousness. Projection takes place when unacceptable impulses are first repressed and then attributed to others; when this happens it can be the basis of paranoia and superstition. For example, people may have aggressive feelings towards other people but cannot recognise and acknowledge this and instead project these feelings onto others and perceive others as feeling aggressive towards them. Displacement occurs when feelings are transferred from an object or person to a substitute which is less threatening to the ego. This process of displacement may lead to a reduction or the avoidance of anxiety. Rationalisation is the process whereby a socially or ethically accepted reason for something that a person has done is unconsciously invented by the ego to protect itself from confronting the real reason for an action, thought or emotion. Regression is a defence mechanism that may take place as an attempt to deal with anxiety or stress by reverting to an earlier developmental stage of thinking or of object relationships that has already been passed through. For example, a teenager may begin to suck her thumb. Sublimation refers to the process whereby unacceptable impulses such as aggressive or sexual energies are transformed into actions that are socially acceptable. Reaction formation takes place when repressed impulses are replaced by thoughts and actions that are the exaggerated opposite of those repressed. Denial or disavowal is the refusal to acknowledge repressed feelings and impulses that are unacceptable or too painful to admit.

Laplanche, J. and Pontalis, J.B. (1973) The Language of Psychoanalysis. London, Karnac Books.

Delinquency

Delinquency refers to juvenile delinquency, a legal designation referring to those offences committed by young people or adolescents, usually up to 16 or 18 years old. In England the age of criminal responsibility is 10, in Scotland, 8. Young people, particularly males, are viewed as sources of crime and disorder, particularly in terms of theft, violence and illegal drug use. Currently, the concerns are the links between truancy, exclusions and crime. However it should be noted that adolescents are victims as well as offenders. Many young offenders have been in local authority care, have been persistent truants and have been permanently excluded from school.

A whole host of biological, psychological, educational and sociological explanations have been put forward for young offending. Biological explanations include genetic influences, low IQ, and temperamental factors. Educational explanations include school factors such as school ethos and poor educational achievement. Family factors include family breakdown, large family size, parental conflict, parental upbringing, parental criminality, physical and sexual abuse, physical and emotional neglect and poor peer relationships. Social factors include economically deprived neighbourhoods, exclusion from opportunities to acquire status and to enter the labour market, deviant subcultures, labelling and moral panics.

Government responses to delinquency include proposals to use curfews for those below ten years old, exclusion zones, fining parents, electronic monitoring (tagging), supervised leisure activities, after-school projects and holiday activity schemes. The government has also aimed to reduce truancy and exclusions through establishing Learning Support Units and Mentoring Programmes in schools and by raising the educational achievement of children and young people in public care.

Psychological responses have been based on cognitive-behavioural approaches and parent management training.

Muncie, J. (1999) Youth and Crime: A Critical Introduction. London, SAGE Publications.
Rutter, M., Giller, H. and Hagell, A. (1998) Antisocial Behavior by Young People. Cambridge, Cambridge University Press.

Delusion

A belief contrary to reality that is not based on evidence and that is resistant to refutation by logical and empirical argument. Beliefs are not held to be delusional if they conform to prevailing social and cultural norms. Delusions are disorders of thought content and can be primary or secondary. Primary delusions arise spontaneously, often commence with misinterpretation and are sustained by a mood of perplexity. Secondary delusions arise out of a pre-existing mood and are a response to environmental cues.

Delusions are common positive symptoms of schizophrenia. Persecutory delusions are particularly common. Other delusions include believing that one is experiencing unwelcome physical sensations, that thoughts are being planted in one's mind, that one's thoughts are being broadcast to or stolen by others and that one's actions and feelings are controlled by others. Delusions can be grandiose, can be preoccupations with sexual concerns and can be imbued with religious significance.

Schizophrenia is treated with antipsychotic or neuroleptic drugs like clozapine, olanzapine and resperidone that help to reduce positive symptoms such as delusions. However cognitive-behavioural therapy can also be used to help reduce delusions. This therapeutic process involves eliciting the delusional beliefs and the clients' reasons for their persistence. On completion clients are asked to consider alternative interpretations for their delusional beliefs.

Haddock, G. and Slade, P.D. (eds) (1996) Cognitive-Behavioural Interventions with Psychotic Disorders. London, Routledge.

Tsuang, M.T. and Faraone, S.V. (1997) Schizophrenia: the facts, 2nd edn. Oxford, Oxford University Press.

Dependence

Dependence occurs where a person has a strong and persistent desire to continue taking drugs. The desire may be to experience the euphoric effects of the drug or to avoid withdrawal symptoms when ceasing to take the drug. Dependence may be psychological or physiological.

Depression/depressive disorder

Depression or depressive disorder is an episodic mood disorder or affective disorder. Everyone experiences changes of mood and feelings of sadness and euphoria; however individuals with depressive disorder experience severe and persistent feelings of sadness, loneliness, worthlessness, hopelessness and guilt such that they cannot function in an appropriate way socially or interpersonally. Alternatively they may feel angry, irritable and aggressive. Sufferers have usually experienced a loss of a significant relationship, of status or of an ability or health. They see the world and the future negatively and are extremely self-critical. In more severe cases depressed individuals may experience auditory hallucinations, lose weight and experience various somatic symptoms.

The major classification systems distinguish between four main mood disorder syndromes: (i) major depressive disorder (also known as unipolar depression), (ii) bipolar disorder, (iii) dysthimic and (iv) cyclothymic disorders. In major, or unipolar, depression an individual experiences severe and persistent feelings of sadness and/or loss of interest and pleasure in activities that were previously found enjoyable. Children experiencing a major depressive episode may appear irritable rather than depressed. In addition, five or more of the following symptoms occurring daily for a period of at least two weeks:

- sleeping difficulties, including not being able to sleep or sleeping all the time;
- changes in levels of activity, including either becoming lethargic or agitated;

- changes in appetite, including either loss of appetite or increase in appetite;
- loss of energy and increasing tiredness;
- negative self-concept and feelings of worthlessness, hopelessness and guilt or shame;
- poor attention and difficulties concentrating;
- suicidal ideas and thoughts of self-harm.

In bipolar disorder, an individual experiences radical and intense swings of mood with episodes of mania, mania alternating with depression and mixed episodes with mania and depression occurring simultaneously. Dysthymic disorders are diagnosed when the individual experiences longstanding mood disorders lasting at least two years for adults and one year for children and adolescents. Symptoms include mild to moderate but chronic depression that results in significant disruption and distress in the individual's life and functioning. Dysthymia usually occurs with other psychiatric and physical conditions and up to 70 per cent of individuals with dysthymia also have a major depressive disorder. This is called double depression. Cyclothymic disorders are diagnosed when there are also chronic hypomanic episodes.

The incidence of depression is high, affecting between five to 20 per cent of the population at some time; and it is more common in women, occurring twice as frequently in females as in males. Depression typically begins in late adolescence or early adulthood although the disorder can occur across all age groups, including children and the elderly. Young adolescents are faced with transitional problems such as separation from parents, individuation, pubertal changes, school transitions and performance challenges. It tends to be a recurrent disorder and around 80 per cent of people who have experienced an episode of depression are likely to have a further episode within a year. The causes of depression are complex and not fully understood. Theories of the causes of depression include genetic vulnerability, biochemical factors, behavioural, cognitive, sociocultural, and systems factors.

- Genetic factors: Twin studies and family studies indicate that depression has a genetic component; individuals with family members suffering with major depression are up to three times more likely to develop depression themselves. More research is required to determine the exact nature involved and to separate environmental from genetic factors.
- Biochemical factors: An imbalance of certain neurotransmitters, the chemicals in the brain that transmit messages between nerve cells, is thought to play a key role in the development of depression. Investigations of the stress response system indicate that depression may be linked to defects in the system. Abnormal levels of cortisol, a key hormone, and sleep abnormalities may indicate that depression is linked to a biological rhythm disturbance. Other theories include dysregulation of the amine or endocrine systems and malfunction of the immune system. A biologically based difficult or inhibited temperament is also a risk factor for depression.

- Behavioural approaches stress the significance of the lack of positive reinforcement in explaining depression. People may lack the social skills necessary for eliciting positive reinforcement from others.
- Cognitive approaches: Cognitive models of depression place an emphasis on the function of negative and dysfunctional thought processes in the development of depression. Most studies have provided evidence that individuals with depression think more negatively than non-depressed people on numerous measures about the self, the past, current and future circumstances. Different theories stress the importance of various constructs such as negative self-schemas of worthlessness and incompetence, low self-esteem, depressogenic and pessimistic attributional style, rumination, passive and avoidant coping responses, learned helplessness and hopelessness among others. Shyness is another risk factor for depression.
- Psychoanalytic/psychodynamic theories: These theories view depression as due to an early trauma that has been reactivated by a recent loss resulting in feelings of powerlessness and dependency. Alternative psychodynamic theories are that an unrealistic ego ideal leads to low self-esteem or uncaring or over-indulgent parents provide models of future relationships that expect abandonment.
- Social/cultural factors: Loss of a parent followed by poor substitute care has been demonstrated to be a reliable predictor of later depression. Furthermore lack of adequate parental care, parental rejection, insecure attachments and negative and unsupportive relationships with parents during childhood have been consistently reported in retrospective studies of adults with depression. Other social factors that have been found to be associated with later depression include low socio-economic status, parental depression, drinking, divorce, family violence, parental mental illness, childhood physical and sexual abuse.
- Family systems: Experience of losses and bereavements in the family, parental absence, abuse, neglect, conflict and frequent changes in placement can all contribute to depression. Negative and pessimistic family belief systems can also play a part.

The treatment of depression has been mainly through psychodynamic therapy, cognitive-behavioural and biological interventions. However, it is important to note that the majority of individuals with depression do not look for treatment and of those who do only 50 per cent go to a mental health specialist. Depression is particularly predictive of suicide, for example diagnosable depressive disorders have been implicated in between 40 to 60 per cent of incidents of suicide.

Psychodynamic interventions aim to identify the early trauma as well as to explore the ambivalent feelings experienced by the individual with depression. Behavioural interventions focus on increasing self-reinforcement and on teaching social skills.

Cognitive techniques are aimed to correct errors in thinking, negative thoughts and attributions. They also include self-reinforcement, activity scheduling, anticipation training, thought-catching, reality testing, cognitive rehearsal and re-attribution training.

Biological treatment has focused on the use of antidepressant medication but other treatments include electroconvulsive therapy, phototherapy, sleep deprivation and physical exercise.

Craig, K.D. and Dobson, K.S. (eds) (1995) Anxiety and Depression in Adults and Children. London, SAGE Publications.

Goodyer, I.M. (ed.) (2001) The Depressed Child and Adolescent, 2nd edn. Cambridge, Cambridge University Press.

Hammen, C. (1997) Depression. Hove, Psychology Press.

Harrington, R. (1993) Depressive Disorder in Childhood and Adolescence. Chichester, Wiley.

Stoppard, J.M. (2000) Understanding Depression: Feminist social constructionist approaches. London, Routledge.

Williams, J.M.G. (1992) The Psychological Treatment of Depression, 2nd edn. London, Routledge.

Contacts

Depression Alliance, Tel. 020 7633 0557.
Manic Depression Fellowship. Tel. 020 7793 2600.
Samaritans, 24 hour helpline 0845 909090.

Desensitisation

Desensitisation refers to a decrease in sensitivity or reactivity to a stimulus. For example, a sudden noise will initially produce a startle reaction the first time but after successive presentations the response will reduce in severity and eventually the reaction will disappear. Desensitisation procedure is a behavioural method frequently used in the treatment of phobias. The method involves two principles: the first requires the pairing of the anxiety-evoking stimulus with the experience of relaxation and pleasure and the second is the systematic progression through an anxiety hierarchy from the least frightening stimulus. For example, a fear of dogs in a child may be gradually overcome by first exposing the child to pictures of dogs, then to toy dogs and so on until eventually the phobia disappears.

Developmental disorders

Developmental disorders are general or specific disturbances in the acquisition of motor, language, cognitive and social skills. They include elimination disorders (functional encopresis and functional enuresis), developmental receptive and expressive language disorders, pervasive developmental disorders (autistic disorder), speech disorder (selective mutism) and gender identity disorders.

Carr, A. (1999) The Handbook of Child and Adolescent Clinical Psychology: A Contextual Approach. London, Routledge.

Rutter, M. and Rutter, M. (1992) Developing Minds: Change and Continuity across the Life Span. Harmondsworth, Penguin Books.

Talay-Ongan, A. (1998) Typical and Atypical Development in Early Childhood: The Fundamentals. Leicester, British Psychological Society.

Developmental perspectives

A developmental perspective focuses on the sequence of changes over the life span of an individual. There are various issues connected to developmental change including how far heredity and the environment influence children, whether children are seen as active agents or passive recipients of social influence and whether developmental change is gradual and continuous or subject to abrupt transitions. Furthermore change can be seen as either quantitative or qualitative, a matter of degree or kind. There is, however, no generally agreed explanation of the processes of normal growth and development and developmental theories include Freudian psychoanalytic (psychosexual stages), Eriksonian psychoanalytic (psychosocial stages), ethological (evolutionary, biological and genetic influences), behavioural (learning and reinforcement history) and cognitive (cognitive developmental stages).

Wenar, C. (1994) Developmental Psychopathology, 3rd edn. New York, McGraw-Hill.

Developmental stages

Developmental stages refer generally to any period of development during which certain characteristic behaviours occur, as for example in the case of attachment. Infants at one year may manifest secure, insecure, resistant, avoidant and disorganised attachment. Common fears of infancy include stranger anxiety (peaks at age 8 to 10 months) and separation anxiety (peaks at age 10 to 20 months).

Diagnosis

Diagnosis is a process whereby a condition, disorder, syndrome or disease is identified and classified. Diagnosis is undertaken by psychiatrists using the two main classification systems available, namely DSM-IV (1994) and ICD-10 (1992). These systems are based on the medical model and for that reason may not find favour with those who adopt alternative perspectives, e.g. cognitive-behavioural or humanistic approaches. The medical model sees disorders or problems as inherent in the person. They are also atheoretical systems in that the systems do not subscribe to any particular aetiology for the disorders. Both DSM-IV and ICD-10 are multi-axial systems recording complex information concerning a number of different aspects of a disorder. There is an emphasis on categorisation of disorders and many of the categories are based on observable symptoms. These systems have been revised and are open to further revision. This has meant a proliferation of categories that have been decided on the basis of agreement by committee.

Furthermore these diagnostic systems are not infallible and neither is their use. The main problems are attaining sufficient inter-judge reliability and validity for disorders. There is a certain degree of arbitrariness and subjectivity in these systems, particularly in terms of cut-off points. In addition, many referrals display comorbidity, i.e. they meet the diagnosis for more than one disorder which may be inaccurate. These problems reflect the fact that emotional and behavioural disorders are not distributed among the general population as distinct categories but rather are the result of interactions or manifest themselves dimensionally. Dimensional approaches have led to two dimensions: one for internalising problems (anxiety disorder) and one for externalising problems (conduct disorder). Extreme scores on the dimensions indicate the severity of a problem leading to a DSM or ICD diagnosis, however many problems may not reach this level of severity but are still referred. Categorical classification may serve to hide the fact that problems are often the results of interactions between people. Furthermore, categorical approaches are susceptible to the labelling and stigmatising of people and the categorisation of disorders does not in itself necessarily lead to a coherent intervention plan.

Diagnosis may also be adversely affected by such factors as diagnostic bias and simply not using the DSM or ICD diagnostic criteria to identify a disorder.

American Psychiatric Association (1994) Diagnostic and Statistical Manual of Mental Disorders, 4th edn (DSM-IV). Washington, DC, APA.
World Health Organisation (1992) The ICD-10 Classification of Mental and Behavioural Disorders: Clinical Descriptions and Diagnostic Guidelines. Geneva, WHO.

Diathesis-stress model

This model states that the occurrence of emotional and behavioural problems are the result of a predisposition (diathesis) interacting with a given stress-evoking environment and the absence or lack of coping skills for dealing with that stress. This idea is not based on any one perspective. There can be biological, cognitive or psychodynamic predispositions (diatheses) for specific problems. A biological predisposition may have a genetic basis as in the case of schizophrenia and depression may have a cognitive predisposition in the form of a depressogenic schema. However having a diathesis or predisposition does not inevitably lead to a disorder or problem. Stress is necessary as a trigger to activate the predisposition or diathesis. The combination of both diathesis and stress are necessary for a problem or disorder to occur. Many factors are required for a problem to develop.

Divorce, separation and behaviour

Divorce is a relatively common event in the family life cycle, between 25 and 33 per cent of marriages end in divorce. Most divorces involve children and the vast majority of children stay with their mother. Most divorced people remarry. Divorce is more frequent among those with low incomes who have psychological problems and who married before they were 20. It is also more frequent if there was a premarital pregnancy. Protective factors include a high income, an absence of psychological problems and marriage after age 30.

The main reasons given for divorce are communication and understanding difficulties between couples, disagreements over roles, responsibilities, constraints and autonomy. Other reasons given include unfaithfulness, substance abuse, emotional immaturity and sexual problems. A cycle of negative cognitions and interactions develops with couples focusing on negative aspects of the relationship until a crisis point is reached.

The possible psychological consequences of divorce include role strain, particularly for women with children, emotional pain, low self-esteem and depression. Further emotional conflict can occur over custody and access to children. However, periods of feeling good can also occur as a result of escaping marital conflict and experiencing a new lease of life.

The possible effects on children include adjustment problems, boys experiencing behavioural problems and girls emotional problems. There may be difficulties at school and with family and peer relationships. However only a minority of children develop psychological problems and only a small number develop problems in adult life due to their parents divorcing. Risk factors for children of divorced parents include being male between three and 18, low ability, a difficult temperament, low self-esteem, insecure attachment, poor parenting, family conflict, abuse, bereavement, poor coping strategies, low self-efficacy, an external locus of control and conflict between divorced parents over parenting, roles and responsibilities. Children in step-families, particularly those in the early teenage years, can be resistant to stepfathers and stepmothers. The main interventions for helping children to adjust to separation and divorce include multisystemic approaches such as a combination of psycho-education about divorce, establishing and agreeing new roles, routines, rules and responsibilities, managing boys' behaviour problems through positive behavioural programmes, parenting skills training, grief counselling and family therapy.

Dopamine hypothesis (of schizophrenia)

There is believed to be a genetic predisposition that influences the development of schizophrenia. This genetic influence may have an effect on the biochemistry of neurotransmitters in particular that of dopamine. The idea is that schizophrenia is due to excess levels of dopamine activity. Drugs effective in treating schizophrenia reduce dopamine by blocking post-synaptic dopamine D2 receptors. Amphetamine psychoses resemble paranoid schizophrenia and are exacerbated by increased levels of dopamine activity. However further research suggested that it was an excess of the sensitivity of dopamine receptors that led to schizophrenia rather than excess levels of dopamine. The effect appears to be related to the positive symptoms of schizophrenia (hallucinations and delusions), negative symptoms (apathy, passivity, few social relationships) are unaffected. However the dopamine hypothesis does not amount to a final theory of schizophrenia as the immediate blocking of dopamine receptors does not reduce positive symptoms. Furthermore, newer drug treatment involves another neurotransmitter called serotonin and a neurotransmitter called glutamate may also be implicated. Additionally dopamine is found to be at normal levels in people with schizophrenia and therefore it cannot be simply a question of an excess of dopamine that leads to the disorder. Drug treatment does not work for all schizophrenics and has side effects for some patients.

Kalat, J.W. (2001) Biological Psychology, 7th edn). Belmont, CA, Wadsworth/Thomson Learning.

Drugs and behaviour

Drugs are chemical substances taken in various forms by individuals with the intention of producing pleasurable physical sensations and pleasurable and altered psychological states of mind. These drugs may be illegal or legal depending on the legal system and on the historical period. Drugs may be used for recreational purposes, to experience altered states of consciousness, to conform to peer groups and to self-medicate. Drug experimentation and recreational use have become common and addiction or dependency has increased.

The prevalence and usage of particular types of drugs varies over time and depends on fashion, availability, price and side effects. Drug taking mostly commences in adolescence and its prevalence is greatest between the ages of 16 and 24. Certain groups manifest higher levels of dependent and higher risk drug use than the general population, e.g. homeless people. Risk factors for dependency include emotional problems, physical and emotional neglect, physical or sexual abuse, parental divorce, parental drug use, hospitalisation, low self-esteem, risk and sensation-seeking behaviour. The effects of a drug can depend on the personality, mood and expectations of the user along with the amount absorbed, the setting and the attitude and behaviour of surrounding people. Pre-existing physical, psychological and psychiatric conditions can be exacerbated by drug taking.

- Alcohol: Produces depressant and stimulant effects in the brain. It adversely affects motor skills, self-restraint, visual and auditory acuity, balance and coordination, concentration and reaction time. Unwanted acute affects include road accidents, domestic violence and violence in public places and events. Unwanted chronic effects include Korsakoff's psychosis (memory loss and confusion), psychiatric problems and risk of suicide.
- Cannabis: Produces a sense of calm, optimism and well being. Inhibitions are reduced or eliminated. Unwanted effects include impaired coordination, concentration and judgement and in extreme cases may produce a temporary toxic psychosis.
- Heroin and opioids: Produce euphoria and optimism and eliminate anxiety and fear. Unwanted effects are few but include reduced appetite, drowsiness and apathy. Accidental overdose is a continual danger due to uncertainties regarding the purity and strength of the dose and mixing with other drugs. Addiction can lead to a lack of self-

concern, infections, accidents and a resort to prostitution in order to purchase supplies. Addicts may have had a disrupted childhood, a history of physical and sexual abuse and a psychiatric disorder that pre-existed their addiction. Opioids are used clinically to treat severe pain. Opioid use is relatively frequent among prisoners. Heroin addiction has grown significantly over the 1990s. Usually heroin addicts have acquired the drug in the first instance from friends rather than dealers. Heroin addicts tend to associate with friends who are users or other heroin addicts. The heroin addict becomes preoccupied with securing fresh supplies and this takes up considerable time and money. Heroin addicts can mature in their 30s and 40s and give up the habit spontaneously.

- Cocaine: Produces stimulant effects in the brain. It produces a sense of well being and of exhilaration, raises self-esteem, improves social skills, increases optimism and energy. Unwanted effects can include impulsivity, impaired judgement, anxiety, panic, aggression, antisocial behaviour, confusion, paranoid delusions and hallucinations. To maintain a continuous intake individuals may spend large amounts of money, selling off personal possessions and getting into debt. Highest rates of cocaine problems occur in men aged 26 to 34. Female crack cocaine users may become involved in risky sexual behaviour in order to purchase supplies. Those who suffer from a psychiatric disorder are at risk of becoming habitual users and use by those who have a psychiatric disorder may exacerbate that disorder.

- Amphetamines: Have similar effects to cocaine and produce feelings of euphoria and pleasure, a decrease in fatigue, an increase in energy and an increase in performance on tasks requiring vigilance or prolonged concentration. They can improve athletic performance and can also suppress appetite. Unwanted effects include amphetamine psychoses in the form of paranoid schizophrenia. Formication (a sensation of bugs crawling under the skin) can also occur as can violent episodes that are unpredictable but these are relatively rare. Methylphenidate (Ritalin) and pemoline (Cylert) forms of amphetamine used clinically to treat children with ADHD. They are central nervous system stimulants. Amphetamines have also been used to treat narcolepsy, a condition of extreme and uncontrollable sleepiness. Use of amphetamines is relatively frequent among prisoners, prostitutes and those who inject heroin.

- Psychedelics and hallucinogens: These drugs produce changes in sensory input and mood, visual distortion, illusions and hallucinations. LSD (lysergic acid diethylamide) is an example of a hallucinogen. Unwanted effects include impaired concentration and performance on tasks leading to accidents. People may develop a sense of invulnerability and engage in risky behaviours. Some experience a sense of losing control and become panicky, agitated and suspicious. A prolonged delusional psychosis or depression and anxiety may also occur in some people.

- Inhalants: Volatile substance abuse (glues, adhesives, aerosols, gas lighter fuels, paint, nail polish remover and room fresheners) spread among teenagers and resulted in fatalities. The effects include exhilaration and excitement. Inhibitions diminish and inhalers feel powerful. Visual illusions and hallucinations may also occur. Unwanted effects include mood swings, disorientation, clumsiness, loss of interest and self-concern and deteriorating school performance. Those who use inhalants frequently often suffer from psychological difficulties, have problems at home, become involved in delinquency and are at risk of taking other types of drugs.

- Ecstasy (MDMA): Produces feelings of euphoria, goodwill, closeness and empathy towards other people. Unwanted effects include clumsiness, poor concentration, drowsiness, anxiety, panic attacks, depression, suspiciousness and hallucinations. Fatal reactions sometimes occur due to the drug's effect along with dehydration and a rapid increase in body temperature but are rare in relation to the large numbers of people taking the drug. Ecstasy is a popular drug in the club scene along with other drugs such as amphetamines, nitrites, alcohol, LSD and cocaine.
- Tranquillizers (benzodiazepines): The most common include temazepam and diazepam; they produce effects similar to alcohol. They are frequently taken in conjunction with other drugs, e.g. with alcohol but also with methadone. Unwanted effects include poor concentration, depression, apathy, clumsiness and the risk of accidents. They are used clinically to treat anxiety and insomnia.

McKim, W. (2000) Drugs and Behavior: An Introduction to Behavioral Pharmacology, 4th edn. Upper Saddle River, NJ, Prentice Hall.
Royal College of Psychiatrists (2000) Drugs: Dilemmas and Choices. London, Gaskell.

Drugs and treatment

Various approaches have been adopted towards substance taking including: harm reduction or minimisation, educational, demand reduction, school-based educational and after-school programmes, mass media, community, work-based based programmes and mandatory drug testing.

Treatment of substance misuse includes cognitive-behavioural counselling, in particular motivational interviewing, pharmacological, contingency contracting, detoxification and rehabilitation.

Robson, P. (1999) Forbidden Drugs, 2nd edn. Oxford, Oxford University Press.

Contacts

Drinkline, national alcohol helpline 0345 320202.
National drugs helpline 0800 776600.
Release, 24 hour helpline 020 7603 8654 (for users, families and friends).

DSM-IV

DSM-IV (1994) stands for the Diagnostic System of the American Psychiatric Association. It was first published in 1952 and has undergone revisions in 1968, 1980 and 1987.

It is a multi-axial classificatory system which rates each person on five different axes. Axes I and II are the main ones. Axis I includes all diagnostic categories other than personality disorders and mental retardation. Axis II comprises the personality disorders and mental retardation. Axis I and II are used to make a diagnosis.

The DSM is a categorical system based on the idea that there are discrete and distinct disorders. DSM diagnoses are constructs because disorders are inferred. There are a number of diagnostic criteria for each disorder that have to be met before a diagnosis can be made. However there is a certain level of arbitrariness in terms of the number of symptoms required for a diagnosis and the level subjectivity with regard to the criteria. There has also been a proliferation of categories up to nearly 300 categories. The categories for homosexuality, hysteria and neurosis have been dropped. Reliability of the DSM system has improved but is still not perfect. Concerns also remain, particularly with regard to subcategories and the more imprecise categories. The cultural expressions of mental disorders also need to be considered in relation to the application of diagnostic systems like DSM IV.

Carr, A. (1999) The Handbook of Child and Adolescent Clinical Psychology. London, Routledge.
Davison, G.C. and Neale, J.M. (2001) Abnormal Psychology, 8th edn. Chichester, Wiley.

E

Eclectic approaches

Eclecticism refers to selecting and utilising different approaches to emotional and behavioural problems. There is no one or overarching approach that is chosen but one that is seen as pertinent and effective for the presenting client. Furthermore there is no theoretical integration of the different approaches. The aim is to choose the most effective approach for the particular client, for the specific problem and context whether that be cognitive-behavioural or humanistic. Eclecticism is preferred because no one approach is seen as capable of addressing all problems and as being appropriate for all clients.

The need for eclecticism is seen as arising from a number of trends: the proliferation of therapies, the perceived inadequacies of particular approaches, demands for brief, problem-focused interventions, the lack of strict adherence to chosen approaches (treatment integrity) and outcome similarities pertaining to different therapies. Evidence that different approaches share certain 'non-specific' factors (e.g. opportunities for release of feelings) in common also contributed towards the growth of eclecticism. An eclectic counsellor or therapist will choose an approach that is perceived as being effective for a particular client with a specific problem in a given context.

It appears that more and more counsellors and therapists are describing themselves as 'eclectic.' Eclecticism differs from integrationism in that integration is where approaches are combined into a new theoretical unity whereas eclecticism maintains theoretical integrity.

Eclecticism has been criticised on a number of grounds: as generating confusion and as making training, supervision and research difficult to undertake.

Woolfe, W. and Dryden, W. (ed) (1996) Handbook of Counselling Psychology. London, SAGE Publications.

Ecological perspective

The ecological perspective looks at the physical, spatial and social environmental influence on behaviour and behavioural problems. The spatial environment refers to the amount of space, spatial density, location, level of crowding and site geography and how they contribute to behaviour problems. Locations are seen as having a special significance, for example the influence on behaviour of particular people and objects in a person's immediate surroundings. People's perceptions of their use of space and the use of space by others influence their behaviour. The physical and biological environment refers to such factors as temperature, light, noise and climate. All these factors are seen as influencing behaviour. The organisational environment refers to factors such as the size, structure and ethos of a particular institution. Problem behaviour is seen as being the result of person-environment interactions. Ecological interventions focus on changing where possible the physical, spatial, locational and organisational environments or aspects of those environments that are found to contribute to behavioural problems.

Bell, P.A., Greene, T.C., Fisher, J.D. and Baum, A. (2001) Environmental Psychology, 5th edn. New York. Harcourt College Publishers.

Ecosystemic perspective

The ecosystemic perspective is based on systems theory and family therapy and sees emotional and behavioural difficulties as the result of interactions between systems or between individuals. Therefore difficulties are not seen as being located simply in individuals or within systems. Rather, individuals and systems involved in interactions all contribute in some way to the emergence and development of those difficulties. The concept of circular causality is paramount rather than that of unidirectional causality. Difficulties are also seen as a function of specific contexts. Individuals can become engaged in a cycle or series of positive or negative interactions. Interpretations and perceptions of behaviour are seen as influencing interactions whether positive or negative. Individuals can interpret what are perceived as negative interactions differently, act on those different interpretations and by doing so can convert a cycle of negative interactions into a series of positive interactions. This process is known as reframing and is one of the main ecosystemic interventions. Other interventions include sleuthing, positive connotation of motive, positive connotation of function and symptom prescription. All these interventions have in common the idea that there are equally valid interpretations of behaviour and that by reinterpreting behaviours in a positive way a cycle of positive interactions and behaviours can replace a series of negative interactions and behaviour. People therefore need to examine their interpretations of other people's behaviour to discover whether changes in interpretation lead to or encourage positive changes in behaviour.

Cooper, P., Smith, C.J. and Upton, G. (1994) Emotional and Behavioural Difficulties: Theory to Practice. London, Routledge.
Molnar, A. and Lindquist, B. (1989) Changing Problem Behavior in Schools. San Francisco CA, Jossey-Bass.

Effectiveness (of therapeutic approaches and interventions)

Controversy regarding effectiveness of psychotherapy began with Eysenck's (1952) critique of psychotherapy where he claimed that the improvement rate post-treatment for neuroses was no better than no treatment due to spontaneous remission. In the following years research on effectiveness by Sloane *et al.* (1975), Smith and Glass (1977), Weisz and Weiss (1993) and Lambert and Bergin (1994) have supported the conclusion that psychological interventions are generally better than no interventions at all. With regard to different approaches, the conclusion is that the outcomes of those approaches are generally equivalent (Smith *et al.* 1980) (Stiles *et al.* 1986).

With regard to interventions for adults, a range of interventions have been found to be relatively effective.

With regard to interventions for children and adolescents, a variety of interventions for specific emotional and behavioural problems have been found to be relatively effective.

- For enuresis, urine-alarm based interventions were most effective; for encopresis, medical care combined with behavioural approaches (shaping and positive reinforcement of toileting routines).
- For ADHD, psychostimulant drug therapy (methylphenidate or Ritalin) combined with social skills training, self-instructional training, parental and school-based contingency management and behavioural parent training.
- For adolescent conduct problems, behavioural parent training, behavioural family therapy and treatment foster care.
- For substance abuse, behavioural family therapy.
- For anxiety disorders, self-instructional training, behavioural and cognitive-behavioural interventions, individually and family focused. For obsessive-compulsive disorder (OCD), individual and parent focused cognitive-behavioural interventions along with the use of the drug clomipramine are advised.
- For depression, cognitive-behavioural interventions are useful.
- For anorexia, outpatient family therapy, and for bulimia nervosa, cognitive-behavioural or interpersonal therapy are effective.

It should be noted that in about a third of child and adolescent cases the available treatments or interventions are ineffective.

Bergin, A.E. and Garfield, S.L. (1994) Handbook of Psychotherapy and Behavior Change, 4th edn. Chichester, Wiley.

Carr, A. (ed.) (2000) What Works with Children and Adolescents? London, Routledge.

Kazdin, A.E. (1988) Child Psychotherapy: Developing and Identifying Effective Treatments. Needham Heights, MA, Allyn and Bacon.

Emotional and behavioural difficulties

There are various definitions of EBD that are based on particular models or conceptions of what constitutes mental health and normal behaviour. These definitions and conceptions may change historically and may vary between different types of institutions, societies and cultures. Mental health is usually regarded as socially and culturally adaptive behaviour. Normal behaviour is usually norm-referenced behaviour and behaviour that is adapted to a particular context such as school and work.

With regard to the SEN Code of Practice EBDs are perceived as existing along a continuum between, at one end, so-called 'normal' naughty behaviour, and at the other, psychiatric disorders. For the term EBD to apply there should be persistent, frequent, severe emotional or behavioural problems occurring within or across particular settings. A child or adolescent with an EBD may show the early symptoms or the actual symptoms of a mental disorder. Where this is suspected the child or adolescent should be referred to an educational psychologist, who in turn would refer to the Child and Mental Health Service if a mental disorder were suspected.

Pupils or students with EBDs tend to be more prevalent among adolescent males and to be living in socially and economically deprived inner city neighbourhoods.

A pupil or student is defined as having a learning difficulty in the sense of a barrier to learning if that difficulty is significantly greater that than of his or her peers. Learning difficulties in the sense of problems with literacy or numeracy may lead to EBD; alternatively EBD may lead to educational failure, lack of achievement or underachievement. The pupil or student with an EBD may also negatively affect the behaviour or achievement of other pupils or students.

The severity or level of EBD may vary across contexts or settings and may also vary depending on teachers' pedagogic and classroom management skills and also their expectations and tolerance levels. EBDs may also be affected by the pastoral organisation, the existence or otherwise of an effective behaviour policy and the overall institutional ethos.

The causes of an EBD can be single or multiple. Causes can be located in the home, within the family, in the child, in the neighbourhood and even in the school. The home may be overcrowded and situated in a socially and economically deprived neighbourhood experiencing delinquency, vandalism, drug taking and dealing. There may be parental conflict or parental mental illness and as a consequence inadequate and inconsistent supervision of children. The parents or parent may be physically, emotionally or sexually abusing their child. The parents may have divorced or separated. There may have been bereavement in the family. The child may be experiencing physical or mental health problems in the form of developmental difficulties. A school may exacerbate EBDs by a purely punitive approach towards those experiencing EBDs. Causes may interact and contribute towards the development of EBDs.

Emotional and behavioural problems that are mental disorders are classified or diagnosed by a psychiatrist using a diagnostic manual such as DCM-IV or ICD-10. If a child, adolescent or adult is diagnosed as having a mental disorder this means that they will meet certain criteria specified in the manual for that disorder.

Emotional symptoms are frequently presented to counsellors and psychotherapists. These may indicate an undiagnosed mental disorder, for example schizophrenia. In other cases there may be distressful feelings accompanying difficulties in relationships at work, school and college or with grandparents, parents, partners, boyfriends, girlfriends, sons and daughters. Alternatively people may feel unhappy over certain aspects of their selves, experiencing low self-esteem and depression as a consequence. These symptoms may in certain cases indicate the beginning of a mental health problem or an actual mental disorder. Whether this is the case depends on a proper, accurate diagnosis by a physician or psychiatrist. There may be underlying physical causes for emotional behavioural symptoms and in certain cases there may be emotional and behavioural symptoms that are the side effects of drug treatment.

Predisposing, precipitating and perpetuating factors

There are predisposing factors that predispose people to develop emotional and behavioural difficulties, precipitating factors that trigger the onset of difficulties and perpetuating factors that maintain the difficulties. These factors can be personal and / or situational.

- Personal predisposing factors include genetic, pre-natal and perinatal factors, the consequences of physical diseases and injuries, low ability, difficult temperament and low self-esteem.
- Situational predisposing factors include negative parent-child interactions, insecure attachment, negative parenting style, parental and family difficulties, marital conflict, delinquent siblings and stressors such as separation, bereavement and child abuse.
- Precipitating factors that can trigger emotional and behavioural difficulties include illnesses, injuries, abuse, bullying, parental conflict, separation, divorce, bereavements, births, adolescence, moving to another school and neighbourhood and loss of friendships.
- Personal maintaining factors include low self-efficacy, an external locus of control, learned helplessness, hostile attributional bias, immature defence mechanisms, poor coping strategies and biological malfunctions.
- Situational maintaining factors include negative family interactions such as insecure attachment, coercion, inconsistent supervision and discipline and unclear and confused communication. Other factors include an absent father, social isolation, family stress and delinquent subcultures.

All these factors need to be assessed in order to arrive at a comprehensive and accurate formulation of emotional and behavioural problems. The existence of protective factors will act to either prevent or reduce the occurrence of emotional and behavioural difficulties. These factors include good physical health, high ability, high self-esteem, high self-efficacy, an optimistic attributional style, mature defence mechanisms, secure attachments, positive family communications and interactions and positive peer relationships.

Presenting symptoms

These are the symptoms that a person, patient or client first brings or 'presents' to a coun-sellor or therapist. At this point it is advisable to consider whether the person is presenting symptoms that may indicate:

- a physical illness or disorder;
- a severe mental disorder;
- suicidal or self-harm tendencies;
- tendency to harm others.

The symptoms presented at the first meeting may not be the same ones presented at a later time or date.

DfEE Publication (2001) Promoting Children's Mental Health within Early Years and School Settings. Nottingham.
Kendall, P.C. (2000) Childhood Disorders. Hove, Psychology Press.
Pianta, R.C. and Walsh, D.J. (1996) High-Risk Children in Schools. London, Routledge.
Winkley, L. (1996) Emotional Problems in Children and Young People. London, Cassell.

Emotional disorders

Emotional disorders are disorders where there is a severe and persistent disturbance of mood. These disorders include anxiety disorders (phobia, panic attacks, generalised anxiety, obsessive-compulsive disorder and post-traumatic stress disorder), eating disor-ders (anorexia nervosa, bulimia nervosa and binge eating), mood disorders (depression, bipolar disorder, manic episodes and suicide).

Emotional intelligence

Emotional intelligence refers to the ability to be aware of one's feelings, managing one's feelings appropriately, marshalling one's feelings in order to achieve one's goals and recog-nising feelings in others. It also includes self-motivation, self-control, persistence, delaying self-gratification, empathy and developing positive relationships with others and social competence. Emotional intelligence is seen as at least as important as abstract or logical intelligence in terms of personal and social adaptation and educational and occupational success.

Goleman, D. (1996) Emotional Intelligence. London. Bloomsbury Publishing Plc.

Environment and behaviour

The influences or effects of the environment on behaviour are related to various medi-ating factors, e.g. heightened and lowered arousal, overload and underload of stimulation, adaptation, perceived control, stressors and physical setting. Too much or too little environmental stimulation leads to strain on our ability to process information. Over-stimulation can lead to difficulties in concentrating, irritability, decreased tolerance and lack of concern for others. Under-stimulation can lead to boredom and the desire for arousal and excitement. Loss of perceived control over the environment leads to unpleasant feelings and negative thoughts and attempts are made to regain control over one's environment. If our efforts to regain control are ineffective then we experience learned helplessness, i.e. we stop trying to regain control, we learn to be helpless and give up.

Stressors include natural catastrophes or disasters, personal events such as unemployment, illness, separation, loss and bereavement and background or ambient events such as pollution, noise, crowding and congestion.

The experience of stress is cognitively mediated through appraisal, i.e. we experience an event as threatening or we do not experience it as threatening, depending on the context or situation. Physiological responses to stress include changes in heart rate, blood pressure, breathing and immune functions. Stress responses may include impatience, irritability, depression and anxiety. Adaptations to stress include psychosomatic illness, cognitive overload or the inability to process given information, a decrease in task performance, withdrawal from or avoidance of social contact and aggression. The after-effects of stress can damage the immune system and lead to health problems. Different types of physical settings influence particular kinds of behaviour.

In terms of environmental factors extremes of noise, heat and cold have been associated with decreases in task performance. Changes in weather (low barometric pressure, wind and humidity fluctuations) have been linked to negative classroom behaviour.

Personal space refers to an individual's concept of body space, a protective, buffer zone that should not be invaded by others. Invasion of this zone is seen as restricting personal freedom, as causing stress and as resulting in compensatory behaviour. Invasions of one's personal space can lead to negative responses such as turning away, avoiding eye contact, fidgeting, mumbling and deterioration in the performance of complex tasks.

Territory refers to the space and neighbourhood of individuals, groups or gangs that is seen as being under their control or ownership. It is usually a visible area with distinct boundaries. The territory is usually 'marked' or personalised in some way indicating that it is controlled or owned. Territoriality can help to establish a group identity and feelings of security; however this may result in the formation of gangs and suspicion of outsiders. Invasion of territory can therefore activate an aggressive response. Disputed territory can also lead to a struggle for dominance and control. Established territories lead to stability in the form of reduced aggression. Territoriality can also be manifested within groups in the form of disputes over shared bedrooms and seating arrangements.

Spatial and social density can also affect behaviour negatively by leading to an increase in stress, over-stimulation, restriction of personal freedom, loss of control and unwanted social contact. Deindividuation occurs where normally responsible individuals become uninhibited within a group or crowd context and as a result engage in negative behaviour.

As regards classroom environments seating arrangements can affect behaviour and high densities can interfere with complex learning. Open plan classrooms can be noisy and distracting environments and windowless rooms may lead to students having negative feelings.

It is important to note that the influence of environmental factors is mediated through individual differences (gender and cognitive appraisal), situation or context (setting and time) and cultural attitudes (concepts of personal space).

Bell, P.A., Greene, T.C., Fisher, J.D. and Baum, A. (2001) Environmental Psychology, 5th edn. London, Harcourt College Publishers.

Ethos

Ethos or organisational culture comprises the approaches or solutions to the internal and external problems of a given institution. It is also the way in which people are taught to perceive, think and feel about the institution and its practices.

The particular ethos of an institution provides order, predictability and meaning to those in the institution. The ethos encompasses shared values and norms of behaviour that are supported by the members of the institution and entails a particular approach to dealing with behavioural problems. These values, norms and approaches may be implicit or explicit. Although there are overarching organisational cultures, there can also be multiple subcultures.

School ethos is said to have an influence on student behaviour. Some see a culture of rewarding pupils, responsiveness to pupil needs, giving responsibilities to pupils, enabling pupils to participate in school decision making and positive teacher role models as contributing to a positive school ethos.

A distinction is also made between an 'incorporative' and a 'coercive' ethos. An incorporative ethos is one where there is minimal, overt institutional control in the form of a reduction of rules that are likely to lead to or foment non-compliance. It is also characterised by a discretionary approach to minor rule infringements, a focus on developing a rapport with pupils, participation by pupils and parents, high expectations of pupils and an optimistic view of school effectiveness. A coercive ethos on the other hand is one where there is excessive control and punishment, an over strict implementation of rules, low expectations and a lack of participation by pupils and parents.

Reynolds, D. and Cuttance, P. (eds) (1992) School Effectiveness: Research, policy and practice. London, Cassell.

Evaluation of behaviour

Behavioural analyses and diagnoses are always based on a particular perspective or perspectives, e.g. behavioural, cognitive, psychodynamic or developmental. Therefore how change is evaluated depends on the methodological approach accepted or used by the particular perspective. The behavioural perspective subscribes to a scientific, empirical methodology; whereas, the psychodynamic perspective depends on psychodynamic interpretations of individual cases made by psychotherapists or psychoanalysts. However, scientific methodology has been applied to perspectives such as the psychodynamic perspective but this type of methodology has not always been acceptable to the practitioners. The developmental perspective sees behaviour as developing and changing over time and as being characteristic of a particular age, stage or phase.

The behavioural perspective evaluates behavioural change in terms of changes in the severity, frequency and duration of overt, observable behaviour relative to a baseline sample of representative behaviour; the cognitive perspective in terms of changes in beliefs, attitudes and attributions; the psychodynamic perspective in terms of the resolution of unconscious emotional conflicts that affect emotional stability or through positively transforming personality structures; the developmental perspective sees change in terms of age-appropriateness or stage or phase appropriateness. Some emotional and behavioural problems are seen as relatively common in childhood and appear and disappear given time.

Behavioural change usually refers to a return to a normative range of behaviour within a given social and cultural context. Criteria of success need to be established in order to determine whether there has been any significant behavioural change. Change that occurs may be statistically significant in terms of an increase or reduction in behaviours but not clinically significant in terms of a return to 'normal' functioning or what observers perceive as 'normal functioning'. Evaluation of behavioural change can be affected by differences over the definition of terms, moderating variables such as the particular characteristics of families and children, lack of treatment integrity, indirect administering of treatment and the timing of the evaluation. It is important to have a no-treatment or waiting list control group for comparison.

Bergin, A.E. and Garfield, S.L. (1994) Handbook of Psychotherapy and Behavior Change, 4th edn. Chichester, Wiley.

Exclusion and behaviour

Excluded pupils refer to those pupils who are excluded for fixed terms or who are permanently excluded from a school. Some children are excluded unofficially or informally and do not therefore appear in official LEA statistics. Pupils are sometimes sent home unofficially as a means of bringing their parents up to school, for not wearing a proper or full school uniform and to avoid being included in a school's official exclusion statistics. Some children are excluded for a very serious one-off incident; others have a long history of incidents that lead to exclusion.

Those disproportionately at risk are upper school pupils (aged 14–15) in secondary schools, pupils in special schools, boys (in particular African-Caribbean boys), children with special educational needs (in particular those with EBD) and children and young people in public care (foster and residential).

Primary school exclusions are relatively rare but rising, most are boys and in older primary age groups and many are seen as having special educational needs. Difficulties often exist in the home and family background of many primary age excluded children in the form of violent relationships, family bereavements and child abuse.

African-Caribbean boys are disproportionately excluded from school, most ethnic minority excluded pupils being boys and many are African-Caribbean boys. Reasons given for this over-representation include institutional and individual teacher racism towards African-Caribbean boys, teachers regarding such boys stereotypically as behaviourally difficult and teachers feeling unable to cope with them. Another reason cited is problematic communication between teachers and African-Caribbean boys. Excluded African-Caribbean boys tend to come disproportionately from single parent families, are often underachieving and are described as having had behavioural difficulties since their early years at school.

Children are excluded for a variety of reasons including fighting, physical and verbal abuse of other children and staff, drug dealing and taking, vandalism, theft, setting off the fire alarm, disruption of lessons and disobedience. Exclusion rates vary between schools that may reflect differences in school policies and practices but also intake differences and catchment area or neighbourhood differences. The highest regional rates of exclusion are from Inner and Outer London.

Increases in exclusions have been attributed to lower thresholds of tolerance in schools, a growing need to cope with disruptive pupils and an actual increasing trend towards more disruptive and violent behaviour.

Exclusion can put children at increased physical and emotional risk and can exacerbate tensions at home. Children who have been excluded from school and who have been in public care are more likely on reaching adulthood to lack GCSE qualifications, to be unemployed and to be homeless.

Children at a high risk of exclusion include:

- Boys, particularly African-Caribbean boys.
- Secondary age, particularly those in the upper school.
- Those who have special educational needs, particularly emotional and behavioural difficulties and also those with learning difficulties.
- Truants.
- Those in public care (foster and residential).

Contributory causes of exclusion that have been suggested include:

- Child-deficit factors, e.g. emotional, behavioural and learning difficulties, low self-esteem and medical problems.

- An academic school curriculum that does not meet the needs of some pupils.
- Whole-school factors, e.g. ineffective behaviour policies and practices.
- Staff factors, e.g. negative attitudes, expectations, communication and poor coping skills.
- Inadequate or insufficient training for teachers in EBD and lack of external support specialists.
- An emphasis on comparative school performance tables that encourages schools to focus on children likely to attain A–C grades rather than children with SEN.
- Senior management teams that subscribe to a culture of exclusion rather than to one of inclusion.
- Family difficulties, e.g. violence, loss of a parent through divorce or separation, bereavement and child abuse.
- Socio-economic factors in the form of high unemployment, low income, limited aspirations and restricted opportunities.

Interventions

Preventative interventions to avoid fixed term exclusions and permanent exclusions, and for permanently excluded pupils being reintegrated into another school, are:

- Addressing pupils' emotional, behavioural and learning difficulties through early interventions in the form of biological treatment and/or psychological interventions.
- Internal exclusion from lessons ('cooling-off' periods).
- Promoting positive behaviour policies and practices in schools.
- In-service training for staff in schools on classroom management and behaviour management.
- Referral to a designated teacher where a child is in public care.
- Referral to a special needs assistant (SNA), learning mentor or learning support unit (LSU) in school.
- Referral to a referral room for time out.
- Referral to external agencies, e.g. EPS and ESWS using a multi-agency approach.
- Whole-school behaviour policies that identify, address and change cultures of exclusions to ones of inclusion. A culture of exclusion is characterised by coercive and confrontational authority, inadequate communications between staff, unreflective staff, lack of differentiation, unidentified and untreated learning difficulties, an inadequate and low status PHSE curriculum and hierarchical and inflexible pastoral systems.
- Referral to an off-site pupil referral unit (PRU) through dual registration.
- Transfer or managed transfer to another mainstream school or to a special school.
- Addressing family difficulties through family therapy and child protection agencies.

Post-permanent exclusion interventions are:

- Referral to an off-site pupil referral unit (PRU). Transfer to another school for a fresh start.
- Addressing any unmet needs.
- Referral to other external agencies.

Blyth, E. and Milner, J. (eds) (1996) Exclusion from School. London, Routledge.
Department For Education (1994) Exclusions from School. Circular 10/94. London, DFE.
Gillborn, D. and Gipps, C. (1996) OFSTED Reviews of Research. Recent Research on the Achievements of Ethnic Minority Pupils. London, HMSO.
Sanders, D. and Hendry, L.B. (1997) New Perspectives on Disaffection. London, Cassell.

F

Fading

A behavioural technique whereby a new stimulus, prompt or cue is presented alongside an old one to which a learned response already exists. The old one is then gradually faded and the new one then acquires control over the learned response.

Family factors

There are many studies that demonstrate that family factors have significant effects on children's behaviour and emotional life. The majority of families do not conform to the traditional nuclear group consisting of a mother, father and around two children. In 1980, the two-parent family existed in only 36 per cent of American households. In 1991, the reported figure for the United Kingdom was 42 per cent. The main family factors that can adversely affect behaviour include:

- divorce or separation;
- marital conflict;
- bereavement;
- number of children, particularly large family size;
- different types of parenting styles, particularly laissez-faire and authoritarian;
- family conflict and stress, particularly that manifested in violent behaviour;
- sibling rivalry;
- lack of social support or social isolation;
- economic and financial distress;
- poverty;
- unemployment;
- overcrowding and poor housing conditions;
- parent with a psychiatric disorder, e.g. depression;
- parent who is a substance abuser, e.g. alcohol;
- having a parent in prison;
- physical illness in the family;
- negative parental attitudes to school and education.

Browne, K. and Herbert, M. (1997) Preventing Family Violence. Chichester, Wiley.
Herbert, M. (1988) Working with Children and their Families. Leicester, The British Psychological Society.

Family therapy

This is a general term which refers to a number of group therapy approaches in which all family members are seen together on the assumption that the identified problem lies not in the individual with the presenting symptom but in the family unit as a whole. The aim of family therapy is to help families to communicate and interact in such a way as to find their own solutions to the presenting problem. This is done through offering various strategies and homework tasks to encourage family members to think, feel and behave differently. As a result of family therapy, more effective communication between family members and more flexible roles within the family are achieved.

There are a large number of major models or schools of family therapy. The communication model has as its basis the view that all behaviour is communication at some level and that all behaviour and communication must be understood within a given context. Furthermore all systems are characterised by rules that tend to maintain and preserve the system, problems being maintained through recurrent patterns of communication. The goal of communication family therapists is to change the recurrent patterns of communication by which the problem is maintained. This is done through defining the problem in clear and unambiguous language, investigating all previous solutions attempted, defining the change to be achieved and formulating and implementing a strategy for change. The defining characteristic of this model is that you change behaviour by changing communication.

The structural family therapy model was founded by Minuchin who described it as a therapy of action. In structural family therapy, the therapist joins the family and participates in all their interactions and observes the roles of its members in an attempt to work actively in restructuring the way the family is organised and how family members communicate. The techniques used may include boundary clarification, for example a mother who treats her teenage daughter as if she were a baby may be surprised to hear her daughter's reply to the question 'how old do you think your mother treats you as – three or thirteen?'

Reframing is another important technique used. It involves changing the emotional and conceptual perception of the problem in such a way so as to force a solution. Strategic family therapy focuses on the dynamics of family interaction and uses techniques to effect change through metaphor, persuasion and indirect influence. It is based on the work of Milton Erickson and further developed by Haley who was originally a communications theorist as well as having worked with Minuchin. He used both the approaches developed by Erickson and the structural directive techniques of Minuchin and incorporated these into a life-cycle framework.

The Milan approach (also known as systemic therapy) views all symptomatic behaviours as serving the function of preserving the family system. The aim of the approach is to establish what are the current systemic rules which maintain the dysfunctional patterns of behaviour. It is a team approach using observers behind a one-way mirror. The first part is a pre-session discussion with the team, followed by a preliminary session with the family during which the observers can interrupt to pose further questions. Further discussion with the team follows during which hypotheses are formulated and further questions planned and then at the conclusion of the family session the therapist returns to the family and presents the team's observations, comments and interventions. This usually reframes the problem and offers a task for the family to be carried out before the next meeting. The final part consists of the team discussing the family's responses to the previous session. This approach is characterised by the therapist taking a neutral position when working with the family and the consistent use of a hypothesis that determines the therapist's questioning.

Dallo, R. and Draper, R. (2000) An Introduction to Family Therapy. Oxford, Oxford University Press.
Goldenberg, I. and Goldenberg, H. (1996) Family Therapy, 4th edn. Pacific Grove, CA, Brooks/Cole Publishing.
Reimers, S. and Treacher, A. (1995) Introducing User-friendly Family Therapy. London, Routledge.

Fantasy

This term refers to the mental processes of imagining objects, symbols or events not immediately present. A distinction between unconscious fantasies (phantasy) and conscious fantasies is usually made.

Fear

Fear is a subjective, emotional condition connected to an existing perceived threat or in anticipation of a perceived threat. There is often intense mental apprehension and sympathetic system, physiological reactions. There is a strong desire to avoid, escape or confront the threat. Fear unlike anxiety is directed towards specific threats. Specific fears tend to decline with age. Fears are extensive among young children but rarely amount to serious problems. The most common fears are fear of spiders and of the dark. Physical responses to fears include breathlessness, palpitations, rapid heart beat and pupil dilation.

Flooding (implosive therapy)

Flooding is a behavioural technique whereby an anxious or fearful client is exposed to the anxiety or fear stimulus at its full intensity for up to one hour. It takes two forms, in vivo or imaginal flooding. Clients after exposure do not experience the expected negative consequences of their anxiety or fears and as a result the client learns that the stimulus is not necessarily threatening.

The basic method is to expose the patient for a long period to stimuli that induce high anxiety and at the same time is prevented from escaping or avoiding the stimuli (response prevention). In vivo flooding is where the client is exposed to the actual stimulus until the client's anxiety peaks and subsides. Imaginal flooding is like in vivo flooding but exposure takes place through the client's imagination.

Flooding is thought to work through a classical conditioning response called extinction or through cognitive restructuring, a change in belief achieved through the experience of coping with the threatening situation.

In vivo flooding has been used to treat obsessive-compulsive disorder and imaginal flooding has been used to treat post-traumatic stress disorder.

Friendship

Friendship can be defined as relationships characterised by relations of cooperation and reciprocity that usually occur between peers. The importance of friendship can be illustrated by the fact that research findings have consistently reported that poor peer relationships, as rated by teachers, are a very reliable predictor of various difficulties in adulthood including truancy, juvenile and adult crime and psychiatric problems. Forming friendships and making friends is a complex and demanding skill and schools can play an important role in facilitating friendships for the isolated and vulnerable child (see entries for Circle Time and Circles of Friends).

There are broadly based developmental stages of friendship which are related to the cognitive, linguistic, emotional and moral development of the child as well as to the play and learning opportunities available. Children as young as 14 months demonstrate an interest in other children and a preference for particular friends. Between the ages of two to four, children engage in parallel play alongside other children rather than fully interacting. Children tend to choose partners of the same sex for play. Friends at this stage are more appropriately described as playmates although there are some studies that provide evidence that some children actively seek each other out. From around the age of six, children begin to make more independent choices and their friendships become more stable. Children demonstrate that they are beginning to understand the nature of friendship as a two-way process and related to the qualities a friend has.

From around the ages of 9 to 13, children's friendships become more intense and are characterised by a greater element of choice as well as an emphasis on shared views and support for each other. In early adolescence, friendships can become even closer and themes of loyalty and the sharing of intimate feelings are dominant. Children and adolescents may form friendships with those in older age groups, this can result in them being exploited, directed into antisocial activities or imitating negative behaviours. However children and adolescents who present behavioural problems may when involved in a supportive role with younger children modify their behaviour due to theresponsible role and caring feelings this type of relationship can evoke.

Erwin, P. (1998) Friendship in Childhood and Adolescence. London, Routledge.
Roffey, S., Tarrant, T. and Majors, K. (1994) Young Friends, Schools and Friendship. London, Cassell.

Functional analysis of behaviour

Functional analysis is a behavioural process undertaken to identify the controlling antecedent and consequences of a given problem behaviour. The aim is to discover empirically the factors that are controlling or causing behaviour over time and across settings. Causes are either direct causes (current events) or indirect (contextual, predisposing or historical) causes.

G

Gender and behaviour

Gender is defined in terms of identity (usually male or female biological sex except in the case of transsexuals), role behaviour (masculine or feminine) and sexual orientation (homosexual, heterosexual and bisexual). Hormones do not directly determine gender identity, sex role behaviour or sexual orientation as psychological and situational factors are also believed to be involved. Sex typing (conformity to socially defined female and male sex roles) and sex stereotyping (attitudes and behaviour regarded as typical of males and females) are other gender-related concepts.

Gender stereotypes are social and cultural beliefs about what it is to be a male or female person. Certain characteristics or traits are seen as typically or essentially male or female. Male traits are often regarded as more desirable than female traits. Parents tend to stereotype their children at an early age and children themselves develop gender stereotypes from the age of two years.

Boys tend to display more verbal and physical aggression in comparison to girls. They tend to dominate teacher time, discussions, play and public spaces. Boys use language as a means not only of communication but also as an instrument of control and domination. They resolve conflicts through the threat or actual use of coercive power. Girls are more likely to use relational language to resolve conflicts. Boys display more behavioural problems than girls, these being expressed in a severe form as ADHD and conduct disorders. They also sexually harass girls through verbal abuse that contains sexually denigrating words or phrases, however girls can also use sexually abusive language about each other. These problems often lead to gender segregation, boys and girls congregating in separate single sex groups.

In childhood mental disorders are more common among boys than girls. For boys these include ADHD and conduct disorders. Girls are more likely than boys to display emotional difficulties such as anxiety and depression. Peer rejection is seen as a factor in contributing to girls' depression along with concerns over body image (shape and weight). During adolescence girls are more vulnerable than boys to depression, eating disorders (anorexia and bulimia) and gender identity disorder but this disorder is still rare in girls.

In adulthood twice as many women as men are diagnosed as having a mental disorder. Reasons given for this 2:1 ratio include a diagnostic bias in psychiatry and women as being more likely to identify emotional problems and more willing to seek and accept support than men. Women particularly vulnerable to depression are those who are low income mothers with three or more young children in stressful circumstances and without social support. Depression also occurs among some mothers after childbirth. Changes around the menopause can also contribute to mental disorders. These changes such as no longer being able to have children, children leaving home or having to care for ageing parents, may have a psychological impact on some women.

Men commit many more violent crimes than women and are much more likely to be involved in violent incidents. Boys who are physically maltreated through extensive and harsh punishment are at risk of becoming violent offenders. Men convicted of murder are also likely to suffer from depression, this being shown by the significant numbers of murderers who go on to kill themselves. Male violence has also been linked to experiences of shame, humiliation and rejection and to imagined or real signs of disrespect. In particular, challenges to stereotypical notions of masculinity are likely to bring forth a violent response in some men. These challenges usually involve calling into question a man's heterosexual orientation. In order to 'save face' some men then resort to violent behaviour.

Gilligan, J. (2001) Preventing Violence. London, Thames and Hudson.
Golombok, S. and Fivush, R. (1994) Gender Development. Cambridge, Cambridge University Press.
James, O. (1995) Juvenile Violence in a Winner-Loser Culture. London, Free Association Books.
Measor, L. and Sikes, P.J. (1992) Gender and Schools. London, Cassell.
Stoppard, J.M. (2000) Understanding Depression: Feminist social constructionist approaches. London, Routledge.

Gender identity disorder

This is a disorder in which the individual feels that they belong to the opposite sex and that their own anatomical sex is not correct. This disorder is sometimes also referred to as transsexualism (in adults). The symptoms in childhood include repeatedly stating the desire to be, or insistence that he or she is the other sex. In boys, a preference for cross-dressing or pretending they are wearing female clothing. In girls, insistence on wearing only stereotypical masculine clothes, a strong and persistent preference for cross-sex roles in make-believe play or persistent fantasies of being the other sex. In adolescents and adults the symptoms include a stated desire to be the other sex, pretending to be the other sex, a desire to live and be treated as a member of the other sex.

People with gender identity disorder frequently experience depression and anxiety. Gender identity disorder is higher in children than in adults; in adults the prevalence is reported as one in 30,000 for men and one in 100,000 to 150,000 for women; whereas for children the figure is about three per cent for boys and one per cent for girls. The causes of gender identity disorder are not known and there is no clear evidence that gender identity disorder is related to hormone levels, chromosomal abnormalities or brain structure. Treatment for gender identity disorder is usually through sex-reassignment surgery. There is some evidence that gender identity can be changed through behaviour therapy.

Davison, G.C. and Neale, J.M. (2001) Abnormal Psychology, 8th edn. Chichester, Wiley.

Generalisation

Generalisation can refer to stimulus generalisation or generalisation of the effects of an intervention beyond the original setting or context.

Stimulus generalisation occurs when an established conditioned or a reinforced response to a specific stimulus is called forth by other similar stimuli. For example salivation conditioned to the sound of a bell can also be called forth by similar noises to the bell.

Generalisation of an intervention occurs where an intervention in one type of setting is effective or works across different settings or contexts. For example an intervention in the school is equally effective in the home. However problems may arise where specific treatments or interventions are only effective within a particular type of closed environment, say a community home, but the effect may not generalise to another setting, say on returning to the neighbourhood.

Generalised anxiety disorder

A generalised anxiety disorder is defined as a chronic state of uncontrollable, diffuse anxiety characterised by constant worry about some harm which the individual fears will happen to themselves or to someone close to them, for example, financial problems, health, work or relationships difficulties. It often occurs together with other anxiety disorders and mood disorders. This disorder is also referred to a free-floating anxiety. DSM-1V classifies generalised anxiety disorder as requiring the following symptoms: excessive worry, over a period of a least six months about a number of life circumstances. A number of physical symptoms may also be reported by the individual with generalised anxiety disorder including excessive perspiration, flushing, heart thumping, stomach upsets, diarrhoea, dry mouth, a lump in the throat. A high rate of respiration and a high pulse is frequently present. The individual with generalised anxiety disorder may also report difficulties relaxing, constant tiredness, muscle pains and aches as well as uncontrollable twitches. Behavioural manifestations are frequently observable such as insomnia, irritability, temper loss and distractibility.

The onset of the disorder is typically in mid-teens or early adulthood and is often triggered by a series of significant life events. Generalised anxiety disorder is quite common and the incidence is high, affecting as many as four to five per cent of the population. It occurs twice as frequently in women as in men.

Suggested causes of the disorder are genetic vulnerability, biological (e.g. hormonal and neurotranmitter levels), behavioural, cognitive and psychological factors.

Perspectives on generalised anxiety disorder

- Biological: Some studies have reported that there is a genetic component in generalised anxiety disorder although not all the data available supports this view. There is also research that has investigated the effect of a group of drugs known as the benzodiazapines which are often effective in the treatment of anxiety. An important neurotransmitter called gamma-aminobutyric acid has been identified. It has been shown to inhibit some nerve impulses and a deficiency in this system may be implicated in the development of generalised anxiety disorder.

- Behavioural: This view stresses the role of learning and sees anxiety as resulting from incorrect learning.
- Cognitive: This view emphasises the importance of the perception of not being in control which is seen as the basis for all types of anxiety. Furthermore, anxious people fear the unpredictability of events, misinterpret harmless events and ambiguous stimuli as dangerous and anticipate future threats They are also over-sensitive to fears of rejection and social embarrassment.
- Psychodynamic: This approach views all the anxiety disorders as neuroses resulting from unconscious conflicts between id impulses and ego actions.

The treatment of generalised anxiety disorder is mainly through psychodynamic therapy, cognitive-behavioural techniques and biological interventions. Biological treatment has focused on the use of anxiolytics (tranquilizers – Valium and Xanax). Behavioural techniques include systematic desensitisation as well as the teaching of relaxation methods. Cognitive methods include the explicit teaching of competence skills and assertiveness through instruction, modelling and/or operant conditioning and the use of exposure techniques. In psychodynamic therapy, treatment focuses on finding out what the ego is attempting to suppress through the psychodynamic techniques of free association, dream interpretation and analysis of resistance and transference. Although improvement does occur symptoms of generalised anxiety persist.

Davison, G.C. and Neale, J.M. (2001) Abnormal Psychology, 8th edn. Chichester, Wiley.

Genetics and behaviour

Behavioural genetics undertakes research into the effects of heredity on behaviour and by elimination the influence of the environment on behaviour. Most mental disorders display complex inheritance. This means that the inheritance of mental disorders is due to the interaction of genetic and environmental influences. This is called a multifactorial vulnerability model. These influences lead to a predisposition to a disorder but do not inevitably lead to that disorder. There can be a range of effects due to the inheritance of a given disorder, mild and moderate symptoms, these being termed 'spectrum conditions', i.e. not the full condition. These spectrum conditions are seen with schizophrenia. Disorders can run in families for many different reasons other than genetic reasons, e.g. sharing a common environment or culture. In the case of schizophrenia, twin and adoption studies are undertaken to determine whether there is a genetic influence and the degree of that influence. Twin studies show that there is a genetic influence with respect to schizophrenia, i.e. having a monozygotic co-twin predicts schizophrenia. However, nearly half of those having a schizophrenic co-twin will not develop the disorder. This indicates an environmental trigger for the co-twin who develops the disorder. A caveat here is that the heritability of a disorder depends on the given sample, their genes along with the given environment. Thus changes in the environment may modify the risks for developing the disorder, an example being mental retardation due to two phenylketonuria (PKU) genes. The development of PKU also depends on the level of absorbed phenylalanine, an environmental factor. Futhermore, schizophrenia-like symptoms can be caused by neurological disorders such as temporal lobe epilepsy and by substance abuse, as with amphetamine psychoses.

Linkage studies have been undertaken to find chromosomal commonalities within affected families that are not shared by unaffected families. It has not been possible to discover how a predisposition for schizophrenia has been transmitted. Some positive linkages have appeared to be been identified, only to be refuted by later studies. Further it is not known what it is that is inherited that predicts risk.

Finally it appears to be the case that mental disorders are the result of interactions between genetic and environmental factors. The diathesis-stress model would seem the appropriate model for investigating the development of mental disorders. This model sees a genetic predisposition for a mental disorder as being triggered by an environmental stressor. The implications for therapeutic intervention are that although biological treatment (drug therapy) is prevalent and indispensable, psychological interventions are also useful and effective and are not precluded for treating mental disorders that have an underlying genetic basis. For example although schizophrenia is treated by antipsychotic drugs or neuroleptics, e.g. phenothiazines, butyrophenones and thioxanthenes, these drugs are not a cure. The drugs reduce the positive symptoms of schizophrenia such as hallucinations but do not have a significant effect on negative symptoms such as sociability. Side effects of the drugs can lead to patients' non-compliance or to them being taken off particular drugs. Other therapeutic approaches have been found to be helpful, e.g. social skills training, cognitive-behavioural interventions and family therapy.

Faraone, S.V., Tsuang, M.T. and Tsuang, D.W. (1999) Genetics of Mental Disorders. New York, Guilford Press.
Plomin, R., DeFries, J.C., McClearn, G.E. and Rutter, M. (1997) Behavioral Genetics, 3rd edn. New York, W.H. Freeman.

Genogram

A genogram is a technique usually associated with a family therapy model from a trans-generational perspective. The technique consists of drawing up a flow diagram or a family map representing the family's biological and emotional processes over generations. A standard format has been developed and symbols are used to represent names, dates, medical and historical life events and emotional relationships between family members. For example, males are denoted by squares, females by circles. Information about marriages, pregnancies, death, birth order, losses through divorce or separation and other life-cycle events is obtained from family members. Emotional relationships including conflict, closeness and distance and other processes are also elicited.

In family therapy, the use of the technique of drawing a genogram performs a number of important functions. In the first place, it may involve the active participation of all family members including children. This results in the drawing up of a genogram becoming both a method of assessment as well as a treatment intervention. The process of working together with emotional material in a safe way can help family members deal with difficult or painful information. A second function is to provide a detailed outline of the family over three or more generations.

Grief

Grief refers to the intense emotional state of mind that follows after the experience of a significant loss. It is a normal and healthy response that takes place after bereavement. Grief has a number of distinct stages. In the first stage, the state of mind can be best described as numbness or shock. In children this may be expressed in various ways, for example, the child may become withdrawn or have outbursts of crying. Another common response can be denial. The next stage is characterised by pining or yearning for the person who has died. A child may become very anxious and search for the dead person or become attached to objects that belonged to that person. Observable behaviours that may occur in children at this stage include signs of anxiety such as bedwetting, sleep disturbances and nail biting. This stage is followed by a period when feelings of despair and sadness dominate. Children may behave in an angry way and reject any help and comfort offered to them. Feelings of guilt are also frequent at this stage and a child may become withdrawn, uncooperative, lacking in confidence and irritable. The final stage is one of reorganisation. The intense feelings previously experienced diminish and the individual begins to plan for a future without the person who has died.

There are individual differences in the way anyone goes through the above stages although it is generally accepted that unless all the stages are worked through the grieving process may not be resolved. It is also now generally accepted that the process of grief is similar in children as for adults. Cultural differences exist, for example in some cultures the grieving process involves public rituals, which may be very demonstrative, whereas in other cultures the process is private. Certain cultures have a fixed period of mourning whereas in others this is not the case.

Interventions for children who are grieving

The key intervention is to make sure that a child who has experienced a loss has available a supportive and responsive adult who can reassure the child that their feelings of grief are normal.

See Bereavement – useful contacts.

Group interventions

Group work with children and adolescents should be considered only if individual work is not appropriate or is impracticable. Group work can be open or closed. Parents/carers need to be approached for permission and the disadvantages need to be considered, e.g. excluding the child from classroom, curricular and other school activities. Groups should never be used as a convenient means of excluding disruptive children from particular lessons.

If planned and used appropriately the group work approach can be beneficial if planned and used appropriately in the following ways:

- Provides opportunities for growth and development through sharing problems and experiences and for practising newly acquired skills and behaviours.
- Enables children to learn new social skills and to increase their self-esteem.
- Enables a larger number of children to be helped and is likely to be economic in time and cost.

Group work may not suit all kinds of children such as those with no self-control, those who are too demanding or who need individual attention, the physically aggressive and destructive, those who are at different levels of development, those who have a mental illness and those having receptive-expressive language disorders.

Group work can be approached from different perspectives, e.g. psychodynamic, humanistic or experiential, solution-focused therapy, behavioural, cognitive-behavioural and developmental. The aims of group work can be therapeutic in order to address specific problems or disorders, counselling for growth and development, psychoeducational for learning or support for those experiencing life stresses and developmental for those experiencing developmental delays.

Planning for group work

Planning for group work requires the following points to be considered and acted on:

- Group leaders (two, one male and one female) need to be familiar with developmental theories and processes, to have counselling skills and to be skilled facilitators.
- Group leaders need to be supervised by experienced group leaders.
- Group leaders can adopt authoritarian, laissez-faire or democratic leadership styles or a mix of styles but democratic leadership styles that involve children in decision making are more likely to achieve group satisfaction and cohesion. Changing leadership styles may be useful at times to provide safety and security or to allow for more open interactions.
- Group leaders need to have strategies at hand for dealing with disruptions, resistance, attention-seeking, manipulative, monopolising and withdrawn behaviour and to deal with confrontations, exclusions and departures from the group.
- Positions on confidentiality issues need to be decided with parents or carers prior to group work.

- Parental or carer permission must be granted in order for children to become group members.
- Children need to be assessed for their suitability for group work using school records, through informal or formal observation in individual and group settings and through the use of assessment instruments.
- Children during group work should learn about their feelings and behaviour and the effects of their behaviour on others; they should also have the opportunity to learn new behaviours.
- Children with similar emotional and behavioural problems should be identified and selected for the group.
- Children should not be coerced or cajoled into group work and should give their informed consent.
- Children who are extremely aggressive, hyperactive or have extremely poor concentration are not likely to be suitable for group work. These children are likely to disrupt, obstruct or dominate group work to the detriment of other children.
- A room in an appropriate setting should be arranged so that it is separate from other school activities.
- Groups may proceed through various stages from preparation and induction, to formation of the group and to termination or closure. Preparation includes assessment and intake protocols. Other stages include group identification, the emergence of sub-groups, individual or sub-group resistance to the group, the development of group cohesiveness and mutuality, preparation for the ending of group work, providing feedback to parents, carers and children and evaluation of group work sessions.
- Limited sessions depending on age should not exceed two hours and should last from eight to ten weeks in duration.
- Sessions should avoid interfering with pupil access to the National Curriculum and other school activities.
- Group size should not exceed 12 members depending on such factors as age, absenteeism, attrition rates and extreme behaviours.
- Group composition should be determined according to the criteria of age, gender, ethnicity and aims. Group work with children from different ethnic minorities needs to be carefully planned to avoid it becoming a forum for the expression of negative opinions about each other's cultures. Groups may need to be single sex rather than mixed to allow uninhibited discussion of sensitive or delicate issues and to avoid dominance of boys over girls.
- Group work can include scheduled activities, role-plays and games to foster and maintain interest as well as be a means of exploring interactions or group dynamics.
- Group work should be formally or informally evaluated, either formatively during the sessions or summatively after the final group work session. Evaluation should focus on the effectiveness of group leadership, on group changes as well as on individual change.

Geldard, K. and Geldard, D. (2001) Working with Children in Groups. Basingstoke, Palgrave.

H

Hallucinations

Hallucinations are defined as perceptions that occur in the absence of a sensory stimulus and as a result not observed by anyone else present at the same time. Hallucinations are usually auditory but can be visual, tactile, olfactory or somatic. Auditory hallucinations, in particular the hearing of voices, are typically associated with a psychiatric disorder, usually schizophrenia although also depression. Visual hallucinations involve the perception of people or objects, etc., where no such person or object is present. Tactile hallucinations may involve tingling sensations. Olfactory hallucinations are usually unpleasant odours such as burning rubber or faeces that no one else can smell. Somatic hallucinations or bodily hallucinations involve the belief that something is happening in the body such as the belief that one is rotting away. The aetiology of hallucinations can include seizures and sleep disorders, substance abuse, neurological damage, reaction to drugs, grief, stress as well as metabolic, endocrine and infectious diseases.

Holistic approaches

This is a general term that refers to any therapeutic approach that focuses on the whole system, organism or person rather than separate elements or functions. The basis of the holistic approach is the view that a complex phenomenon cannot be understood by an analysis of the constituent parts alone and it is therefore opposed to reductionism. It is necessary to understand how the whole person functions in terms of thoughts, feelings and behaviour and how they interrelate to form that person. There is an emphasis on encouraging people to take responsibility for their own growth and development by enabling people to discover and draw on their own inner resources. Both person-centred and gestalt counselling approaches are examples of holistic approaches to therapy.

Hormones and behaviour

Hormones are chemical messengers produced by endocrine glands and released into the blood stream where they flow to a particular receptor and produce a specific effect. They have an effect on sexual functioning, sexual development, physical growth as well as on emotional responses such as stress. The relationship between hormones and behaviour is complex. For example testosterone and oxytocin can influence sexual behaviour yet sex offenders have approximately normal levels of testosterone.

Kalat, J.W. (1998) Biological Psychology, 6th edn. Pacific Grove, CA, Brooks/Cole Publishing.
Silber, K. (1999) The Physiological Basis of Behaviour: Neural and hormonal processes. London, Routledge.

Humanistic perspective

The humanistic perspective is a holistic approach that developed in the 1960s and is often contrasted with behaviourism and psychoanalysis. The focus is on the self and on the whole person. The aim is to avoid examining the pathology of behaviour and mental states but rather to encourage the optimal development or growth of a person.

All individuals are regarded as trying to grow or develop into fully functioning people. Self-actualisation or self-fulfilment is seen as a fundamental human need. People strive to create or construct meaning for themselves of the world around them. People are seen as involved in a process of becoming and therefore labelling and categorising are best avoided. Humanistic counsellors facilitate individual growth by encouraging people to develop through drawing on their own resources and by identifying constraints to growth. People are seen as capable of self-reflection and therefore as having responsibility for their choices and the ability to choose alternatives. There is often a tension between how people see themselves as and how others see them and as a consequence a need to reconcile these differences. Finally people are not reduced to their feelings or their thoughts but are seen as experiencing the world through the interaction of both their thoughts and feelings. Existing behaviour is not therefore determined by the past but is the result of how people give meaning to the past, present and future.

People are not assessed through labelling them but through understanding their experiencing, i.e. how they attribute meaning to events in their lives. In terms of interventions the focus is on facilitating the development of self-awareness and awareness of others' thoughts and feelings. The counsellor is required to become aware of how people make sense of their world, the meanings they attribute to the actions and behaviour of others and the feelings they evoke. The counsellor avoids making assumptions or judgements about the ways in which people interpret the world and considers both thoughts and feelings. It is hoped that through self-actualisation people will become more open to experience, i.e. develop more self-understanding and build on their strengths.

Nelson-Jones, R. (2001) Theory and Practice of Counselling and Therapy, 3rd edn. London, Continuum.
Woolfe, R. and Dryden, W. (eds) (1996) Handbook of Counselling Psychology. London, SAGE Publications.

I

Identification

Identification is seen as a conscious or unconscious mental process whereby people identify with another person or with a group. People identify, i.e. take on or fuse with the perceived characteristics or attributes of the person or group.

Idiographic approach

The idiographic approach to personality research focuses on the individual as a unique person and rejects the idea that there are general laws or traits that apply to individuals. This approach is the opposite of the nomothetic approach.

Impulsivity

Impulsivity is a general term that refers to the tendency to act first without thinking things through. A well-known experiment called the Marshmallow Test was conducted with four year olds who were offered the choice of one marshmallow immediately or two if they were able to wait a few minutes while the researcher left the room. Around one third of the children took the one marshmallow within a few seconds, the remaining children waited and received two marshmallows when the researcher returned. All the children were followed up 12 to 14 years later. Significant differences on a number of behavioural as well as other measures were found between the two groups. The youngsters who at the age of four had managed to defer gratification and waited for the two marshmallows were as adolescents described as more socially competent, self-assertive, personally effective and able to cope well with the stresses of life. This group also had more success academically. In contrast, the group who were unable to wait were as adolescents perceived as easily upset, coping poorly with stress, had negative self-image and were prone to overreaction.

Impulsiveness is also used to denote one of several overlapping concepts viewed as part of a condition known as attention deficit hyperactivity disorder.

Inhibition

Inhibition refers to any process that restrains, prevents, diminishes or prevents certain responses. For example fear or anxiety can inhibit performance or the expression of wishes or desires.

Reciprocal inhibition is a theory that regards emotional difficulties as being produced through a maladaptive learning process, these difficulties arising in an anxiety- provoking situation. Reciprocal inhibition is the basis for unlearning learned emotional difficulties, e.g. fears and anxieties. The aim of the reciprocal inhibition approach is to inhibit, reduce or prevent anxiety by encouraging people to engage in behaviour that inhibits their anxiety and thereby reduces the connection between their anxiety and the anxiety-producing situation. People are gradually exposed to anxiety producing situations and then asked to engage in behaviour that would inhibit anxiety in those situations. Systematic desensitisation is the intervention that is based on the principle of reciprocal inhibition.

Intelligence and behaviour

In terms of scores on IQ tests there is a tendency for recidivist delinquents to have a lower IQ score than non-delinquents. In part the explanation for this finding is seen as the result of a failure of educational achievement. Children with reading difficulties are more likely to truant and therefore to engage in delinquent activities. However pre-school low IQs are linked with increased risks of disruptive and delinquent behaviour. Therefore both low IQ and poor educational achievement are both seen as associated with delinquent activity. Low IQ is closely connected to a risk of hyperactive and inattentive behaviour and truancy.

Feldman, P. (1993) The Psychology of Crime. Cambridge, Cambridge University Press.

Interactional model of behaviour

An interactional model of EBD has as its focus the positive and negative interactions between systems such as the family, school and groups and between individuals such as the child, his and her peers, and the significant adults in the child's life. The interactional approach regards EBD as the result of negative interactions that take place in a context and not simply as deficits residing within the child or adolescent. It also sees individual behaviour as a function of person-situation interactions. These interactions can be assessed through observation, interviews, checklists, rating scales and questionnaires and through sociometry. Changes can only be brought about across and between all those different systems involved in and contributory towards the identified or referred behaviours. Interactional interventions therefore aim to change, alter or modify what is often a cycle of negative interactions through encouraging positive interactions. An example of an interactional approach is the ecosystemic perspective that uses the family therapy technique of reframing to promote positive interactions.

Cooper, P., Smith, C.J. and Upton, G. (1994) Emotional and Behavioural Difficulties: Theory to Practice. London, Routledge.

Internalisation

Internalisation is a mental process whereby people come to accept particular beliefs, attitudes and values as their own. This process is usually seen as one whereby one's parents' values are internalised. In psychoanalytic theory the superego is believed to develop through a process of internalisation.

Intervention

An intervention is a process whereby an attempt is made to change people's thoughts, feelings and behaviour from a pre-existing state. Interventions are based on or informed by particular perspectives or approaches, e.g. cognitive-behavioural, psychodynamic or biological. Psychologists, counsellors or psychiatrists implement or enable others, including at times clients themselves, to implement interventions.

Before interventions are selected a period of assessment is undertaken in order to arrive at a baseline or at least some idea of the extent and severity of the current problems that the client manifests. Assessments are also used to establish targets, goals or aims of the intervention.

Interventions are often evaluated through the use of assessment instruments, personality tests or self-report measures. Some types of interventions may not have been evaluated or there may exist disputes over evaluation or the appropriate evaluation methodology for the type of intervention considered.

In some cases spontaneous remission occurs, the client improves without any treatment. Interventions may have limited or no effect and may result in negative side effects. They may also be implemented without regard to necessary preconditions or suggested guidance and therefore lack what is termed treatment integrity.

People, both recipients and implementers, may avoid or evade interventions. Finally interventions may face practical problems of personnel, time and cost in terms of particular contexts or institutions.

Ayers, H., Clarke, D. and Murray, A. (2000) *Perspectives on Behaviour: A Practical Guide to Effective Interventions for Teachers*, 2nd edn. London, David Fulton Publishers.

Mace, C., Moorey, S. and Roberts, B. (eds) (2001) *Evidence in the Psychological Therapies: A Critical Guide for Practitioners*. Hove, Brunner-Routledge.

Interviews and interviewing

An interview can be defined as any verbal interaction between one or more people with an individual or a group of people with the aim of obtaining information that will form part of an assessment process. The approach adopted in interviewing people will depend on the chosen perspective, e.g. biological, behavioural or cognitive.

Interviewing parents, teachers, young people and children is a key element in the process of both diagnosis and assessment and is a necessary prerequisite to formulation and intervention. Interviews may vary from being very highly structured with a pre-agreed set of questions to relatively unstructured and open-ended dialogues in which the client is encouraged to talk about the issue presented in any way he or she chooses.

A number of important considerations relating to ethical, cultural issues and confidentiality have to be acknowledged in the conduct of interviews. Professionals may not share the linguistic or cultural background of a client and if they are not sensitive and aware they run the risk of producing ill-informed formulations. Generally, the method of interview will reflect the theoretical perspective held by the person holding the interview. Behavioural approaches will focus on overt, observable and measurable responses whereas cognitive approaches will focus on thoughts, beliefs and attributions. However, in all cases, it is necessary to establish the purpose of the interview, to decide on the people to be interviewed and also decide on methods of obtaining information and at the same time develop positive rapport and accurate empathy.

Herbert, M. (1998) Clinical Child Psychology, 2nd edn. Chichester, Wiley.

Introjection

Introjection is a mental process whereby elements of the external world including relationships are taken over and become internal representations within the self.

Irrational thinking and beliefs

Irrational thinking and irrational beliefs are terms used in Rational-Emotive Behaviour Therapy (A. Ellis) to describe beliefs that negatively influence people's feelings, behaviour and other thought processes. These beliefs are seen as arising from a biological predisposition towards irrational thinking. Irrational thinking and beliefs contribute to self-defeating feelings and behaviour. Modification of these beliefs can enable people to overcome their emotional and behavioural problems. People are helped to challenge, refute and replace those beliefs with self-enhancing beliefs.

Irrational beliefs are absolutistic and rigid and take the form of 'musts', 'shoulds' and 'oughts'. These beliefs are not usually empirically or logically consistent and as a result they often have harmful emotional and behavioural consequences. Many types of irrational thinking take the form of over-generalisations. Examples of irrational beliefs are that:

* one must be loved and approved of;
* one must be totally competent;
* one must view things as catastrophic if frustrated;
* one has little or no control over one's feelings;
* one must be anxious and preoccupied with any threat;
* avoidance is better than taking on one's responsibilities;

- the past has to determine one's current feelings and behaviour;
- if solutions are not found then life must be terrible;
- happiness can be achieved through passivity or inaction.

People who subscribe to absolute 'musts' are inclined to:

- 'awfulising', believing things are totally bad if things are not as they should be;
- 'I-can't-stand-it-it is', things are totally unbearable if things do not turn out as required;
- 'damnation', failure to attain things we must have leads us to condemn ourselves or others.

The emotional consequences of irrational thinking and beliefs are unhealthy or self-defeating negative emotions that include anger, depression, shame and anxiety. In order to overcome their emotional problems people need to accept that they disturb themselves through their irrational thinking and are responsible for the continuance of their emotional difficulties if they continue to subscribe to irrational beliefs.

The aims of the counsellor should be to help people identify their irrational beliefs and then to empirically, logically and pragmatically dispute or challenge those beliefs. The counsellor's role is an active and directive one. People are asked to provide evidence for their beliefs and the consequences of not receiving what one thinks one must have. Furthermore people are encouraged to stop thinking in terms of absolute 'musts', 'shoulds' or 'oughts'. They are also required to look at their emotional and behavioural problems using an ABC analysis. 'A' stands for an activating event (an individual's perceptions and inferences), 'B' stands for rational and/or irrational beliefs and 'C' stands for emotional and/or behavioural consequences of those beliefs.

Yankura, J. and Dryden, W. (1994) Albert Ellis. London, SAGE Publications.

Isolation

Social isolation can be defined as a situation in which an individual feels alone and without anyone with whom they can share their feelings or thoughts. Teachers and parents can support the child who presents as an isolate by formulating interventions that involve the child in a safe way. For example, the child could be asked to carry out a task that is perceived as having high status and could be allocated a 'helper'. This may result in a friendship developing.

L

Labelling and behaviour

Labelling theory states that the labelling, assigning or attribution of deviant categories to individuals leads to a self-fulfilling prophecy. This theory sees no act as intrinsically deviant. Labelling is the result of a value judgement about other people's behaviour by people in positions of authority or power. Those in authority have the power therefore to define what acts are deviant and to apply the label as they see fit, consistently or inconsistently. These labels change according to historical, cultural and social contexts. Labelling is seen as acting to amplify or increase the growth and level of deviance and ends up in stigmatising those so labelled. Individuals who are labelled may decide to identify with the label and so continue or increase their level of deviance. They may also feel stigmatised and react by engaging in further deviance as they have nothing to lose from committing further acts of deviance.

Language and emotional behavioural difficulties

Children who have experienced delayed or disordered language development are vulnerable to developing emotional and behavioural difficulties. The reasons for this are inextricably linked with the fact that communicating effectively through language fulfils important needs. If a child is less able to understand what others want or less able to explain what they need, the result will inevitably be frustration. In addition, language plays a critical role in the development of children's social and self-regulatory behaviour. Children with a variety of speech and language impairments are at increased risk as their language abilities fall behind those of their peers. Although there are individual differences in the rates at which all children develop speech and language skills, the majority are able to achieve milestones within expected limits. Those that do not may have a language delay or a language disorder. Language delay refers to the fact that the individual's speech and language skills are following the normal sequence and pattern of development but at a slower rate than that expected of the majority of children. Language disorder refers to speech and language skills that are characterised by atypical and unusual development.

Language is a highly complex system which involves auditory, phonological, pragmatic, articulation, listening, attention control, semantic and grammatical components. These processes interact and difficulties in one area are likely to affect other parts of the system. Current diagnostic criteria distinguishes between expressive language disorders, receptive language disorders and specific speech articulation disorders (also referred to as phonological disorders).

The prevalence of language and communication difficulties is generally thought to be between five to ten per cent of children when they begin attending school although estimates vary depending on criteria used. The incidence of severe and specific language disorders is rarer, affecting one child in every one thousand. The causes of language disorders are not understood. More boys than girls experience language disorders.

There are different views as to the reason why there is an association between language problems and emotional behavioural difficulties. Some emphasise the link between language development and the individual's ability to regulate their behaviour and to exert control over the environment. If language development is delayed/disordered a child may present with challenging behaviour such as temper loss and an intervention may focus on the behaviour without checking whether language difficulties are an underlying cause. Another view is that children with language disorder may experience rejection by peers and have fewer opportunities for social interactions. This can then result in the individual developing emotional and behavioural problems. An alternative perspective is to view language and behavioural problems as symptoms of an underlying cause such as neurological immaturity. As many mothers of children with language disorders report high levels of stress it has also been proposed that psycho-social stressors may co-exist with language impairments and result in psychiatric disorders.

Ripley, K., Barrem, I. and Fleming, P. (2000) Inclusion for Children with Speech and Language Impairments. London, David Fulton Publishers.

Rutter, M., Taylor, E. and Hersov, L. (eds) (1994) Child and Adolescent Psychiatry Modern Approaches, 3rd edn. Oxford, Blackwell Scientific Publications.

Learned helplessness

This concept is based on experiments carried out by M. Seligman (1975) and his colleagues. They observed that dogs exposed to uncontrollable and inescapable electric shocks later failed to take action to escape or to stop the shocks even when a fairly obvious way of doing so was available. They concluded that in the first part of the experiment when the shocks were inescapable that the dogs had learned that the electric shock was uncontrollable. In the second part of the experiment the dogs acted on this assumption even when they could attempt to escape or avoid the electric shocks. In other words they had learned that they were helpless.

Learned helplessness was formulated as a way of describing the expectation of helplessness and lack of control that was generalised to new situations. Seligman applied this concept to depression by hypothesising that depression, like learned helplessness, was a reaction to inescapable or apparently inescapable situations or events over which the person has no control. Research has also shown that continual exposure to academic failure contributes to learned helplessness, withdrawal, lack of persistence and unwillingness to attempt new learning tasks. Parents and teachers can help to prevent learned helplessness by not only praising their children's successes but also by not attributing failures to a lack of ability and by not being overly concerned about the odd failure.

Seligman, M.E.P. (1975) Helplessness: On depression, development and death. San Francisco, CA, W.H. Freeman.

Learning difficulties and behaviour

Learning difficulties in the form of reading, writing, spelling and communication difficulties are often associated with a risk of developing emotional and behavioural difficulties. Children of average and higher ability can manifest learning difficulties (specific learning difficulties or dyslexia) as well as children of lower ability levels (mild, moderate or severe difficulties).

Children, adolescents and adults who experience learning difficulties are at risk of developing behavioural difficulties particularly if they have low self-esteem. Children and adolescents with learning difficulties can be stigmatised and may become socially isolated. They can also face discrimination in terms of offered options within the National Curriculum and also due to the operation of the hidden curriculum (negative attitudes, undifferentiated or low status materials and separatist organisation of learning). Students may be typified as 'thick' or unintelligent, unwilling to learn, unrewarding and difficult to teach. Discrimination may lead to students developing low self-esteem, feeling that they are failures, resulting in poor motivation and low achievement. Schools may emphasise the cognitive-intellectual domain at the expense of other domains such as the aesthetic, emotional, physical, thus putting these students at a disadvantage. The lack of differentiation in lesson delivery and materials may also adversely affect students with learning difficulties but differentiation in itself may also create a stigma of separation and low status.

Some students with learning difficulties may engage in off-task behaviours, may be less responsive, more easily distracted and more passive than students without learning difficulties. These behaviours may result from negative learning experiences in the past and the present.

Where learning difficulties are associated with emotional and behavioural difficulties, teachers and schools should focus on intervening in terms of:

- curriculum content and materials;
- teacher attitudes, teaching style and methods;
- differentiated groups, tasks and levels of work;
- problem solving approaches;
- oral work;
- the use of information technology;
- classroom organisation, resources, learning assistants, helpers and class size.

Behaviour and classroom management techniques are essential which means:

- knowing names of the students;
- using attention-gaining signals – noise, light as well as voice;
- stating verbally and writing on the board clear and concise instructions;
- having equipment and materials ready for immediate use;
- managing transitions within lessons between one set of activities and another;
- monitoring behaviour through constantly scanning the classroom while seeking out opportunities to acknowledge students' positive behaviour;
- mentally noting antecedents and consequences of behaviour (the ABC analysis), that of teachers and students;
- non-verbal as well as verbal cueing – gestures, looks and prompts;
- teacher mobility around the classroom – checking work and behaviour;
- counselling students outside or after the lesson – focus on the actual offence, avoid labelling, shaming, humiliating, screaming or being sarcastic;
- positive reinforcement of on-task behaviour and where possible ignoring off-task behaviour;
- modelling positive behaviour for students;
- time-out from positive reinforcement.

Emerson, E. (1995) *Challenging Behaviour: Analysis and intervention in people with learning difficulties.* Cambridge, Cambridge University Press.
Farrell, P. (1997) *Teaching Pupils with Learning Difficulties.* London, Cassell.
Montgomery, D. (1990) *Children with Learning Difficulties.* London, Cassell.

Learning theory

Learning theory regards emotional and behavioural difficulties as being largely the consequence of a particular type of learning process mediated through environmental factors. Hereditary or genetic factors set limits to the amount of learning that can be achieved. However those emotional and behavioural difficulties that have genetic components may be amenable to learning processes. These processes include classical conditioning, operant conditioning and social learning. People learn inappropriate or undesirable behaviour or fail to learn appropriate or desirable responses or behaviour. People are encouraged to learn appropriate responses or behaviour through learning techniques such as positive reinforcement, negative reinforcement, punishment, extinction, systematic desensitisation and modelling.

Domjan, M. (1998) *The Principles of Learning and Behavior,* 4th edn. Pacific Grove, CA, Brooks/Cole Publishing.

Locus of control

A person's locus of control refers to the particular type of perception or expectation the person has as to the origin of positive or negative reinforcement for their emotional or behavioural difficulty. Some people have an internal locus of control (internals), meaning that they think they have the ability to control events. Other people with an external locus of control (externals) think that events that happen to them are the result of chance or luck, influences they have no control over. Thus internals are more likely to make an effort to change things, believing they have control, whereas externals are more likely to feel powerless to change things, believing they have no control.

Rotter, J.B. (1966) *Generalized expectancies for internal versus external control of reinforcement. Psychological Monographs, 80 (Whole No. 609).*

Loneliness

Loneliness can be defined as a persistent longing for human interaction in the form of friendship and companionship. Loneliness is not the same as being alone. Many if not all individuals enjoy solitude some of the time. Loneliness is associated with feelings of desperation, depression, impatient boredom and self-criticism. The affection and intimacy that friendships provide are lacking and as a result the practical assistance, nurturance, companionship that all individuals need are not available. This can lead to the individual retreating from the social world and becoming withdrawn and passive. Research has established that children who are rejected by their peers and who have no friends are vulnerable to developing mental health problems when they are adults. Their academic attainments may be poor, they may begin to truant and to become involved in delinquent behaviours. However, there are significant differences between individuals regarding the extent to which they need friends and any interventions need to be sensitive to this. The interventions and strategies will need to address the perceptions and behaviours of others as well as helping the individual concerned to acquire the necessary skills to initiate and sustain friendships such as listening skills, communication and social skills.

M

Maintaining factors

In the behavioural approach maintaining factors are those factors that serve to maintain a person's current emotional or behavioural difficulties. Current behaviour is due to existing maintaining conditions, the past is seen as having an indirect influence on current behaviour. Current behaviour is modified through changing its maintaining conditions.

There are other kinds of personal maintaining factors such as cognitive, psychodynamic and biological. Cognitive factors include low self-efficacy beliefs, attributional bias, external loci of control, cognitive distortions, irrational beliefs and inadequate coping strategies. Psychodynamic factors include immature defence mechanisms, e.g. repression, denial, displacement, projection and splitting. Biological factors include high levels of physiological arousal, abnormal neurotransmitter functioning and hormonal imbalances.

Maintaining factors are often connected to particular contexts, for example the family system, e.g. negative interactions between parents, parents and children and between siblings. These negative interactions may take the form of inappropriate reinforcement, insecure attachment, punitive and inconsistent parenting, infrequent caring and supervision, emotional over-involvement or disengagement, unclear communication in the form of mixed messages and child abuse.

Maternal deprivation

Bereavement or the loss of love or a confiding relationship is a powerful source of stress throughout life. Conversely a caring, close relationship is protective. Children (particularly ages six months to four years) admitted to hospital or a residential nursery after separation from their parents initially display acute distress, tearfulness, restlessness, fretting, irritability and become sad, apathetic, aggressive and destructive. But after a time, a few days or weeks, children settle down. After returning home children may become temporarily unsettled and display fearfulness of separation but also hostility towards their parents. Repeated hospital admissions and separations from parents can enhance the risk of emotional problems.

With regard to bereavement, children's grief reactions (numbing, pain, pining and yearning, agitation, insomnia, anger and sadness) are similar to adults' but reactions appear to be less intense and briefer than in adults.

Parental divorce or separation may lead to children being at risk of developing behavioural difficulties in the form of aggression, impulsivity, disobedience and negative interaction with peers. However, only a minority of separated children are likely to display difficulties. These difficulties are particularly likely if parental conflict continues after separation, and are more severe among boys than girls. Boys tend to display externalising problems such as aggression whereas girls display internalising problems such as anxiety. Specifically with regard to maternal deprivation, children in general do not experience emotional and behavioural difficulties if mothers are out at work as long as the carer-child relationship is stable and caring. Separation only leads to the risk of emotional and behavioural problems and delinquency if it is the consequence of parental or family conflict. Children post-separation will benefit from the preservation of normal routines with regard to home, school and friendships and from inter-parental cooperation.

Rutter, M. (1972) Maternal Deprivation Reassessed. Harmondsworth, Penguin Books.

Medical conditions and behaviour

Medical or physical conditions can be associated with or caused by psychological and psychiatric disorders. Certain degenerative disorders such as Parkinson's disease and Huntington's disease are associated with depression and dementia. Creutzfeldt-Jakob disease is a degenerative disorder that leads to dementia. Epilepsy is a neurological disorder characterised by recurrent generalised (entire brain) or partial (part of the brain and simple or complex) seizures due to a spontaneous and abnormal discharge of neurons in the brain.

Complex partial seizure is the most common adult type of seizure. Prior to this type of seizure there can be unusual experiences such as déjà vu and jamais vu, mood states (fear, panic and depression) and automatic behaviours such as lip smacking. In the case of temporal lobe epilepsy sufferers are likely to experience changes in sexual behaviour (hyper or hyposexuality). Conversations and writing are likely to be ponderous and pedantic. Religiosity may be pronounced and schizophrenic-like episodes may occur. Brain tumours can cause delirium. Head injuries or traumas commonly occur in individuals aged 15 to 25 years and in males more than females. The most common consequences are cognitive impairments such as decreased concentration, increased distractibility, impaired learning and motivation and behavioural impairments such as depression, impulsivity and aggression. Endocrine disorders such as thyroid disorders (hyper and hypothyroidism) and adrenal disorders (Cushing's syndrome) can lead to psychological symptoms. AIDS, an immunodeficiency, viral, infectious disease can lead to mental disorders such as dementia, delirium, anxiety and depression.

Down's syndrome is a learning disability, a genetic disorder associated with chromosomal abnormalities, mostly trisomy 21 (an extra chromosome) but also mosaicism and translocation. Main characteristics include visual awareness and visual learning skills alongside poor motor coordination, speech and language difficulties, short-term auditory memory problems, writing and spelling difficulties and problemsolving difficulties. As regards behaviour difficulties there are no specific difficulties related solely to children with Down's syndrome. However they do possess a vulnerability to certain behaviour problems, in particular the adoption of avoidance and attention-seeking strategies.

Contacts

British Epilepsy Association, Anstey House, 40 Hanover Square, Leeds. Helpline 0800 309030.
Down's Syndrome Association, 155 Mitcham Road, London SW17 9PG. Tel. 020 8682 4001.
National Society for Epilepsy, Chalfont St Peter, Gerrards Cross, Bucks. Tel. 01494 873991.

Medical model

The medical model generally refers to the approach taken by psychiatry and clinical psychology towards emotional and behavioural difficulties or mental disorders. It is based on the idea that there is an underlying medical reason for these difficulties and disorders analogous to physical illness. Therefore the assumptions are that:

- there are identifiable, discrete biologically based categories of difficulties and disorders;
- there is disruption or malfunctioning of biological processes in the brain or the body, e.g. of neurotransmitters like norepinephrine, serotonin and dopamine;
- there are genetic factors that contribute to the causes of difficulties and disorders;
- there are biochemical, physiological, neurological or endocrinological factors that contribute to difficulties and disorders.

Treatment is mainly through the prescription of psychotropic drugs for the various difficulties and disorders, e.g. stimulants like methylphenidate (Ritalin) for ADHD.

Medication and behaviour

Medication or drug therapy, while addressing the main presenting symptoms of mental disorders, may have side effects on some individuals. Drug treatment is usually prescribed for mental disorders such as anxiety, schizophrenia and mood disorders such as depression, depending on age. Side effects may be counterbalanced by the benefits of being on the drug. Alternatively the individuals may have to be taken off the drug because of severe side effects. Furthermore prescribed drugs may not have any therapeutic effect on some individuals or they may not affect all the presenting symptoms. It can also be the case that some problems are not amenable to drug therapy and that some people are non-compliant with regard to taking drugs. Drugs themselves do not effect a cure but ameliorate symptoms that enable sufferers to return to a normal life. Termination of drug therapy can lead to the reappearance of the disorder.

Aldridge, S. (2000) Seeing Red and Feeling Blue. London, Arrow Books.
Lader, M. and Herrington, R. (1990) Biological Treatments in Psychiatry. Oxford, Oxford University Press.

Mentoring and behaviour

Mentoring in schools is a relationship between a mentor and pupil(s) whereby a mentor provides learning and behaviour support to a referred pupil(s). Mentoring comprises a range of functions including assessment, problem solving, mediation, role modelling, facilitation and confidence building.

Mentors need to be trained in a number of approaches to behaviour. These could include behavioural, cognitive and person-centred counselling approaches. They could also help the process of inclusion by supporting the reintegration of permanently excluded and special school EBD pupils into mainstream schools. These functions can enable pupils to raise their self-esteem and to self-regulate their behaviour.

The role of a mentor needs to be considered in relation to the roles of and expectations of teachers, pastoral staff and the pupils themselves. This is important in order to avoid role conflict between teachers and mentors.

Voluntary mentoring is where volunteers, from areas other than education such as business and commerce, act as role models to provide learning support for pupils and students while encouraging them to raise their aspirations.

Liverpool Excellence Partnership. Primary Learning Mentor Training: Trainer Manual, DfEE.

Modelling

Modelling is based on social learning theory and is both an explanation for how emotional and behavioural difficulties can be learned and an intervention or therapy for modifying or changing inappropriate behaviour.

Social learning theory states that behaviours can be learned through observation or imitation. Observational learning enables people to learn behaviours directly without proceeding through trial-and-error learning. This form of learning involves four cognitive processes or preconditions: attention, retention, motor reproduction and motivation.

* In order for observational learning to occur people must direct attention towards the modelled behaviour. The amount of attention depends on the attractiveness and status and even the age of the model. The amount learned also depends on the complexity of the behaviour demonstrated, existing behavioural repertoires and the ability to process the information provided.
* The observed behaviour must be retained or remembered in the form of symbols or words so that the behaviour can be rehearsed and reproduced appropriately on future occasions.
* The observed behaviour must then be translated into appropriate action. This in turn depends on knowing and understanding the main responses that make up the observed behaviour and being aware of the accuracy with which it is performed. Behaviours may need to be broken down into a series of small steps, actions or tasks that are finally integrated into the full behaviour.
* Finally motivation is necessary if the observed behaviour is to be attended to, retained and rehearsed.

Models can have five main effects:

- They can demonstrate new types of behaviour or new arrangements of behaviour.
- They can provide prompts or cues for behaviours to be performed.
- They can show or indicate the positive or negative consequences of particular types of behaviours. Positive consequences lead to motivation or imitation of observed behaviours whereas negative consequences lead to lack of motivation or avoidance of those behaviours. Anxiety can also be reduced when positive consequences occur.
- They can initiate or facilitate similar behaviours.
- They may provide the criteria for self-reinforcement especially when those criteria are unclear or unknown.

Modelling therapy or interventions are usually combined with behaviour rehearsal, i.e. practising the observed, target behaviours. Modelling interventions can be used in skills and social skills training in order to rectify deficits, in self-modelling through video recording, in assertion training and fear or anxiety reduction through coping or mastery models.

The upshot of successful modelling is an increase in perceived self-efficacy, the belief that one can be successful at a task or can perform desired behaviours. Modelling is a brief therapy that is cost effective, relatively easy to implement in different settings, is relatively acceptable and unintrusive and is an aspect of many behavioural interventions.

Spiegler, M.D. and Guivrement, D.C. (1998) Contemporary Behavior Therapy, 3rd edn. Pacific Grove, CA, Brooks/Cole Publishing.

Moral reasoning retraining

Moral reasoning retraining is based on Kohlberg's (1963) stage theory of moral reasoning. Level 1 (Preconventional) stages 1 and 2 are based on coercion and the exchange of favours. Level 2 (Conventional) stages 3 and 4 are based on approval, expectations, traditional values and patriotism. Level 3 (Postconventional) stages 5 and 6 are based on human rights and universal values of conscience, justice and equality.

The aim of moral reasoning retraining is to move antisocial children and adolescents from immature moralities (superficial, egocentric and selfish moralities) to mature moralities (mutuality and social conscientiousness) through peer group discussion of moral dilemmas and problem situations such as substance abuse, negative peer and family relationships. The focus is on cognitive distortions and how they impact on moral reasoning. The procedure is to introduce a problem situation, encourage a group ethos of mutuality, cooperation and conscientiousness, provide perspective-taking opportunities, challenge negative viewpoints and finally consolidate mature moralities.

Kohlberg, L. (1963) The development of children's orientations towards moral order: Sequence in the development of moral thought. Vita Humana, 6.

Motivation and behaviour

The term motive can refer to an internal state or state of arousal or an external event that initiates or directs action or behaviour. Motivation may refer to physiological drives, to needs, to emotional states, to incentives and to unconscious processes. People give reasons, excuses and justifications for their actions or behaviour by referring to motives. In some cases people rationalise their behaviour by concealing unacceptable reasons for their actions by citing socially acceptable motives.

There are various approaches to motivation: drive (Freudian) theory, behavioural (stimulus–response) theory, need theory, goal theory, cognitive theory, attributional theory, self-actualising theory and motivational style.

Drive theory states that an internal state of arousal or instinct drives people to reduce or eliminate a state of tension. Tension is connected to pain and tension reduction is connected to the elimination of pain. Tension reduction is also associated with pleasure. Drive theories are both tension reduction and hedonic (pleasure-pain) theories. Freudian theory is an example of a drive theory that is based on sexual and aggressive drives that have a source, an aim and an object. People attempt to satisfy their sexual and aggressive impulses in a variety of idiosyncratic ways. The ways in which people satisfy their drives are the bases for their particular character or personality. Conflicts that arise in attempting to satisfying drives may evoke anxiety and neurosis unless defence mechanisms come into play that prevent this anxiety from emerging. People's sexual and aggressive drives need to be satisfied in socially acceptable ways if they are not to lead to antisocial, deviant or criminal behaviour.

Behavioural, in particular operant theory, sees people as being motivated through positive reinforcement of specific behaviours. Behaviour that is positively reinforced or rewarded will be strengthened, i.e. repeated. In order to motivate people it is necessary to find incentives or rewards that will induce them to perform desired actions or behaviours. People are therefore seen as being extrinsically motivated.

Need theory sees motivation as the satisfaction of certain needs. Satisfaction of these needs will lead to a reduction in tension. These needs can be primary (physiological) or secondary (acquired). Some examples of primary needs are food, water and sex and some secondary examples are achievement, affiliation, nurturance and dominance. Environmental factors can have an affect on particular needs through allowing or denying their satisfaction. People who have a need for achievement may find that the environment they live or work in prevents them from satisfying their need for achievement. People should be analysed in terms of needs-environment congruence or fit, the extent to which the needs of people are met by their environment.

Goal theory focuses on goal-directed behaviour. People choose goals that they then pursue. The kinds of goals people pursue can be included under the general categories of leisure, power, self-improvement, relationships and stress-reduction. Within these categories there are more specific goals that reflect idiosyncratic choices. The goals people choose to pursue are often characterised by high value, positive feelings and a high probability of achievement. Sometimes people do not achieve their goals. This may be due to external factors but can also be due to internal factors, mainly problems with volition.

Cognitive theories focus on cognitive processes such as thinking and reasoning about the external world. People try for example to predict the future and reduce uncertainty. They develop hypotheses that are tested to see if they are confirmed or disconfirmed. The results of these hypotheses influence behaviour.

Another cognitive theory is attributional theory that focuses on causal explanations for events. This involves considering certain dimensions such as internal or external locus of control and stability of causality. For example, success or failure might be attributed to ability, effort or luck. Another dimension is controllability. People might see certain qualities or attributes as controllable, e.g. physical appearance, but others such as intelligence as not controllable. Different types of causal attribution may lead to related types of emotion such as guilt or shame and anger or sympathy. Another cognitive theory sees educational failure as due to different motivational styles, namely helpless and mastery motivational styles. Helpless-oriented people see setbacks as permanent failures whereas mastery-oriented people see setbacks as temporary and as challenges or opportunities for future success.

Self-actualisation theories see people as wanting to develop and realise their full human potential. People are intrinsically motivated, i.e. they wish to pursue their interests for their own sake rather than for any reward. Incentives are not considered necessary for learning. External constraints and rewards are seen as diminishing intrinsic motivation. Controlling and pressuring approaches are also seen as producing negative outcomes as compared to strategies that encourage self-control and self-determination.

Galloway, D., Rogers, C., Armstrong, D. and Leo, E. (1998) *Motivating the Difficult to Teach*. London, Longman.
Pervin, L.A. (1996) *The Science of Personality*. Chichester, Wiley.

Motivational interviewing

First described by W. R. Miller in relation to treating problem drinkers and then developed further by W. R. Miller and S. Rollnick (1991).

Principles

- Person-centred type of counselling basis: empathy, acceptance and unconditional positive regard.
- Active role of pupil and teacher, teacher as facilitator mobilising a pupil's internal strengths.
- Avoidance of confrontation and argument. Avoidance of diagnostic labelling.
- Collaboration or partnership between teacher and pupil.
- Pupil is encouraged to accept responsibility for changing and the need to change.

- Internal attribution is also encouraged, i.e. attributing success to one's own efforts rather than to another's actions, luck or circumstances.
- Resistance is regarded as pupil feedback indicating counsellor expectations of change are too high at the stage required.

Aims

The main aim is to elicit ambivalence and facilitate pupils' resolution of that ambivalence. The term ambivalence refers to the conflicts that pupils experience over changing their behaviour.

- Promote pupil self-esteem and self-efficacy.
- Promote pupil knowledge of their problems and concern about their problems and illuminate discrepancies between pupil goals and current behaviour.

Model stages

- Pre-contemplative: Pupils do not acknowledge they have behavioural difficulties. The pupil is not aware of a difficulty or may not accept that it is a difficulty. Pupils may be reluctant or resistant to changing their behaviours. In such cases pupils should be helped to an informed choice regarding the consequences of not changing their behaviour.
- Contemplative: Pupils consider that they may have behavioural difficulties and that change may be desirable. Pupils should be made aware of the positive and negative consequence of change as well as the positive and negative aspects of the behavioural difficulty. Pupils considering change do not necessarily decide to change.
- Determining or deciding: Pupils decide to change behaviour or not to change their behaviour but at any time they may change their minds. This stage should ensure that the pupil is equipped with skills that will effect change and that barriers to change are identified along with responses that can circumvent those obstacles. A plan should be drawn up to specify the targets to be achieved and the action pupils need to perform in order to achieve those targets.
- Active change: Pupils put decision to change their behaviour into practice. They should confirm their desire to change and they should also receive feedback and positive reinforcement depending on progress made.
- Maintenance: Pupils maintain their changed behaviour through receiving feedback and positive reinforcement and through feeling that the changes they have made are beneficial.
- Relapse: Pupils revert to their original behavioural difficulties. There does not necessarily have to be a pessimistic response to relapse as it may mean that further attempts need to be made before change becomes permanent.

Some counselling techniques used in motivational interviewing:

- Selective or differential active listening to pupils.
- Reframing positively pupils' negative responses to the interviewer.
- Reflecting the feelings underlying pupils' statements.
- Reflecting pupils' internal mental conflicts.
- Encouraging pupils to discuss the pros and cons of changing their behaviour.
- Deliberately exaggerating pupils' responses and deliberately understating pupils' responses in order to encourage particular reactions.
- Provoking responses by denying pupils' difficulties.

Miller, W.R. and Rollnick, S. (eds) (1991) Motivational Interviewing: Preparing People to Change. New York, The Guilford Press.

N

Nature and nurture

There is an ongoing debate and controversy about the relative influences of nature (heredity) and nurture (environment) on human behaviour but there is a consensus that both nature and nurture contribute to behaviour. However, certain points should be considered first, namely that:

- A trait can be modified but also be heritable, which is to say that even when a trait is highly heritable the environment can still be very influential, as for example with height.
- Heritability refers to the variability in a trait, i.e. a consequence of differences in heredity or alternatively the different claims as to the relative degrees to which heredity and the environment contribute to the variation between individuals in a population for a particular trait. It should be noted that heritability refers to populations and to the differences between individuals in the population, not to the particular traits of the individuals themselves. It also refers only to the specific trait observed within the particular population in the given environmental setting. Heritability does not equate with inherited nor with unchangeability. Heritability estimates are helpful in determining whether there is any hereditary basis for differences in traits.
- Heritability estimates vary according to place and time.
- As environments improve heritability increases as the only source of differences in an optimum environment would be genetic.
- It is generally agreed that heredity and the environment influences particular traits. However disagreement occurs over the relative contributions of nature and nurture to those traits. In actuality people inherit a predisposition to particular traits or diseases that require environmental triggers in order for them to manifest themselves.
- There are other biological influences on development besides heredity, e.g. infections in the intrauterine environment.
- Behaviour appears to be influenced by many genes rather than by a single gene but defective, single genes can adversely affect behaviour.
- Environmental influences are divided between shared and non-shared experiences. Non-shared environmental influences (peers, neighbourhood and school) appear to have a greater influence than shared (home) influences.
- Traits that are considered as partially inherited include temperament, extroversion and introversion, intelligence (IQ), hyperactivity, autism and schizophrenia.

Ceci, S.J. and Williams, W.M. (eds) (1999) The Nature–Nurture Debate: The Essential Readings, Oxford. Blackwell Publishers.

Negative reinforcement

Negative reinforcement is a process in operant conditioning. Negative reinforcement takes place when a response stops or prevents the occurrence of an environmental event. If the response occurs then the stimulus is terminated or withdrawn, if the response does not happen then the stimulus continues.

Procedures in which responses terminate or prevent aversive stimuli occurring are examples of negative reinforcement. There are two kinds of negative reinforcement, escape and avoidance. Escape occurs where an aversive stimulus can be terminated by a response, e.g. by turning off something and by leaving situations. The response is reinforced or strengthened by termination of the aversive stimulus. Avoidance occurs where a response prevents the occurrence of an aversive stimulus. Negative reinforcement in both cases leads to an increase in responses or behaviour.

The term 'negative' does not refer to an unpleasant outcome but simply to the removal of an aversive stimulus. Negative reinforcement is different from punishment although both include aversive stimuli. With punishment the response is followed by the delivery of an aversive stimulus leading to a reduction in the response. In the case of negative reinforcement the response either terminates or prevents the delivery of an aversive stimulus and as a result leads to an increase in that response. Although negative reinforcement is a process that maintains behaviour it is rarely used as a behavioural technique for changing behaviour.

Spiegler, M.D. and Guivrement, D.C. (1998) Contemporary Behavior Therapy, 3rd edn. Pacific Grove, CA, Brooks/Cole Publishing.

Nomothetic approach

Nomothetic refers to general explanations of common factors in people behaviours contrasted with explanations of unique behaviours.

Normal behaviour

Normal behaviour is contrasted with abnormal behaviour. Behaviour is often judged normal according to its:

- statistical frequency;
- how far it conforms to social or cultural norms;
- how far it does not cause personal distress or stress;
- how far it does not cause stress or distress to others;
- how far working and personal relationships are successful and unimpaired;
- proportionality in respect of responses to stressful or unpleasant experiences.

What is perceived as normal and abnormal behaviour can vary historically, socially, culturally and according to a particular group, setting or context. Normality may be what is ideologically (politically or religiously) acceptable. The attribution of normality and abnormality can simply be a function of the power or authority a person or a group possesses. The labelling of people as normal or abnormal may be inconsistent or inaccurate even according to current norms or even when applying diagnostic categories. Issues and controversies arise with regard to defining normality and abnormality with respect to cultural and ethnic differences. However there are similarities across societies and cultures in terms of what are regarded as the main mental disorders (schizophrenia, depressive and anxiety disorders) but there may be differences with regard to the normality of people's beliefs. It should be remembered that at times many people have their behaviour assessed, diagnosed or described as 'abnormal'. However this 'abnormal' behaviour may be temporary, of short duration and developmental in nature.

O

Obesity

Whereas anorexia and bulimia are considered as psychiatric disorders, obesity is generally regarded as a medical condition, albeit one which is overlaid with powerful social and cultural beliefs and assumptions. Obesity is a weight-related disorder and can be defined as an excessive amount of body fat. This is measured by calculating the Body Mass Index whereby weight in kilograms is divided by height in metres squared. As different people have varying body shapes BMI is not an exact measure and several bands have been devised ranging from underweight through desirable weight to overweight, obese and morbidly obese. Obesity is currently considered to be a major and increasing problem and its incidence has risen dramatically. In 1980 the percentage of obese men and women in the United Kingdom was 6 and 8 per cent respectively; in 1998 it had risen to 17.3 and 21.2 per cent. The prevalence of obesity increases with age up to around 65 and then decreases. A number of factors appear to predispose an individual to becoming obese. Obesity has been demonstrated to have a genetic component; it is more common in some ethnic groups and its incidence is higher in industrialised countries. The causes of obesity are complex and involve many factors including genetic, cultural, socio-economic, and medical.

Genetic factors

Evidence that obesity has a genetic component is contained in twin studies as well as studies of adopted children who were found to have weight patterns similar to their birth parents rather than their adopted parents. Children with two obese parents have approximately 70 per cent risk of becoming obese in comparison to 20 per cent of children whose parents are not obese. The extent of the influence of genetic factors ranges from more than 50 per cent to as low as 5 per cent but the precise genes involved have yet to be identified and it is very likely that there is a multigene factor. Genetic factors do not control how fat a person becomes but they influence the person's predisposition to obesity.

Cultural factors

Studies in the USA have demonstrated that Black and Hispanic groups are at greater risk of obesity than White Americans. These differences are likely to be a result of a combination of socio-economic, cultural and genetic factors. In Western industrialised societies obesity is stigmatised. Surveys demonstrate that people who are overweight are perceived as lacking in self-control, lazy, stupid, poorly organised and weak-willed. Even with the same qualifications, they are less likely to succeed in obtaining a place at college and less likely to be offered jobs.

Socio-economic factors

In contemporary Western societies, the increasing rates of obesity can be viewed as in part the result of the process of industrialisation. Specifically, relative abundance of food, diets that contain large amounts of fat and sugars and an increasingly sedentary lifestyle are significant factors. The reason for the higher number of obese individuals from lower socio-economic background is likely to be related to the higher calorific content of cheap food.

Medical factors

Obesity increases the likelihood of a number of medical problems, including digestive illnesses, cardiovascular diseases, adult-onset diabetes and cancer. There are a few medical conditions that increase the likelihood of becoming obese, for example, hypothyroidism and Cushing's syndrome. These conditions can be diagnosed through blood tests and appropriate treatment usually corrects the problem. There are also certain drugs such as some antidepressants and antihistamines that can contribute to changes in body weight and fat distribution.

Treatment

The treatment of obesity includes behaviour therapy, cognitive-behavioural therapies, drug therapies, group therapy, psychotherapy, relaxation and imagery techniques, as well as traditional dietary interventions and surgical interventions.

Gordon, R. (2000) Eating Disorders: Anatomy of a Social Epidemic, 2nd edn. Oxford, Blackwell.
Thompson, S. (1993) Eating Disorders: A Guide for Health Professionals. London, Chapman and Hall.

Contacts

Eating Disorders Association. Helpline 01603 621414 (9.30 a.m. to 6.30 p.m., Monday–Friday).
Overeaters Anonymous. Various locations across the UK. Tel. 07000 784 985

Object

A psychoanalytic term that refers to an object meaning a person or part of a person to which another person directs their desire or behaviour towards. A bad object (internal or external) is one that is disliked or feared. A good object (internal or external) is one that is liked and approached.

Object relations

Object relations theory is a psychoanalytical theory that sees a person's need to relate to other objects as paramount. This theory sees a person's primary need as one of relating to others. It is in contrast to instinct or drive theory. This theory sees the satisfaction of drives and instinctual processes as foremost.

Object relations theory sees the internal mental world as populated by the self, its objects and their relationships. The relationship between these internal objects serve as models for future relationships. Transitional objects and phenomena are half-way objects (a comforter such as a teddy bear) that facilitate separation from the mother. These objects enable children to move from infantile self-love to love for others and from dependency to independence.

Observation

The behavioural approach to assessment is mainly based on formal, empirical observation. This type of observation is seen as a way of avoiding speculation and high levels of inference and as a means of accumulating verifiable evidence for assertions about behaviour. Observation is considered a necessary precondition of achieving a relatively objective description of specific and overt behaviours. Precise definitions of overt behaviour are agreed before observing behaviours. Observations are undertaken systematically in a naturalistic or real-life setting such as the home and school. This type of observation is based on measuring or quantifying the frequency, duration and intensity of behaviours. It provides a means of establishing a pre-intervention baseline through arriving at a representative sample of behaviour. Observation schedules are used as a means of recording observations such as behaviour frequency counts, fixed interval sampling, behavioural checklists and ABC charts.

Observers need to be familiar with agreed definitions of behaviour such as what constitutes physical or verbal aggression and with the methods of measuring and recording behaviours. The aim is to achieve a high level of observational accuracy or inter-observer reliability.

There are various difficulties with this type of observation, namely subject reactivity, observer error, observer drift, observer bias and impracticality. Reactivity occurs where people observed are aware of being observed and as a result behave differently. In order to avoid reactivity it is advisable to become familiar with the setting and for those observed to become accustomed to observation. Observational errors arise when definitions of behaviours are imprecise and recordings of behaviours are inaccurate. Observer drift occurs when observers deviate from the agreed definitions of behaviour when observing behaviour. Bias can occur even when definitions are precise. Observers who have preconceptions about what they expect to observe are likely to display bias and skew their results. Finally observation may often be impracticable in that it is both labour and time intensive and behaviours may only be performed infrequently. It is often necessary for reasons of practicality to choose a time and place when and where the behaviours are most likely to occur and when and where they are least likely to occur.

Ayers, H., Clarke, D. and Ross, A. (1996) Assessing Individual Needs, 2nd edn. London, David Fulton Publishers.

Ollendick, T.H. and Hersen, M. (eds) (1984) Child Behavioral Assessment. New York, Pergamon Press.

Silva, F. (1993) Psychometric Foundations and Behavioral Assessment. Newbury Park, CA, SAGE Publications.

Obsessive-compulsive disorder (OCD)

Obsessional-compulsive disorder is characterised by obsessional thoughts, compulsive behaviours and secondary or associated anxiety and depression. It occurs along a spectrum or continuum from mild to severe. Obsessions can occur with or without compulsive behaviour. Sufferers themselves view their obsessive behaviour as out of character and as absurd.

Obsessional thoughts consist of words, phrases and beliefs that invade sufferers' minds even though they try to exclude them. They feel compelled to think these thoughts even though they resist them. These thoughts and beliefs are often concerned with contamination, catastrophes and exact order and are also aggressive, obscene or blasphemous. Obsessional images are vivid and are frequently violent or sexual in nature. Obessional ruminations are endless internal debates over intrusive ideas and beliefs. Obsessional doubts are where sufferers constantly worry over whether they have turned things off, whether they have harmed or damaged other people or whether they have done the right thing. Obsessional impulses are where sufferers feel and struggle with urges to perform violent or embarrassing acts. These acts are not performed but the mental conflict is very unpleasant. Obsessional rituals occur when sufferers engage in repeated, unproductive activities such as touching, counting, checking, cleaning and washing. These rituals are repeated again and again until the sufferer feels they have been performed correctly. Obsessional phobias develop when thoughts and rituals become more intense in certain settings. Eventually sufferers become phobic about these settings and avoid them in order to escape the accompanying thoughts and rituals.

OCD sufferers often feel anxious and become depressed as a result of the strain of experiencing the disorder. Parents and family members may feel compelled to conform to obsessional requests or requirements. OCD is a disorder that is much less prevalent than anxiety disorder and is found equally among men and women. The most common time of onset is late childhood or early adolescence and is often connected to a stressful event. Men tend towards checking compulsions whereas women tend towards cleaning compulsions. A significant number of adult sufferers have experienced OCD symptoms before the age of 15 years. OCD symptoms may co-occur in other disorders such as tic disorders (Tourette's syndrome), eating disorders, ADHD, delays, enuresis, encopresis and schizophrenia. Most sufferers improve within a year but a minority experience partial or complete remissions over months or several years.

There are several perspectives on the causes of OCD, the main ones being biological and psychological. There is a preponderance of OCD among families within which the disorder is diagnosed so there may be a genetic predisposition. It has been suggested that OCD may be the consequence of biological problems, namely basal ganglia disease or levels of the neurotransmitter, serotonin in connection with both dopamine and acetylcholine. The psychoanalytic approach focuses on the defence mechanism of undoing that enables sufferers to control anxiety through performing a compulsive ritual that undoes or eliminates their undesirable urges. The cognitive-behavioural approach focuses on classical conditioning and irrational thinking as causes of OCD preceded by a marked vulnerability to obsessional thoughts and compulsive rituals. Systems approaches focus on those factors that may operate in families to maintain compulsive behaviour such as becoming involved in the sufferer's rituals, possessing and expressing inadequate or erroneous information about the condition, expressing open criticism and seeing the sufferer only as a problem.

There are various interventions for OCD based on particular perspectives or combinations of perspectives such as biological, cognitive-behavioural, behavioural and ecosystemic. The biological approach uses serotonin reuptake inhibitors (clomipramine or fluoxetine) to reduce fear. The cognitive-behavioural approach uses psychoeducation (changing catastrophic interpretations) along with modelling. The behavioural approach uses exposure along with response prevention to manage anxiety. The ecosystemic approach uses reframing to externalise OCD as a common problem for all to address rather than it being seen as simply a sufferer's behavioural problem.

Parents are trained to avoid using coercion or blame, to practise exposure and response prevention, to use positive reinforcement and reframing.

De Silva, P. and Rachman, S. (1998) Obsessive-Compulsive Disorder: the facts, 2nd edn. Oxford, Oxford University Press.

Oedipus complex

The Oedipus complex is a Freudian psychoanalytical term that refers to unconscious conflicts arising from the desire to sexually possess the parent of the opposite sex and to get rid of the parent of the same sex. The complex is resolved through identification with the same sex parent and the rejection of the parent of the opposite sex until a similar substitute is found in a sexual partner in adult life. The choice of a partner who resembles one's father or mother is determined by a father or mother fixation at the Oedipal phase.

Operant conditioning

Operant conditioning is one of the main learning theories developed by B. F. Skinner (1904–90) and is based on E. Thorndike's (1874–1949) law of effect which states that behaviour followed by rewarding consequences is repeated and behaviour followed by punishing consequences is reduced or terminated.

Operant learning occurs when behaviours operate on the environment in such a way that they produce certain consequences. Behaviour is linked to or determined by its consequences. There is no need to refer to cognitive or unconscious processes given that behaviour is controlled by its consequences. There are contingent, empirical relationships between behaviours and the consequences of those behaviours. Behaviours that have rewarding consequences are likely to increase and those behaviours are said to have received positive reinforcement. If certain behaviours do not receive positive reinforcement then those behaviours are not likely to increase. Discriminative stimuli are external events that inform people that if they perform certain behaviours then particular consequences will ensue. A reinforcing stimulus or reinforcer is defined as any event that follows an operant response and that increases the likelihood of its recurrence. If a person praises a person on each occasion the person performs a task or behaviour well and the person responds to praise by increasing the tasks and behaviour then the praise is a reinforcer. A biological or primary reinforcer is one that is naturally pleasant, such as food, or one that is naturally unpleasant, such as pain. A conditioned or secondary reinforcer is one that has become associated with a biological reinforcer. Generalised reinforcers are ones associated with a range of biological reinforcers and can be material, such as money, or non-material, such as attention, praise and affection. Positive reinforcers are rewarding or pleasant stimuli that increase behaviours whereas negative reinforcers are aversive stimuli which when withdrawn following appropriate responses increase behaviours. People who need to be encouraged can either be praised for commencing their on-task behaviour or they can stop being criticised when they commence their on-task behaviour. Both types of reinforcers result in an increase in on-task behaviour. Punishment occurs when an aversive stimulus is applied after a response and results in a reduction in the response. There is also continuous and partial (intermittent) reinforcement and various schedules or reinforcement, interval and ratio schedules.

Shaping or successive approximation is a method of bringing about target behaviours not being performed through reinforcing similar behaviours to the target behaviours.

Operant theory states that emotional and behavioural difficulties are the consequences of reinforcement or punishment. Fears and anxieties can be seen as being the result of being punished in certain situations or being reinforced for avoiding those situations. Depression can be seen as due to the loss of positive reinforcement as in bereavement or unemployment or ineffectual attempts to remove one's self from unpleasant or punishing situations.

Operant interventions are primarily based on the use of positive reinforcement. Negative reinforcement is rarely used and punishment is avoided if possible. Punishment is avoided if it is ineffective or if it has undesirable side effects. Positive reinforcement is the preferred option and refers to rewarding appropriate or desired behaviours or approximations to those behaviours such that those desired behaviours increase. It should be noted that inadvertent positive reinforcement of undesired behaviours is possible. In these situations positive reinforcement should cease. Positive reinforcers can be material (preferred activities) or non-material (praise) and used with individuals or groups and in a token economy. Opportunities for positive reinforcement need to be maximised. Positive reinforcement is more effective at first if delivered immediately and continuously after the desired behaviours are performed.

Domjan, M. (1998) *The Principles of Learning and Behavior*, 4th edn. Pacific Grove, CA, Brooks/Cole Publishing.

Spiegler, M.D. and Guivrement, D.C. (1998) *Contemporary Behavior Therapy*, 3rd edn. Pacific Grove, CA, Brooks/Cole Publishing.

Oppositional defiant disorder (ODD)

Oppositional defiant disorder (ODD) is a type of conduct disorder more commonly manifested by young children, especially those in the pre-school period. The main symptoms are frequent temper loss, anger, resentment, vindictiveness, disobedience, arguing with and defying adults, particularly parents, and blaming others. These symptoms need to be manifested over a period of six months and to be more frequent than average before the diagnosis can be made. The symptoms are more evident in situations involving adults and peers. The antisocial aspects of conduct disorders such as delinquency are not apparent in the case of ODD. ODD is more common in boys than girls.

Organic brain disorders and behaviour

Brain disorders are relatively rare in children and are likely to be caused by genetic factors, pre-natal and postnatal problems. Brain disorders are diagnosed through neurological assessment, e.g. an EEG or CT or MRI scanning. It should be noted that some brain disorders are reversible as in the case of epilepsy. Brain disorders may be the result of injury, accidental and non-accidental, infections, metabolic problems and severe malnutrition. Children with brain disorders are more likely to have mental disorders than the general child population. However children with brain disorders do not necessarily have mental disorders and those with mental disorders do not necessarily have brain disorders. Children that have brain disorders along with mental disorders do not manifest a single type of disorder. However, autistic and hyperactivity disorders appear over-represented. Children with brain disorders often appear to parents and teachers as oppositional and irritable, displaying temper outbursts and high levels of distress. Particular types of neurological disorders are associated with certain types of mental disorders, e.g. Sydenham's chorea with OCD and tuberous sclerosis with pervasive developmental disorders.

Brain disorders can lead to negative psychological and social consequences in the form of low self-esteem, peer rejection, unrealistic expectations and overprotection.

There is a wide range of specific brain disorders that are associated with a greater risk of mental disorders. These include Rett's syndrome (screaming attacks and unprovoked laughter), epilepsy (at greater risk for a conduct or emotional disorder), cerebral palsy and head injuries. However, children with brain disorders can grow out of mental disorders as well as develop them. Child mental disorders may be coincidental with brain disorders and also secondary to the brain disorder.

The treatment of the mental problems of children with brain disorders does not have to be exclusively from the biological perspective but can also can be based on behavioural approaches.

Goodman, R. and Scott, S. (1997) Child Psychiatry. Oxford, Blackwell Science.
Kaplan, H.I. and Sadock, B.J. (1996) Concise Textbook of Clinical Psychiatry, 7th edn. Baltimore, MA, Williams & Wilkins.

P

Panic disorders

Panic disorder refers to the occurrence of panic attacks. These attacks are abrupt and consist of feelings of intense apprehension that may also be associated with breathlessness, palpitations, dizziness, trembling, nausea, chest pain, choking, derealisation (a feeling of having loss contact with reality), depersonalisation (feelings of being out of one's body) and paraesthesias (unusual skin sensations). Sufferers may also feel that they are about to die or that they are going mad.

Panic attacks are common in anxiety disorders. Panic attacks can occur frequently, often occur in specific situations and are frequently cued or triggered by specific stimuli and they usually last for minutes rather than hours. They can even occur in uncued situations when people are relaxed or asleep. More women than men are affected. Panic attacks are very rare in pre-adolescents. Generally panic attacks begin during adolescence and are particularly related to stress. Panic disorder can occur with or without agoraphobia. It can also co-occur with depression, generalised anxiety disorder and alcoholism.

The various perspectives on panic disorders include the biological and the cognitive-behavioural perspectives. The biological approach regards panic disorders as being caused by physical problems (e.g. mitral valve prolapse syndrome) in a minority of cases and as possibly involving genetic factors as it tends to run in families. It may arise partly as a response to autonomic overactivity. Certain chemicals such as yohimbine (an alpha-adrenergic antagonist that increases sympathetic activity) and carbon dioxide can induce attacks. Certain drugs such as imipramine and SSRIs can reduce attacks. Antidepressants such as SSRIs (Prozac) and tricyclics such as Tofranil and anxiolytics such as alprazolam have helped to reduce attacks. Drug treatment has to be continuous and can have side effects such as weight gain and raised blood pressure.

The cognitive approach regards panic disorders as due to people catastrophically misinterpreting the physical sensations they experience. Sensations of normal anxiety are misinterpreted as indicating imminent physical (heart attack) or mental (insanity) collapse. People who experience panic attacks develop an intense fear of losing control particularly in public.

The behavioural techniques of exposure and desensitisation have been used to treat panic disorder with agoraphobia. Cognitive interventions include psychoeducation about the nature of panic attacks, identifying triggers, encouraging the use of distraction and helping sufferers to question or challenge their catastrophic cognitions.

Clark, D.M. and Fairburn, C.G. (1997) Science and Practice of Cognitive Behaviour Therapy. Oxford, Oxford University Press.

Dobson, K.S. and Craig, K.D. (eds) (1996) *Advances in Cognitive-Behavioural Therapy*. London, SAGE Publications.

Rachman, S. (1998) *Anxiety*. Hove, Psychology Press.

Paranoid schizophrenia

Paranoid schizophrenia refers to a type of mental disorder that is characterised by delusions (beliefs that resist empirical or logical refutation). The contents of delusions are often influenced by cultural beliefs and are also culturally relative. These facts become important in terms of diagnosis. Sufferers may feel they are being spied on, cheated, followed, conspired against and maligned.

Delusions of persecution are the most common but sufferers may also experience grandiose delusions (exaggerated notions of who they are, their power and influence) or delusional jealousy (unfounded notions about their partner's infidelity). Auditory hallucinations may co-occur with the delusions. Ideas of reference may also be present. This refers to sufferers interpreting trivial insignificant events or people's actions as possessing personal significance and as referring to them in a way that is personally threatening. Paranoid delusions can occur in children when they are suffering from schizophrenia but schizophrenia is rare before late adolescence.

In the case of the prolonged use of large doses of amphetamines a paranoid psychosis can develop that may resemble paranoid schizophrenia. It subsides after the drugs are stopped but may last for months.

Carr, A. (1999) *The Handbook of Child and Adolescent Clinical Psychology: A Contextual Approach*. London, Routledge.

Gelder, M., Mayou, R. and Geddes, J. (1999) *Psychiatry*. Oxford, 2nd edn. Oxford, Oxford University Press.

Parenting styles and behaviour

A variety of parental and parenting factors contribute to the socialisation of children. These factors include warmth and responsiveness, e.g. praising and encouraging positive behaviour. On the other hand hostile parents are hypercritical, punitive and belittling or are indifferent towards their children. Uncontrolling parents give their children space to develop and to learn self-control and self-discipline. On the other hand controlling parents inhibit their children's development by establishing too many restrictive and inflexible rules and regulations. Uninvolved parenting (extremely lax, indifferent, uncaring and rejecting) tends to be associated with children who display high levels of aggression and serious problems at school and become antisocial and delinquent in adolescence.

Certain types of behaviours are associated with particular parenting or child-rearing styles. Authoritarian parenting (punitive, restrictive and coercive) tends to be associated with moody, unfriendly and unhappy children. Permissive parenting (lax, undemanding, unrestrictive and laissez-faire) tends to be associated with selfish, impulsive and aggressive children, especially boys. By contrast, authoritative parenting (firm, flexible, guiding, responsive and consultative) tends to be associated with motivated, high achieving, sociable, confident.

Authoritative parenting requires parents to be warm, to communicate care and concern, to explain their decisions rationally, to listen to their child's point of view, to set realistic standards and make realistic demands and allow their children some autonomy.

Advice to parents on bringing up children

Parents should:

- Display emotional warmth towards their children and set aside time to engage in leisure activities and to discuss achievements with them as well as problems.
- Be clear about their own principles, values and their rationale. Avoid hypocrisy. Be clear as to the rules and limits that they want to establish for their children and make sure they understand what they are. Rules and limits should have an underlying rationale that is justifiable.
- Be firm, consistent and clear with respect to infringement of rules and limits and use appropriate and proportionate non-violent sanctions where necessary. Avoid using violence or threats of violence to enforce rules or to punish for infringements of rules. Restraint should only be used where children are being dangerous to themselves or others.
- Reinforce effort as well as good behaviour with non-material rewards (praise and smiles) and material rewards (preferred trips and activities).
- Ensure that children are adequately supervised and monitored, particularly out of doors and in terms of their friends and acquaintances.
- Remember that at times it is to be expected that children test limits and boundaries and rebel against parental authority. Children are asserting their autonomy but at the same time wish to be reassured that parents are there for them even when they are being disobedient.
- Remember at a certain age adolescents become self-conscious about themselves and also about their parents.
- Be fair and equal in dealing with siblings. Do not show favouritism. Assign appropriate family responsibilities to children according to age, ability and maturity.
- Show an interest in their child's school activities and attend parents' evenings.
- Be clear about their own attitudes and values regarding sexual activities and drug taking and discuss them with their children. Make sure their children are aware of the possible consequences of sexual and drug taking activity.

Contact

Parentline Plus. Tel. 0808 800 2222 (offers support to anyone parenting a child).

Peer group

Peer groups refer to those individuals who associate together and are of the same age or at the same emotional and behavioural levels. The formation of peer groups can occur as young as three years but with the advent of adolescence these groups become much more cohesive and intimate. Peer groups enable children to practise social skills and to build close relationships and manage conflict. Children learn to make social comparisons and to validate their beliefs and attitudes.

Children seek out and associate with others who are similar in beliefs, attitudes and behaviour. In adolescence children rely on their peers for support as they question parental or adult rules and demands. Conflicts develop over dress, chosen friends, smoking and the use of recreational drugs. These conflicts are often a means of testing boundaries and parental affection as well as tolerance. Peer rebellion is often over-exaggerated as most adolescents conform to their parents' core demands and confine their rebellion to minor issues.

Peer relationships can be disrupted through children moving out of the neighbourhood or through changing school. Friendships and peer relationships are often in a state of flux and may form, break up and reform over a brief period.

In the pre-school years children who are insecurely attached tend to be socially isolated and negative towards their peers and provoke peer rejection or else they seek out friendship but are ineffective through lack of interpersonal skills. Children are rather egocentric until the age of seven or eight and tend to focus on other children in terms of appearance and possessions. During this period there exists a tendency to make external attributions in order to explain the behaviour of others. Dispositional attributions come later. After this age children tend to focus on sharing, friendship obligations and attributing attitudes and traits to friends.

Children who develop empathic understanding are more likely to be popular and to have positive peer relationships. The development of empathic understanding involves role-taking abilities that are further enhanced through positive interactions with friends. In adolescence, trust, loyalty and respect grow in importance, along with the sharing of secrets and problems. Socially isolated or rejected children are more at risk of developing delinquency in later life.

In adolescence children become preoccupied with relationships with peers and tend to become concerned with their appearance and that of others. Being underweight or overweight can be causes of low self-esteem and affect children's social standing in the eyes of their peers. Similarity becomes a criterion for peer group selection. Cliques develop that associate in school and in particular neighbourhoods. These cliques may become exclusive and rebuff outsiders. Most of the time may be spent in 'hanging around' rather than in directed or structured activities. Most peer groups continue to remain single sex in the school years. Adolescent girls tend to form emotional relationships with a few close, intimate female friends. They stress trust, loyalty and confidentiality in their relationships and any infringement often results in conflict. Adolescent boys also stress trust and loyalty but are often preoccupied with shared interests and activities such as football and computer games. However in adolescence the development of cross-sex relationships and groups of same-sex peers interact with each other, leading at times to the emergence of mixed-sex couples and related conflicts.

Peer relationships may be affected by factors such as physical attractiveness, physical disabilities, shyness, loneliness and the loss of friendships. Problematic peer relationships can be addressed through behavioural (positive reinforcement and shaping), cognitive-behavioural (self-instruction, self-reinforcement and modelling) social skills, problem solving (role-taking), peer tutoring (paired role models and cross-age tutoring) and assertiveness training programmes. These programmes need to consider the relevant social contexts otherwise the effects of these programme will fail to generalise to those contexts.

Erwin, P. (1998) Friendship in Childhood and Adolescence. London, Routledge.

Personal construct perspective

Personal construct theory is a cognitive theory developed by George Kelly (1905–67) and is based on the idea of 'constructive alternativism' which means that people are able to construe or interpret their own thoughts and behaviour, that of others and the world around them in alternative or different ways. There are alternative ways of interpreting actions and behaviours. People when observing people and their behaviour construe similarities and differences and it is this construing that leads to personal constructs.

The personal construct approach explains the behaviour of people through putting oneself in their place and by seeing the world through their perspective. People are seen as scientists and different types of behaviour can be thought of as experiments or ways of testing hypotheses or predicting events. The aim of this approach is to understand the way people construe or interpret events and to help people reconstrue or reinterpret events. The past and the future do not determine our behaviour since it is the way that we construe the past and future that influences our behaviour. Construing and constructs are seen as bipolar and involve experience as well as thought. Constructs are formed through perceiving two elements that are similar in comparison with a third element that is a contrast. An example would be observing two people being aggressive and a third person being gentle leading to the construct aggressive-gentle. Core constructs are fundamental to personal identity. Constructs can be preverbal (not spoken), verbal (spoken) or submerged (unavailable for verbal expression). People's behaviours express an interrelated hierarchy of constructs and any change in those constructs can lead to change in other constructs. Leaning occurs when we reconstrue events. Tight construing occurs when people always construe events in the same way regardless of the situation whereas loose construing occurs when people construe events according to the situation. People seek validation and the expansion of their constructs.

Emotional and behavioural problems occur when people's constructs are continually invalidated or incorrectly predicted. People rigidly adhere to their system of constructs out of anxiety, fear and threat. This means that people's ways of construing are static and ineffective and as a result they are not able to predict events satisfactorily. They are not able to think of different ways of construing events that would enable them to behave more satisfactorily.

Anxiety is defined as a situation where people's constructs do not satisfactorily apply to events or the actions of others and as a result they feel they lack the necessary constructs. Fear is where a new construct is on the verge of forcing itself into people's systems of constructs. Threat is defined as the awareness of impending fundamental change in people's core constructs or self-identity. Hostility is defined as the continual effort to find evidence for a construct that has already failed rather than considering that change is necessary.

People's constructs may be excessively permeable or impermeable, i.e. ignoring differences that exist between events or people or rejecting events or people that cannot be easily pigeon-holed. Constructs can also be excessively tight or loose, i.e. people construe events and people the same way regardless of circumstances (as in obsessive-compulsive disorders) or construe events and people randomly regardless of the situation (as in psychoses). Constriction occurs when people excessively narrow their construct systems (as in depression) and dilation is when people excessively expand their system (as in mania).

The treatment of people's emotional and behavioural difficulties is through helping people to reconstrue; some constructs need replacing, some need to be added, some tightened, some loosened, some made more permeable and some more impermeable. Altogether people need to be better scientists, to be encouraged to form new constructs or alternatives, to test out new hypotheses, to present themselves in new ways, to construe themselves in new ways and to behave in new ways. People need to be in a position where they are able to make more accurate predictions.

Kelly's Role Construct Repertory Test (Rep Test) is a means of identifying people's constructs through direct questioning. It elicits people's construct system based on the way in which two elements are similar and different from a third. The test describes people in terms of both structure as well as content of their constructs.

Fransella, F. (1995) George Kelly. London, SAGE Publications.
Kelly, G.A. (1955) The Psychology of Personal Constructs, vols 1 and 2. New York, W.W. Norton.

Personality

There is no one definition but the term personality is used to refer to a particular person's pattern of thoughts, feelings and behaviour. Personality is a disposition to think, feel and behave in a particular way. There are individual differences between the ways people think, feel and behave. There are various approaches to the study of personality: type, trait, behaviourist, cognitive-behavioural, social learning, humanistic, psychodynamic, situational and interactionist. They differ respectively according to their focus on types of temperament, characteristic and enduring ways of thinking, feeling and behaving, on overt and observable behaviours, on cognitive processes, on interpretation and choice, on unconscious processes, on regular responses to similar situations (traits) and interactions between traits and situations.

Trait theories of personality are based on factor analysis and aim to identify and measure the underlying predispositions that constitute particular types of personality. Another aim is to predict the behaviour of people with similar traits across different situations. Trait theorists have concluded that five traits (the 'Big 5') constitute personality, namely extroversion, agreeableness, conscientiousness, emotionality and intellect. All trait theories regard personality as stable across situations and that it is possible to predict people's behaviour in any situation. However, situationists claim that it is difficult to predict people's behaviour across different situations on the basis of their traits. Situationists explain people's behaviour by external events and situations rather than by predispositions.

Interactionists on the other hand claim that in order to explain people's behaviour we need know how people's traits and the situations they find themselves in interact. Various types of situation appear to override traits: strong situations where there are few alternatives to choose from (these act to minimise trait differences), imposed situations where there are few or no choices available and situations where little or no reflection occurs.

Behaviour is now often explained by referring to both traits and situations, i.e. interactions between people's predispositions and situations. There is an advantage in focusing on situations because where emotional or behavioural problems occur it is their expression in a given situation that is of importance in terms of adapting feelings or behaviour.

Personality can also be viewed from a social cognition perspective. This perspective sees personality as being formed through information processing strategies that individuals use when addressing particular situations. The focus is on people's perceptions and inferences. Causal attribution occurs when people decide whether people are the cause of their own behaviour. If people appear to have the ability and are seen to be making an effort then the behaviour is attributed to them but if ability and effort are not involved then it is attributed to the situation. Attribution can also be extended to include responsibility. If people are judged as intending their behaviour then a 'correspondent inference' is made, if not then a 'non-correspondent' inference is made instead. People are more interested in establishing responsibility than cause and in cases where people act against our interest or authority we are more likely to make correspondent inferences. Therefore the social cognitive perspective regards people's perceptions of other people's behaviour as being affected by cognitive biases or heuristics (hasty types of decision making). The Fundamental Attribution Bias occurs when we hold people responsible for their behaviour rather than the situations they find themselves in. Decisions may be based on memories of previous incidents (the representative heuristic), on what springs to mind first (the availability heuristic) and on what appears to confirm rather than disconfirm our opinion (the confirmation bias heuristic). Overall the tendency is to attribute responsibility to people rather than to people's situations. However the opposite can occur, i.e. where people tend to attribute the causes of behaviour to dispositions rather than to situations. This self-serving bias operates where people attribute the responsibility for positive outcomes to themselves and the responsibility for negative outcomes to external situations.

Brunas-Wagstaff, J. (1998) Personality: A Cognitive Approach. London, Routledge.

Hindle, D. and Smith, M.V. (eds) (1999) Personality Development: A Psychoanalytic Perspective. London, Routledge.

Kline. P. (1993) Personality: The Psychometric View. London, Routledge.

Matthews, G. and Deary, I.J. (1998) Personality Traits. Cambridge, Cambridge University Press.

Monte, C.F. (1999) Beneath the Mask: An Introduction to Theories of Personality, 6th edn. Fort Worth, TX, Harcourt Brace College Publishers.

Pervin, L.A. (1996) The Science of Personality. Chichester, Wiley.

Personality disorder

Personality disorders are pervasive and persistent difficulties that affect the personality as a whole. These difficulties adversely affect social and personal relationships and cause personal distress. The term personality disorder is mainly applied to adults rather than to children or adolescents.

Antisocial personality disorders can include the following characteristics: unstable work behaviour, failure to plan for the future, financial recklessness, habitual lying, impulsive behaviour, abusive parenting, unstable marital relationships, a tendency to violence, a strong tendency to blame others and an absence of remorse. This type of disorder is more common among men than women and often co-occurs with substance abuse. This disorder is believed to have genetic and environmental components. This disorder is defined as only applying to adolescents over 18 years old; before 18 the term applied is that of conduct disorder.

Borderline personality disorder is characterised by pervasive and persistent instability in personal relationships, self-esteem, feelings and impulses. It also includes suicidal behaviour and the lack of anger control.

Schizotypal personality disorder is a pervasive pattern of feelings and behaviour that include being uncomfortable with and being unable to maintain close personal relationships.

Schizoid personality disorder includes an inability to experience pleasure in normal activities, being emotionally frigid, indifferent to praise and criticism, an inability to express positive or negative feelings, social isolation, a preference for one's own company, an insensitivity to social conventions and excessive introspection and fantasy.

Carr, A. (2001) Abnormal Psychology. Hove, Psychology Press.
Gelder, M., Mayou, R. and Geddes, J. (1999) Psychiatry, 2nd edn. Oxford, Oxford University Press.

Pervasive developmental disorders (PDD)

The main characteristics of these childhood, early onset disorders are difficulties in reciprocal social interactions, language and communication problems and a limited, narrow, stereotyped pattern of interests, activities and behaviours. These disorders include autism, Rett's syndrome or disorder and Asperger's syndrome. The main characteristic of these disorders is a failure in acceptable social interactions with other people. Some of these children with PDD manifest average or above average ability but others often have impairments in cognitive functioning.

Carr, A. (1999) The Handbook of Child and Adolescent Clinical Psychology: A Contextual Approach. London, Routledge.

Phobic disorders (phobias)

Phobic states or disorders are characterised by a persistent, pervasive and unfounded fear of specific objects, activities or situations. The unfounded fear results in avoidance of the specific objects, activities or situations. Intense fear leads to personal distress and affects social relationships.

* Specific fears include animals, the dark, heights, enclosed or open spaces, medical treatments, crowds and public transport. Agoraphobia, the fear of being in public places is uncommon in childhood and early adolescence. Specific fears are common in childhood, particularly fear of animals and fear of the dark. Girls report experiencing more fears than boys. Children experiencing specific fears may be treated using behavioural techniques such as flooding, systematic desensitisation and modelling.
* However social phobia, the intense fear of being under public scrutiny in some way can occur in late childhood or adolescence. Social phobia can occur when a person is asked to perform certain activities in public. The fear is of being embarrassed publicly and being negatively evaluated by other people. Children with social phobia may be treated through family and group based approaches. The aim is to expose children to challenging public situations and to provide feedback regarding the adequacy of their performances. Children are given social skills training where they lack the necessary social skills to perform in public situations.

- School phobia or school refusal occurs when children are frightened to leave home due to anxiety or depression. It affects boys and girls equally. School refusal is different from truancy. It mainly occurs during early adolescence but also occurs when starting school or on transition to a new school. These children experience separation anxiety, fear of leaving the safety and protection of the home. They can also complain of a number of physical symptoms particularly at breakfast times, e.g. poor appetite, nausea, vomiting, stomach pains, diarrhoea and insomnia. If pressured to attend school these children may physically resist, plead or burst into tears. In a number of cases school refusal may be exacerbated by family factors such as family disorganisation, parental over-protectiveness or poor liaison with school. These children often have difficulties coping with social relationships with other children, changes of school routine, particular subjects like Games and PE and new teachers. School refusers can also become angry, resentful and aggressive when frustrated. Generally they are of average or above average ability and therefore able to cope with curricular demands. In certain cases school refusal is indicative of separation anxiety or a specific phobia regarding a particular teacher, child or subject at the school.

Treatment may require the parents to be firm and insistent that the child returns to school with the active support of teachers on arrival. Gradual systematic desensitisation may also be appropriate where the parent's or the child's anxiety is severe and where the child has been absent from school for a long period of time. Where the child is absent for a long time the child is in danger of falling behind with school work, of losing contact with friends and of non-attendance being reinforced by constant attention at home. A transition period in a pupil reintegration unit can be helpful prior to returning to school. Transfer to a new school does not usually help solve the problem of school refusal. Most school refusers return to school depending on age, severity of symptoms and the timing of the intervention.

Goodman, R. and Scott, S. (1997) Child Psychiatry. Oxford, Blackwell Science.
Herbert, M. (1998) Clinical Child Psychology, 2nd edn. Chichester, Wiley.
King, N.J., Hamilton, D.I. and Ollendick, T.H. (1988) Children's Phobias: A Behavioural Perspective. Chichester, Wiley.
Spiegler, M.D. and Guivrement, D.C. (1998) Contemporary Behavior Therapy, 3rd edn. Pacific Grove, CA, Brooks/Cole Publishing.

Physical conditions and behaviour

Physical conditions for a variety of reasons can become associated with psychological problems or psychiatric disorders:

- Physical conditions may become associated with problems or disorders by coincidence and vice versa.

- In particular, depression and anxiety are associated with physical conditions. The experience of psychological problems such as depression, anxiety and relationship difficulties may lead people to develop unhealthy habits and to harm themselves through self-mutilation or by over- or undereating.
- People when depressed or anxious may not seek medical assistance for a physical problem nor comply with medical treatment when diagnosed.
- People can become depressed and anxious when diagnosed or when treated for a serious or terminal illness, e.g. side effects of surgery, pharmacology, chemotherapy and radiotherapy.
- People may become anxious due to the direct physiological influence of a physical condition such as with some endocrine disorders (hyper and hypothyroidism).
- People may have accidents due to the effects of depression and anxiety and after those accidents (brain injuries) may experience increased anxiety and depression.

Vague, ill-defined and unexplained physical symptoms (tension headache and non-cardiac chest pain) may be due to psychological problems and the misinterpretation of physical sensations may lead to disorders such as panic attacks. However, unexplained physical symptoms may be due to undetected or unidentified physical causes and not be of psychogenic origin. For this reason it can be dangerous to assume that physical symptoms are necessarily psychogenic if no physical cause can be identified.

Pica

Pica refers to the eating of substances that do not provide nutrition. These include soil, paper, string, leaves, paint, hair, insects, pebbles and sweet wrappers. It can be associated with developmental delays or inadequate supervision by parents. It frequently accompanies mental disability and is then referred to as a feeding disorder of infancy or early childhood.

Play and behaviour

The concept of play includes cognitive, emotional and behavioural processes. It can be exploratory, communicative, expressive, social, educational and creative.

Play is seen as an essential or critical requirement for positive emotional and behavioural development. It enables children to organise their emotional experiences and to cope with separations from primary carers. Play also provides opportunities for children to acquire, develop and practise social skills such as taking part, taking turns, sharing, exploring, discovering, enjoying themselves, self-regulating their behaviour and empathising with others.

Very young children engage in solitary play, parallel and onlooker play whereas older children engage in cooperative play. Children also engage in fantasy, creative and pretend play. Children who are not able to play with others or to play properly are at risk of developing emotional and behavioural problems. They are likely to experience rejection and isolation. Play therapy aims to provide opportunities for catharsis for those children who have emotional and behavioural difficulties that in part result from a lack of critical play in the past. The Nurture Group is one means by which such children can be given play opportunities in order to compensate for the absence of such opportunities.

Sayeed, Z. and Guerin, E. (2000) *Early Years Play. London, David Fulton Publishers.*
Talay-Ongan, A. (1998) *Typical and Atypical Development in Early Childhood. Leicester, The British Psychological Society.*

Playground behaviour

Playground behaviour is increasingly perceived as problematic due to the incidence and prevalence of bullying, the contest for space and dominance within public areas and the existence of a machismo playground culture. Public space is often the site for antisocial behaviour. This may be the case because playgrounds and other public spaces provide opportunities for miscreants to avoid surveillance and supervision. Gender differences may manifest themselves in playgrounds, for example boys often preferring large open spaces in which to play games, particularly football, and girls may as a consequence prefer peripheral areas. Boys may dominate playground areas and other public spaces thereby confining girls to peripheral areas.

The most common types of misbehaviour include verbal abuse (general, racist and sexist), teasing and fighting. Verbal abuse may escalate to physical conflicts between individuals, between an individual and a group and between groups. Conflicts may take the form of inter-ethnic conflict in some schools. Play fighting may be difficult to distinguish from aggressive fighting. Children can also experience rejection and isolation in the playground possibly due to a lack of social skills on their part but also because of other pupils' power assertion, dominance or rejection.

Interventions

- Whole-school policy, a playground policy: Involving all staff (teaching and non-teaching) and should relate to all public spaces. Elements of a policy should include conflict resolution, mediation and monitoring. Anti-bullying, anti-sexist and anti-racist policies will all have a bearing on playground behaviour.
- Landscaping: Providing an attractive and interesting physical environment, decorated, litter-free areas with different levels, places to shelter, climb and explore, shady areas, trees, plants and fixed play equipment.
- Training lunchtime supervisors: Improving status, clarifying roles, responsibilities and procedures and improving liaison between teachers and supervisors.
- Conflict resolution for teaching and non-teaching staff: Identifying, exploring and

resolving different types of conflicts (over resources, values and needs). Conflicts over needs are often paramount. Conflicts can be a learning experience and should be regarded as problem solving exercises for all the participants to a conflict.

• Altering the length and number of break times in order to reduce the time available for behaviour problems and conflicts to emerge.

• Providing different play areas for boys and girls thus enabling girls to own and use different play areas as their own.

• CCTV surveillance of public spaces to monitor the use of public spaces and to identify and record antisocial behaviour.

Blatchford, P. and Sharp, S. (eds) (1994) Breaktime and the School: Understanding and Changing Playground Behaviour. London, Routledge.

Positive reinforcement

Positive reinforcement is a behavioural technique. Operant responses are affected by their consequence. If the consequences are desirable or favourable then the behaviour leading to those consequences is likely to be repeated in the future. If the consequences are undesirable then the behaviour is not likely to be repeated in the future. This observable relationship is called the law of effect and is the basis of operant conditioning.

A reinforcer or reinforcing stimulus is any event which is a consequence of an operant response and which increases the likelihood of its recurrence. The reinforcer is contingent on the response. A positive reinforcer is observed to increase the frequency and duration of a given behaviour. A child starts to work, the teacher praises the child's behaviour and the child's work rate increases. The teacher has positively reinforced the child's behaviour. An operant response has to be made first before positive reinforcement can occur. There is no need to consider why positive reinforcement has occurred. All that is necessary is to establish empirically or observationally that positive reinforcement leads to an increase in desired, appropriate or adaptive behaviour. There is no need to make assumptions about what is pleasurable or unpleasurable for a particular person. Reinforcement is seen as relative, not absolute, as illustrated by the Premack Principle where the opportunity to perform a more probable behaviour will act to reinforce a less probable behaviour. This occurs where for example a child stays in his seat as a result of being given the opportunity to watch more television.

Positive reinforcement can be of either desired or undesired behaviour. The term 'positive' itself does not refer to it being good or bad but what serves to increase *any* behaviour, good or bad.

Spiegler, M.D. and Guivrement, D.C. (1998) Contemporary Behavior Therapy, 3rd edn. Pacific Grove, CA, Brooks/Cole Publishing.

Positive symptoms

This term refers to the positive symptoms of schizophrenia. The symptoms include delusions, hallucinations and in some cases of schizophrenia symptoms of disorganised thought and speech.

- Delusions or irrational or unfounded beliefs are common positive symptoms. They comprise beliefs that one is the unwilling recipient of physical sensations and of intrusive thoughts. They also comprise beliefs that one's thoughts are being broadcast or are being forcibly extracted or that one's feelings or behaviour are being controlled. Delusions can also occur in mania and depression.
- Hallucinations are sensations experienced in the absence of external stimulation. They are more often auditory than visual. Auditory hallucinations can take the form of believing one's thoughts are being spoken by another, that voices can be heard arguing and that voices are commenting on one's behaviour.

Post-traumatic stress disorder (PSTD)

This type of anxiety disorder became identified in relation to adult reactions to stress, particularly those experienced in the Vietnam War. It was first categorised as a disorder in DSM III in 1980 and in this instance a cause was identified, namely a traumatic event or stressor. PSTD comprises distressing recollections of traumatic events, avoidance of anything internal or external associated with those events and symptoms of physiological arousal. The abrupt onset and the dangerousness of the trauma determine the severity of the symptoms. Severe stress leads to an increase in psychiatric problems. The occurrence of PSTD depends in part on personal vulnerability. Children, old people and people with psychiatric disorders are particularly vulnerable. PSTD may last for four years and may recur on anniversaries of the trauma. However not everybody exposed to trauma develops PSTD. Prevalence rates vary from 10 to 30 per cent.

PSTD is characterised by symptoms that result from extremely distressing events outside normal experience such as war, natural disaster, torture, physical and sexual abuse and murder. The most frequent trauma is bereavement. Natural disasters appear to produce less emotional disorders than technological disasters. Deliberate violence appears to produce the severest problems. These symptoms can be delayed or protracted. The main symptoms include severe anxiety, irritability, insomnia, poor concentration, avoidance of associated stimuli external and internal, detachment, emotional numbness, intrusive flashbacks and distressing dreams or nightmares. Many children and adolescents experience depression, anxiety and stress following a life-threatening trauma.

Children who experience a traumatic event are often frightened to go to sleep or to sleep alone, fear separation from parents and fear they are going mad. Younger children often re-enact the trauma in play activities. Traumatic events can adversely affect academic performance. However family support and other factors can both mediate and moderate the symptoms of PSTD.

The treatment of PSTD is through psychoeducation, family support, providing opportunities for children to tell and recount thoughts, feelings, dreams through the use of various art media such as drawings and paintings and the use of cognitive and desensitisation techniques. Avoidance strategies can lead to problems with anger control and emotional regulation. Cognitive-behavioural techniques are also to treat the symptoms of PSTD such as intrusive imagery and avoidance behaviours. These techniques include problem solving, thought-stopping, cognitive restructuring, desensitisation, relaxation techniques and exposure. Drug therapy is not central to the treatment of PSTD but antidepressants and tranquillisers are prescribed where there are comorbid or associated disorders such as depression and anxiety.

Kinchin, D. and Brown, E. (2001) Supporting Children with Post-traumatic Stress Disorder. London, David Fulton Publishers.

Scott, M.J. and Stradling, S.G. (1992) Counselling for Post-Traumatic Stress Disorder. London, SAGE Publications.

Yule, W. (ed.) (1998) Post Traumatic Stress Disorder: Concepts and Therapy. Chichester, Wiley.

Problem solving perspective

The problem solving perspective aims to enable children and adults with emotional and behavioural difficulties to approach their problems through structured problem solving programmes. Children and adults are perceived as lacking or possessing inadequate problem solving skills that are essential for positive social interactions. The aim of these programmes is to enhance problem solving, i.e. how to think, not what to think. Problem solving approaches have both cognitive and behavioural components and are multi-stage in structure.

- The problem solving skills training of T. J. D'Zurilla (1986) is based on a five stage model. The five stages are orientation (being aware of the problem), problem definition and formulation, positing alternative solutions, decision making and verification (testing the solutions). People are trained to prevent initial impulses, to recognise problems, to brainstorm alternatives, think about consequences, plan solutions and evaluate the solutions.
- The interpersonal cognitive problem solving skills training of M.B. Shure and G. Spivack (1978) focuses on alternative thinking, consequential thinking and means-end thinking. The aim is to improve sensitivity to others' feelings, to develop information-gathering skills and to understand others' motivation.

D'Zurilla, T.J. (1986) Problem-solving Therapy. New York, Springer Publishing Co.

Shure, M.B. and Spivack, G. (1978) Problem-Solving Techniques in Child Rearing. San Francisco, CA, Jossey-Bass.

Projective tests

Projective tests are controversial personality tests that are based on the psychoanalytic idea that people who respond to ambiguous stimuli reveal unconscious aspects of their personalities. It has been also been claimed that these tests can be used to diagnose mental disorders or for detecting propensities towards criminality or for detecting sexual abuse. The most commonly used of these tests include the Rorschach inkblot test, the Thematic Apperception Test and the Draw-a-Person Test.

In general, questions have been raised regarding the validity and reliability of projective tests. In particular, incremental validity has been questioned, which means that these tests may not add anything over and above what is obtainable by other means such as interviews. Contextual influences are also seen as affecting scoring, e.g. ethnicity, sex and the way in which the test it is administered.

They are still widely used as assessment instruments even though their validity and reliability have been challenged. This is because of the claims by users that they are useful in clinical settings, that they are productive in terms of probing unconscious aspects of personality and of exploring unstructured responses and that they are a rich and unique source of data. An emphasis is placed on users having adequate training and expertise in administering the tests in order to avoid invalid and unreliable assessments and diagnoses.

Kline, P. (1993) *The Handbook of Psychological Testing*. London, Routledge.
Murphy, K.R. and Davidshofer, C.O. (1998) *Psychological Testing: Principles and Applications*, 4th edn. London, Prentice-Hall.
Rust, J. and Golombok, S. (1999) *Modern Psychometrics*. London, Routledge.

Prosocial behaviour

Prosocial or helping behaviour can be egoistic or altruistically motivated. Altruism or helping others can be explained from different perspectives. Biologically it can be seen as an innate predisposition based on kin selection and reciprocity. Personality factors may be seen as fostering prosocial behaviour, e.g. empathy, an internal locus of control, a sense of social responsibility and a just-world belief. Prosocial behaviour is also fostered when people are in a good mood, an affect-priming model. Instead of focusing on antisocial or negative behaviour one can focus on positive or prosocial behaviour. Prosocial behaviour includes helping, caring, sharing, cooperating and sympathising with others. People do show altruism and empathy. However empathy does not necessarily lead to altruism. Children in the second year begin to show signs of empathy and begin to act altruistically. Young children are observed to take an interest in others' activities, like imitating and joining in those activities, and enjoy receiving praise and recognition. In middle childhood role-taking skills increase and children distinguish between their own feelings and the feelings of others. They feel compassion.

Prosocial behaviour is encouraged through providing clear and explicit rules, through expressing one's beliefs and approval with conviction, through attributing prosocial qualities, through modelling and through a warm, accepting, empathic caring relationship.

Psychiatric disorders of children and adolescents

A number of psychiatric disorders have their onset in childhood or adolescence, e.g. schizophrenia, mood disorders, personality disorders, eating disorders and substance induced disorders.

Findling, R.L., Schultz, S.C., Kadshani, J.H. and Harlan, E. (2001) Psychotic Disorders in Children and Adolescents. Thousand Oaks, CA, Sage Publications.

Psychiatric perspective

The psychiatric perspective applies the medical model to mental disorders, seeing mental disorders as medical problems. This perspective searches for underlying physical (biochemical, physiological, neurological) causes of mental disorders and also biological treatments for mental disorders.

Psychiatrists diagnose mental disorders using diagnostic manuals, mainly DSM IV and ICD-10. These manuals categorise disorders according to specific criteria but do not assign causes except for PSTD. Medically based assessment techniques include CT scan, MRI and the PET scan to investigate brain anomalies. There are also neuropsychological and psychophysiological tests to investigate neurological and physiological dysfunctions. Psychometric tests like the WISC are used to investigate cognitive functions such as thinking and reasoning processes. Projective tests like the Rorschach inkblot are also used by some psychiatrists to probe unconscious processes.

Psychiatry is mainly concerned with severe mental disorders (psychoses) such as schizophrenia and manic-depression and severe forms of anxiety, depression and addiction. Biological treatment or drug therapy is the main intervention used for psychoses. Psychotropic drugs include anxiolytics (anxiety reducing), antipsychotics (controlling psychotic symptoms), antidepressants (controlling depressive symptoms) and psychostimulants (controlling ADHD). Depending on the psychiatrist's viewpoint psychological interventions are also used particularly for minor conditions, these include behavioural, cognitive-behavioural and psychodynamic techniques. There are various specialisms within psychiatry such as child and adolescent psychiatry and forensic psychiatry.

Barker, P. (1995) Basic Child Psychiatry, 6th edn. Oxford, Blackwell Science.
Gelder, M., Mayou, R. and Geddes, J. (1999) Psychiatry, 2nd edn. Oxford, Oxford University Press.
Stone, J.H., Roberts, M., O'Grady, J. and Taylor, A.V. with O'Shea, K. (2000) Faulk's Basic Forensic Psychiatry, 3rd edn. Oxford, Blackwell Science.
Tyrer, P. and Steinberg, D. (1993) Models for Mental Disorder: Conceptual Models in Psychiatry, 2nd edn. Chichester, Wiley.

Psychoactive drugs

Psychotropic drugs are used to treat mental disorders. However, in practice drugs are frequently used along with psychological interventions. For drugs to be effective they must enter the brain in appropriate amounts. This depends on such factors as absorption, metabolism, excretion and crossing the blood-brain barrier. Other factors affecting drug treatment include the effects of drug interactions, drug withdrawal and compliance. Different types of drugs can have serious side effects.

The main types of psychotropic drugs are:

- anxiolytics (minor tranquillisers) reduce anxiety;
- hypnotics produce sleep;
- antipsychotics (major tranquillisers) control delusions, hallucinations and agitation;
- antidepressants relieve symptoms of depression;
- psychostimulants control ADHD.

Psychoanalysis

Psychoanalysis, also known as the psychodynamic approach, originally developed through the works of Sigmund Freud and is termed Freudian or classical psychoanalysis. However, various schools of psychoanalytic theory and practice developed from and reacted against various elements of Freudian psychoanalytic theory and practice. The main schools are Jungian, Adlerian, Object Relations, Ego psychology, Self psychology, neo-Freudian and Lacanian.

Classical psychoanalysis comprises the following main elements:

- Psychological determinism is the theory that thoughts and feelings are influenced by unconscious processes manifested in the form of slips of the tongue and pen (Freudian slips), dreams and neuroses. Unacceptable thoughts and feelings are repressed.
- The topographical model of the mind divided the internal world into the unconscious, preconscious and the conscious. The later structural model divided the mind into three functions, the id, superego and ego. The id refers to the basic innate sexual and aggressive drives, the superego refers to the conscience and ideals and the ego refers to the rational, reality based self. The ego's task is to control the id. Conflict occurs between the pleasure principle and the reality principle. Defence mechanisms function in order to resolve this conflict. They include repression, denial, projection, reaction formation, rationalisation, displacement, conversion, regression, avoidance and sublimation.
- Unconscious processes are processes that exist below conscious awareness but which influence behaviour. Memories of early childhood events and desires that are unacceptable to the ego are repressed. The unconscious always tries to gratify basic drives.
- Unconscious motivation is the idea that unconscious motives can be used to explain

people's conscious attitudes, beliefs and reasons for engaging in certain types of behaviour.

- Innate biological drives such as sexuality and aggression are seen as having a major influence on behaviour and for considerable periods of time people struggle with biological drives in their internal worlds.
- Early infant development influences development in adolescence and adult life. Children proceed developmentally through psychosexual stages (oral, anal, phallic, latency period, genital), eventually reaching a watershed in the form of resolution of the Oedipus complex (boys) and Electra complex (girls). Problems with development may take the form of fixation (arrested development) and regression (return to an earlier stage of development).
- Developmental issues emerge during the pre-Oedipal period and the Oedipal period. The pre-Oedipal issues include forming secure attachments to parents, learning to cope with separations and absences, learning to cope with feelings and developing a stable sense of self.
- Psychoanalytic therapy involves dream analysis, interpretation, free association, transference and counter-transference. It involves understanding the psychodynamics of a person's inner world and helping that person to become aware of and develop insight into the nature of the unconscious conflicts that are causing emotional and behavioural difficulties.

Bateman, A. and Holmes, J. (1995) Introduction to Psychoanalysis: Contemporary Theory and Practice. London, Routledge.

Freud, S. (1986) The Essentials of Psycho-Analysis: The Definitive Collection of Sigmund Freud's Writing. London, Penguin Books.

Psychodynamic

Psychodynamic is a term that refers to emotional conflict or conflicts taking place within a person's internal, unconscious world or mind. Conflicts can arise over unacceptable sexual and aggressive feelings. These feelings may not be within conscious awareness and may manifest themselves in the form of neuroses such as anxiety and obsessive-compulsive disorders or psychosomatic symptoms.

Bateman, A., Brown, D. and Pedder, J. (2000) Introduction to Psychotherapy: An outline of psychodynamic principles and practice, 3rd edn. London, Routledge.

Psychogenic

This term refers to a psychological disorder where there is no known organic or physical cause.

Psychological dependence

This term refers to a psychological dependence on a specific drug or drugs. This type of dependence is characterised by a persistent and pervasive desire to obtain and use a specific drug or drugs. It is contrasted with physiological dependence where biochemical reactions caused by the drug or drugs themselves induce continued drug use. However, there is a connection between the two, and both forms of dependence need to be considered in order to explain addictive behaviour.

Psychoneuroimmunology

Psychoneuroimmunology is the study of the way in which psychological factors, especially stress, affect the immune system and how the immune system affects the central nervous system.

Psychopathology

In psychiatry or abnormal psychology the study of abnormal behaviour, mental or psychiatric disorders. Defining mental health or mental illness can be problematic, value-laden and subject to historical, social and cultural influences. Definitions and classifications of mental disorders are based on psychiatric diagnostic, manuals in particular DSM IV and ICD-10. Controversies have arisen over the validity and reliability of diagnostic systems.

With regard to the causation of mental disorders the focus and emphasis in psychopathology is generally on the medical model and the search for the underlying genetic, biological and neurological bases for mental disorders. Controversies have arisen over the extent of the genetic basis for mental disorders. The treatment of mental disorders is often physically or biologically based, in the main using psychotropic drugs to treat specific disorders, e.g. anxiety, depression and schizophrenia. Other physical treatments include electroconvulsive therapy (ECT) used to treat severe depression and psychosurgery used to treat severe obsessional disorder. Controversies have arisen over physical and psychological side effects and the effectiveness of specific physical and biological treatments.

There are no physical cures for mental disorders; however, alleviation of symptoms does occur such that patients may return to normal functioning but there may be unpleasant side effects associated with the treatment.

Gelder, M., Mayou, R. and Geddes, J. (1999) Psychiatry, 2nd edn. Oxford, Oxford University Press.
Johnstone, L. (2000) Users and Abusers of Psychiatry, 2nd edn. London, Routledge.
Lemma, A. (1996) An Introduction to Psychopathology. London, SAGE Publications.

Psychopathy (psychopath)

The term psychopathy is a legal concept that refers to antisocial behaviour and in particular the thoughts and feelings that can become associated with that behaviour. Antisocial behaviour involves a conduct disorder, e.g. truancy, theft, violence, arson and vandalism, being reckless, impulsive and lacking in remorse. At times psychopaths may experience short-lived psychotic periods. Psychopaths do not experience shame or anxiety, manipulate and exploit others and behave irresponsibly, impulsively and cruelly towards other people. They do not show remorse and have a complete lack of feelings for others. Many persistently break the law regardless of punishment. They commit a wider range of offences than non-psychopathic offenders, receive more convictions and spend a longer time in prison than other offenders.

A number of factors are thought to contribute to psychopathy, including parenting (harsh discipline and parental rejection), being able to ignore fear-inducing stimuli and a lack of empathy. It should be noted that the term psychopathy does not refer to a particular disorder but rather to a problem in relating positively to other people, particularly in taking account of their feelings and needs. There is no general agreement about the best way of treating psychopaths or whether they are effective treatments. However, psychopaths have been treated in prisons (Grendon Underwood and Parkhurst Prisons) and in special hospitals (Broadmoor and Henderson Hospitals). Individual therapeutic approaches have included psychodynamic and cognitive approaches. Medication is also used to treat associated symptoms such as anxiety but it is not a cure.

Prins, H. (1995) Offenders, Deviants or Patients?, 2nd edn. London, Routledge.

Psychophysiological disorder (psychosomatic disorders)

Psychophysiological disorders are physical symptoms that are caused by or exacerbated by emotional problems, e.g. hypertension, headache and gastritis. However, it is now thought that any illness can be affected by psychological factors such as stress. Stress and anxiety can induce and exacerbate physical symptoms, e.g. headaches.

Psychosis

The term psychosis is used in psychiatry to refer to a major mental disorder where contact with reality or insight into the condition is seriously impaired, e.g. schizophrenia and dementia. Psychoses are divided into two types: functional and organic. In organic psychoses there is an identifiable physical cause or abnormality in the brain, e.g. dementia. In functional psychoses no underlying physical cause has been discovered but genetic and biochemical studies indicate that there may be physical causes at work, e.g. schizophrenia.

Psychotherapy

Psychotherapy is a term that encompasses a whole range of non-biological and non-behavioural therapies that involve or depend on a therapeutic relationship or alliance between a therapist and a client. This special relationship is used to achieve therapeutic goals. The relationship and its use depend on the theoretical and practical bases of the particular psychotherapy. Current psychotherapies include psychoanalytic and humanistic approaches. It should be noted that the term therapy is used in connection with behaviour therapy, cognitive-behavioural therapy and even drug therapy. However, in those cases the actual relationship between the therapist and the client is not paramount and is not used therapeutically. The therapist in this context is seen primarily as using behavioural and cognitive techniques or drugs to help the client to change maladaptive behaviours or cognitions. This does not mean the nature of the relationship between therapist and client is irrelevant, as rapport is necessary in any therapy, but it does mean that the relationship itself is not used therapeutically.

It should be noted that the term psychotherapy is often a synonym for the term counselling. With regard to the effectiveness of psychotherapy there is a consensus that psychotherapy is effective in the sense that it is better than no treatment and that different therapies are equally effective. However, it should be noted that spontaneous remission does occur such that emotional and behavioural difficulties can decrease or terminate without therapeutic intervention.

Punishment

Punishment is the most frequent behavioural intervention used by many schools and parents. Punishment is defined as the delivery of an aversive stimulus after an undesired behaviour or the taking away of a pleasurable object or activity or privileges (response cost). It can be physical or psychological. Punishment is said to have occurred where a decrease or termination of the undesired behaviour has occurred. It is popular because the results are immediate and is often effective but the long-term effect may be limited. Punishment may have adverse consequences:

- simply suppresses the behaviour;
- does not state what the desired behaviour should be;
- models aggressive behaviour;
- produces resentful and vengeful behaviour;
- elicits fear, tension, stress or withdrawal;
- leads to physical and emotional abuse;
- evokes dislike and avoidance.

From the behavioural perspective punishment should be used as a last resort after positive reinforcement fails. Where punishment is used, guidelines should be followed:

- specific rules and the consequences of their infringement should be discussed, reviewed and posted;
- provide models of desirable behaviour;

- punish immediately and proportionately;
- punish consistently, not capriciously or erratically;
- punish the behaviour not the person;
- punish fairly;
- punish without losing control;
- do not threaten punishment without intending to carry it out;
- do not depend solely on punishment, use positive reinforcement as well;
- do not punish the group for the offences of an individual;
- do not combine punishment with expressions of affection or warmth;
- do not harp on past misbehaviour;
- do not humiliate or condemn the person.

Emerson, E. (1995) Challenging Behaviour. Cambridge, Cambridge University Press.

R

Rational-emotive behavioural therapy (REBT)

REBT is a therapy created and developed by Albert Ellis. This approach focuses on thinking, inferring, deciding and acting and regards emotional and behavioural difficulties as arising from beliefs, interpretations and evaluations of life events. People are largely seen as responsible for creating their own emotional and behavioural difficulties. The basic theoretical principles underlying REBT are that:

- People have a biological tendency to develop strongly held beliefs or hypotheses about themselves, other people and the external environment.
- Beliefs can influence thoughts, feelings and behaviour. Some beliefs are self-enhancing, others are self-defeating. These different types of beliefs can be identified and modified.
- Rational beliefs are self-enhancing whereas irrational beliefs are self-defeating and contribute to emotional and behavioural difficulties.
- Irrational beliefs involve absolute and rigid demands in the form of 'musts', 'have to's' and 'ought to's'. These beliefs are often empirically false and logically invalid. Irrational beliefs increase the likelihood of adverse emotional and behavioural consequences, e.g. anxiety, depression, guilt, shame and anger. Irrational beliefs lead to certain positions namely 'awfulising', 'I-can't-stand-it-itis', and 'damnation'. The consequences of irrational beliefs include unhealthy negative emotions such as anger, anxiety, shame, guilt and depression whereas the consequences of rational beliefs are healthy negative emotions such as concern, sorrow, regret and annoyance.
- Psychological problems arise from ego disturbance or absolutistic demands directed at one's self or discomfort disturbance or absolutistic demands directed at conditions.
- An ABC analysis or model can be applied to emotional and behavioural difficulties. A = an activating event including perceptions and inferences, B = rational and irrational beliefs and C = emotional or behavioural consequences. A, B and C can overlap and influence each other.

The REBT approach to therapy is active-directive, psychoeducational, multimodal and based on the following principles:

- People mainly choose to disturb themselves about the unpleasant things that happen to them.
- It is current beliefs that disturb people, not the past.
- Change requires effort and practice as there is no magical way to effect change.
- An ABC assessment.

- People should aim to change their irrational beliefs through disputation. Disputation requires identifying, debating and challenging irrational beliefs through testing them empirically, logically and pragmatically.

Ellis, A. (1962) Reason and Emotion in Psychotherapy. New York, Lyle Stuart.

Ellis, A., Gordon, J., Neenan, M. and Palmer, S. (1997) Stress Counselling: A Rational Emotive Behaviour Approach. London, Cassell.

Yankura, J. and Dryden, W. (1994) Albert Ellis. London, SAGE Publications.

Reaction formation

A psychoanalytic defence mechanism through which an unacceptable impulse, desire or feeling is controlled by an exaggeration of an opposite more acceptable proclivity. The original unacceptable impulse has been repressed into the unconscious but is likely to re-emerge given certain situations. An example would be where a person having underlying aggressive feelings towards another person becomes excessively concerned about the welfare of that person.

Reading difficulties and behaviour

Reading difficulties tend to affect males more than females and are more prevalent among children of manual workers rather than white-collar workers. They are also more common in the inner city than in suburban areas.

There is a reasonably strong connection between reading difficulties, conduct disorders, hyperactivity and juvenile delinquency. Conduct disorders or emotional and behavioural difficulties may interfere with learning processes, particularly reading. Alternatively reading difficulties may lead to emotional and behavioural difficulties. Where reading difficulties and conduct disorders occur together, problems during adolescence are likely to deteriorate. These can take the form of increasing truancy and educational failure (inadequate or a lack of leaving qualifications), unemployment and delinquency.

Reality principle (and pleasure principle)

A psychoanalytic term contrasted with the pleasure principle. The id, the origin of biological drives such as aggression and sex, operates according to the pleasure principle, i.e. immediate gratification without restraint or inhibition. The id disregards reality and is demanding, impulsive, irrational, illogical, amoral, and totally pleasure seeking. The ego operates according to the reality principle and attempts to satisfy the id's impulses in accordance with the demands of reality. The gratification of desire is delayed until an optimum time when gratification can be obtained without harmful consequences. The id's drives may be blocked, diverted or gradually satisfied.

Regression

Regression is a psychoanalytic defence mechanism through which a person avoids anxiety by returning to an earlier, primitive or infantile libidinal, sexual or ego stage of development. Earlier infantile patterns of behaviour continue to exist and provide alternative ways of behaving. Regression as a defence is not total and it is possible for regression to result in further anxiety.

Reinforcement

Reinforcement is a behavioural term used to describe any stimulus, event, action or behaviour which is dependent or contingent upon the response that preceded it and which serves to increase the relative probability of that response. An operant response is an external, observable behaviour that is performed by a person – swimming, talking, fighting and praying – and is not elicited by any specific, eliciting stimuli but can be said to operate on the environment. The response must occur before the reinforcing stimulus in order for reinforcement to take place. The reinforcing stimulus is therefore contingent on the response. Where a person produces work and receives praise resulting in an increase in work output, reinforcement has occurred. A reinforcer strengthens or increases the behaviour it follows.

A reinforcer is defined empirically and pragmatically by its effect on behaviour, if it increases the likelihood of that behaviour then reinforcement has occurred.

- Positive reinforcement strengthens behaviours by increasing their frequency, e.g. a person praised for helping others increases helping others in the future.
- Negative reinforcement strengthens responses by also increasing their frequency but through the withdrawal of a negative reinforcer, e.g. a person stops or avoids criticism for being lazy by working hard, increasing work output in the future.
- Punishment occurs when an aversive stimulus follows a response and leads to a reduction in the frequency or termination of that response, e.g. a detention is given for swearing. Punishment may also be the withdrawal of a positive reinforcer, e.g. swearing leads to the TV being switched off.
- Extinction occurs when positive reinforcement is withheld until the previously positively reinforced response decreases or terminates, e.g. teacher no longer pays attention to shouting out.
- Shaping occurs when successive approximations to a specific behaviour are positively reinforced, e.g. praising each action or step that eventually leads to a person swimming.
- Partial reinforcement is where reinforcement is delivered according to certain schedules, time schedules or interval schedules and response-based schedules or ratio schedules.

Domjan, M. (1998) The Principles of Learning and Behavior, 4th edn. Pacific Grove, CA, Brooks/Cole Publishing.

Relationships and behaviour

There are various perspectives on the formation, development and breakdown of relationships.

The learning or behavioural approach to relationships is based on classical and operant conditioning. The learning approach based on classical conditioning sees the breakdown of relationships as due to the association of others with painful, stressful and unsatisfying events even if they are not directly the cause of those events. On the other hand, people may develop relationships with each other because they share experiences of common adverse situations. The learning approach based on operant conditioning sees the breakdown of relationships as due to the effects of diminishing rewards, punishment or disapproval that emanates from other people.

Relationships perceived as unrewarding, negative and stress-inducing are likely to break down. However, people may be altruistic and disregard the negative and unrewarding aspects of relationships.

The social exchange approach is an economic theory that sees relationship breakdown as being due to high costs being combined with low rewards. There are rewards but these do not offset the high costs of maintaining the relationship. Relationships perceived as providing little in the way of benefits in return for high levels of investment are likely to disintegrate. However, people do not necessarily maintain a balance sheet of costs and rewards of relationships, nor would they want to (e.g. as in altruism).

The social equity approach sees relationship breakdown as being due to people feeling that they are receiving too little or too much from a relationship, in other words the relationship is perceived as inequitable or disproportionate in relation to their inputs. Relationships break down where people perceive there is a deficit in benefits or even an excess of benefits.

However people may try to restore equity in an inequitable relationship by reducing their inputs or by convincing themselves that they are getting their just deserts. On the other hand, people may not be solely or overly concerned or preoccupied with the amount of benefits they do or do not receive from relationships. The attachment style approach sees relationship breakdown as due to the type of attachment manifested in early childhood, i.e. an avoidant or ambivalent (anxious or insecure) attachment in early childhood. Those who are avoidant become remote, distrustful and unresponsive towards others. Those who are anxious or insecure become uncertain about the attitudes, feelings and responses of others. Attachment styles are seen as relatively stable or enduring but in a significant number of relationships styles do undergo change.

Duck, S. (1988) Relating to Others. Milton Keynes, Open University Press.
Duck, S. (1998) Human Relationships, 3rd edn. London, SAGE Publications.
Dwyer, D. (2000) Interpersonal Relationships. London, Routledge.

Relaxation training

Relaxation training is a behavioural technique, an example of alternate response training. This form of training is used to control anxiety. The aim is to train a person to engage in responses that are incompatible with an undesired response such as anxiety. Relaxation is a response that is incompatible with anxiety. A person is trained to relax. In behaviour therapy a person is trained to tense and relax specific groups of muscles. Alternately tensing and relaxing muscles enables people to discriminate or differentiate between different levels of relaxation. Relaxation techniques enable people to develop self-control over their anxiety.

Repetition compulsion

Repetition compulsion as a general term refers to an irrational compulsion to repeat behaviours. As a psychoanalytic term it refers to a person repeatedly returning to a past trauma or upsetting event and reliving that event. An analyst leads a person to revisit and re-experience the past trauma in order for the person to gain insight into that trauma. This process is called working through. In some analytic relationships a person's failure to sustain the relationship is attributed to repetition-compulsion, the wish to preserve the status quo.

Repression

Repression is a psychoanalytic term that refers to an unconscious mental process or defence mechanism that protects a person from unacceptable and unavoidable wishes, desires, impulses and memories that would produce anxiety or guilt if they entered consciousness. Repression is a process. In the first stage, the stage of primal repression, a repressed desire or impulse is fixated or prevented and does not undergo any further development. The second stage is called primary repression and is directed against any derivatives or associated ideas connected to the primally repressed impulses. Finally in secondary repression any reminders of what has been previously repressed are also repressed. What is repressed is not inactive but continues to exert an influence on consciousness through dreams, slips of the tongue and pen, mistakes and emotional problems. The analyst attempts to bring repressed desires and impulses to the surface or into consciousness so that they can be understood and controlled.

Resistance

Resistance is a psychoanalytic term referring to the many ways people prevent unconscious and unacceptable impulses, desires and memories surfacing or entering into consciousness. It is a defence mechanism in that it protects the person from bringing up or acknowledging unacceptable desires and impulses. However, these unacceptable impulses and desires still strive to enter consciousness and may do so in a disguised form through symptoms. Resistance takes many forms including:

- repression resistance, denying the need to know about unconscious impulses and desires;
- transference resistance, an hostility or indifference to the relationship with the analyst;
- superego resistance, where people accept their condition with no apparent desire to change or improve it.

The aim of the analyst is to interpret the person's resistances in order to enable the person to gain insight and to overcome the unconscious conflicts that underlie resistances.

Reward

Reward refers to any object or activity that produces a state of physical or mental pleasure or satisfaction in a person. The term reward is often used as a synonym for a positive reinforcer. The state of pleasure may be of short or long duration, of lesser or greater intensity. Rewards can be tangible, e.g. food, drink, money, or social, e.g. praise, smiles and caresses. What a particular person finds rewarding can only be discovered through experience, observation or self-report, it cannot be assumed a priori. People can be motivated by the thought of receiving rewards and it is often hoped that rewards will increase desirable or appropriate behaviours. Rewarding desirable behaviour is seen as a positive alternative to punishment and negative reinforcement. The aim of rewarding is to reward specific behaviours, not the person.

Ritalin

Ritalin is an example of methylphenidate, a stimulant drug used to treat ADHD in children (not under four years of age) and adolescents since the 1960s. The drug is contra-indicated where there is a high risk of cardiovascular disease, tic disorders and Tourette's syndrome. The drug is given orally in short acting and sustained-released tablet forms at an optimal dose level. It is usually taken in the mornings and afternoons. The optimal dose level should be determined by the collection of objective data (teacher or parent ratings, exam and test results and direct observation), as should treatment efficacy. There may be considerable variation in responses to doses but generally speaking higher doses have the greatest effects. The effects stop once drug treatment ends. Even on the drug there can be days when behaviour is bad.

Ritalin is the most frequent drug treatment of ADHD. There is short-term improvement in concentration, attention, classroom behaviour and social relationships with adults and peers and reductions in aggressive and impulsive behaviour in 70 to 80 per cent of cases. This improvement occurs across all settings. The remaining 20 to 30 per cent either show no change in behaviour or their behaviour worsens. However, educational achievement may not improve over the long term.

A question remains as to how far an ADHD student's classroom behaviour is normalised by drug treatment, a question of clinical significance compared with statistical significance. Teachers' reports indicate that normalisation of classroom behaviour does occur but it is recommended that other interventions will be required at the same time as drug treatment.

There are possible side effects, the most frequently reported being the temporary loss of appetite and insomnia. There is also a risk that Ritalin can be used as a recreational drug. Mild types of ADHD may be treated by behaviour modification, especially operant techniques, and these techniques should be used prior to drug treatment and as an adjunct to such treatment.

Drug treatment requires parental commitment and proper parental supervision.

In cases where children are antagonistic towards drug treatment various forms of non-compliance will occur, nullifying the approach.

S

Schedules of reinforcement

The term schedules of reinforcement refers to how many or which responses or behaviours will be reinforced. Positive reinforcers are delivered according to a schedule or plan.

- Continuous reinforcement takes place when behaviour is reinforced on every occasion. This type of reinforcement is used when the behaviour is just being acquired or is just developing. It is not advised for long-term use due to the problem of satiation.
- Intermittent reinforcement occurs when behaviour is reinforced only on some occasions. The advantage of this type of reinforcement is that resistance to extinction is greater when reinforcement is terminated. Another advantage is economic: for a few reinforcers a higher number of responses are achieved, less time is required, there is less interruption and satiation is less likely.

Intermittent reinforcement can be delivered on a ratio schedule (number of responses) or an interval schedule (time elapsed). Both these schedules are fixed, i.e. the same requirement on every occasion. However the requirement can be variable, i.e. different on each occasion.

A fixed-ratio schedule is one where a reinforcer is delivered for an unvarying number of responses, an example being piecework payments. A variable-ratio schedule states that reinforcers are delivered after a particular number of responses but the number varies in an unpredictable way, examples being angling, playing a slot machine.

A fixed-interval schedule requires an interval or period of time to elapse before a reinforcer is delivered, e.g. checking to see whether one has any post. A variable-interval schedule states the average length of the intervals needed for reinforcement, e.g. quiz tests given to student by teachers.

Schools and behaviour

School ethos can influence behaviour, although intake differences still play a part in influencing behaviour in schools. Punitive, coercive and exclusive school policies are likely to exacerbate antisocial behaviour and generate various forms of resistance, e.g. disruptive classroom behaviour, vandalism and graffiti. Rigid streaming is likely to lead to the development of a lower stream anti-school culture. Schools that reward positive behaviour and provide children with opportunities to exercise responsibility (as in school, year and form councils) are more likely to encourage positive attitudes and behaviour among their pupils.

Efficient and effective pastoral and referral systems also serve to prevent and reduce behavioural problems through early identification and intervention. Senior management systems characterised by strong and authoritative pastoral leadership combined with collegial and consultative approaches to staff management lead to effective and positive whole-school behaviour policies.

Where the school buildings and decor are kept decorated, repaired and free of graffiti antisocial behaviour is likely to be reduced. Teachers who provide positive role models for pupils are likely to encourage their pupils to emulate them. Efficient and effective classroom organisation, preparation and punctuality are likely to prevent or reduce disruptive behaviour. Schools may also decide to install CCTV in order to deter and detect disruptive and antisocial behaviour in school corridors and in the playground. However misbehaviour and exclusions still occurs in schools equipped with CCTV.

Intake differences can have a significant impact on school behaviour in terms of an imbalance of children with EBD, of children with learning difficulties and of children permanently excluded from other schools. Boys' schools can be more problematic than girls' schools given that boys display more behavioural problems than do girls. Schools that are undersubscribed may find themselves in a downward spiral of falling rolls while at the same time having to accept a disproportionate number of children with behavioural problems from other schools.

Comparisons between schools in terms of differences in behaviour are usually made on the basis of exclusion rates (fixed term and permanent) and unauthorised attendance rates. In terms of fixed term exclusion figures and non-attendance these can be affected by the ways in which schools compile figures, record absences and resort to unofficial exclusion. Schools may avoid permanently excluding a child by persuading parents or carers to send their child to another school. The parents or carers may themselves feel under such pressure that they decide to transfer their child to another school before the child is excluded. However, similar problems with the child may resurface in the new school, leading to further exclusions and further moves. Schools may be wary of accepting 'problem' children from other schools as these children can be perceived as putting at risk the receiving school's academic results and good reputation for discipline and behaviour. As a consequence they may resort to delaying or obstructive measures such as 'no places available', 'the long waiting list' or simply 'no response'. Schools may, in other words, wish to 'export' their problem children, and avoid 'importing' problem children from other schools.

Sanders, D. and Hendry, L.B. (1997) New Perspectives on Disaffection. London, Cassell.

Selective mutism

Selective mutism is a psychiatric disorder characterised by a child persistently failing to speak in specific settings. Typically, the child is able to speak in the home and to certain people, usually parents. The child who is selectively mute usually does not speak in the school setting and/or in certain other social situations. The incidence of selective mutism is rare; persistent selective mutism lasting for at least six months occurs at a rate of 0.7 per

1,000. Many children are initially reluctant to speak or very shy when they first start attending school. For example, in a group of four- to five-year olds who had started school, 7.2 per 1,000 did not speak. Twenty months later, only one child still did not speak. Selective mutism is slightly more common in girls than in boys as demonstrated by research which found a sex ratio of 40 per cent boys to 60 per cent girls.

The exact cause of selective mutism is not known although a number of factors that may predispose children to developing this disorder have been identified. These include

- having controlling or oppositional tendencies;
- having poor peer relations;
- being excessively shy;
- being socially isolated.

Some evidence also points to maternal over-protection, greater family discord and environmental stressors as predisposing factors. Current interventions for the treatment of selective mutism favour focusing on the symptoms and potential for change rather than delving into possible causes. The first step involves a thorough analysis of the contexts in which the problem does not occur as well as where it does, as well as identifying the resources in the home and in the school setting which can be used to support change. The persistence of this disorder can be due to the child's non-verbal communication being reinforced by both adults and children. Adults tend to employ a pattern of verbal interaction that does not require the child to speak and children tend to either reduce their verbal interactions with the child or to stop speaking to the child altogether.

Behavioural approaches use techniques such as

- shaping, i.e. rewarding the child for any behaviours that approximate speech;
- situation fading, i.e. moving the child and the person to whom the child does speak to settings where the child does not usually use speech;
- individual fading, i.e. gradually introducing new individuals to the child in settings which are familiar to the child;
- reinforcement sampling is another intervention that has been used. This involves allowing the child to play with a reward for a short time – later, this reinforcer can later be earned through speaking.

Herbert, M. (1998) Clinical Child Psychology Social Learning, Development and Behaviour, 2nd edn. Chichester, Wiley.

Schizophrenia

Schizophrenia is a psychiatric or mental disorder characterised by hallucinations, thought disorder, delusions and inappropriate emotional responses. It is found in all parts of the world and in all ethnic groups. The development of schizophrenia can be very insidious in early life. The average age of onset is 18 to 25 for men and 26 to 40 for women.

Positive symptoms in the acute form include hallucinations, ideas of persecution, delusions of reference, withdrawal and impaired social and working relationships. However not all sufferers experience all of these problems.

There may be deterioration in appearance and behaviour, e.g. social withdrawal, isolation and awkwardness, inappropriate emotional expression and a flattening of mood. Speech may become difficult to understand and thinking may become disordered or preoccupied with pseudo-scientific or mystical ideas. Hallucinations are frequent and tend to be auditory rather than visual. Some sufferers experience other kinds of hallucinations, including somatic, olfactory and gustatory. Sufferers hear voices that appear to give commands, discuss or make comments about the sufferer. Delusions are common and take the form of persecutory delusions, delusions of reference (being referred to), delusions of control (being controlled by an outside source) and delusions of thought (having thoughts inserted by others or broadcast to others). As regards cognitive functions, attention and concentration are impaired and there is often a lack of insight into the condition.

Negative symptoms in the chronic phase include lack of motivation, inactivity, neglect of personal hygiene and appearance, movement disorders (catatonia, stupor and excitement) and repeated movements, blunted or flattened emotions, hallucinations, delusions, impaired attention and concentration and lack of insight.

It should be noted that hallucinations and delusions can be symptoms of other disorders, e.g. depression, anxiety and organic disorders. The content of hallucinations frequently reflects the cultural context of the sufferer.

Childhood schizophrenia manifests the same sort of symptoms as adult schizophrenia but diagnosis may be more complicated due to children's limited cognitive skills. However, it has been identified in children as young as five years but is rare before seven years. Males are more likely to develop early onset schizophrenia. Childhood and adolescent schizophrenia is likely to be preceded by speech and language delay and poor social adjustment. After puberty is reached there is an increase in the incidence of schizophrenia and late adolescence is the main time of onset. Its development is often insidious and it can be difficult to diagnose. Most childhood schizophrenics suffer from auditory hallucinations. Delusions and thought disorders are also common, as are emotional blunting and social withdrawal.

Diagnosis of schizophrenia is through the application of the criteria found in DCM IV and ICD-10. Certain symptoms characterise schizophrenia, these are called Schneider's 'first rank' symptoms and occur in 70 per cent of schizophrenic sufferers. These symptoms are hearing voices, hallucinations, thought withdrawal, thought insertion or thought broadcasting, delusions and feelings or behaviour as being determined externally. Other disorders can display some schizophrenic symptoms, e.g. organic conditions (encephalitis, amphetamine abuse, temporal lobe epilepsy, delirium, dementia), mood disorder and personality disorders.

Schizophrenia runs in families and concordance rates for the condition are about 53 per cent for identical twins and 15 per cent for fraternal twins. These concordance rates indicate a genetic component but also indicate that other factors are responsible for schizophrenia. Many people who suffer from schizophrenia do not have relatives suffering from the condition. The mode of genetic inheritance is currently unknown.

Various biological theories about the origin of schizophrenia have been proposed including the neurodevelopmental hypothesis, the dopamine hypothesis and the glutamate hypothesis. The neurodevelopmental hypothesis states the pre-natal or neonatal abnormalities impair brain development; however this hypothesis awaits further verification. The dopamine hypothesis states that excess activity at particular types of dopamine synapses leads to schizophrenia. This hypothesis is based on the observation that antipsychotic drugs like phenothiazines block dopamine receptors and also drugs like amphetamine can induce some of the positive symptoms of schizophrenia. However, the dopamine hypothesis is not yet confirmed. The glutamate hypothesis states that there is insufficient activity at the glutamate synapses. The drug phenycyclidine (PCP) inhibits glutamate-type receptors and also produces both the positive and the negative symptoms of schizophrenia. The glutamate hypothesis also awaits confirmation.

Environmental factors are thought to play a part in exacerbating schizophrenia. These factors include stressful life events and expressed emotions such as hostility when sufferers return to their families.

The treatment of schizophrenia is mainly through antipsychotic drug therapy such as Chlorpromazine (conventional) and Clozapine (atypical). Compliance with medication can be poor and there can be adverse side effects such as extrapyramidal effects (involuntary movements and restlessness), tardive dyskinesia (muscle movements of the face) and agranulocytosis (deficiency in making normal number of white blood cells).

Cognitive theories of schizophrenia state that there is either an underlying cognitive deficit, in particular an attentional deficit that produces delusions, hallucinations and thought disorders, or alternatively a cognitive bias in the form of irrational beliefs. Cognitive-behavioural therapy is directed at empirically challenging the irrational beliefs and inferences that are seen to lie at the root of delusions.

Davison, G.C. and Neale, J.M. (2001) Abnormal Psychology, 8th edn. Chichester, Wiley.
Tsuang, M.T. and Faraone, S.V. with assistance of Johnson, P.D.C. (1997) Schizophrenia: the facts. Oxford, Oxford University Press.

Contacts

Hearing Voices Network. Tel. 0161 228 3896.
National Schizophrenia Fellowship. Advice line 020 8974 6814 (10 a.m. to 3 p.m., Monday–Friday).
Schizophrenia – A National Emergency (SANE). Helpline 020 7724 8000.

School refusal (phobia)

School refusal is the reluctance or refusal to leave home for school. The child refuses to go to school, or after departing for school returns home. School refusers complain that they are frightened or that they are suffering from physical conditions such as headaches and stomach disorders. It mainly occurs at the age of five or six on commencing school, at 11 when starting secondary school and in the early teenage years. School refusal is equally common among boys and girls. Secondary school refusers tend to be more persistent.

When attempts are made to force the child to school they often become resistant, uncooperative and angry. The onset of school refusal may be abrupt or gradual triggers; may include a change of school or teacher, absence from school or the loss of a friend. School refusal may be a symptom of separation anxiety. In some cases there is a specific phobia related to bullying, a disliked or feared teacher, or of a particular subject like physical education.

Family factors may contribute to school refusal, such as inadequate discipline and supervision and emotional over-protectiveness and parental collusion. School refusal is to be differentiated from truancy. Truants absent themselves from school without parental permission and often engage in delinquent activities.

School refusers are of average ability and do not experience difficulties with school work. There is usually a history of separation problems when first attending school.

Behavioural approaches are used to treat school refusal. Parents are asked to be consistently and persistently firm in encouraging their child to return to school. Parents should use positive reinforcement to encourage school attendance in the form of rewards and they should avoid positively reinforcing attempts to remain at home. If the child has been absent from school for a long period then a systematic desensitisation approach is indicated. This involves gradually approaching and entering the school in successive and discrete steps or stages. Family therapy approaches can also be used to encourage parents to set clear boundaries and to avoid over-involvement and over-protectiveness. Tuition in the home setting is inadvisable as it can encourage all parties to avoid addressing the problem and positively reinforces the pupil in staying at home. Transfer to another school is also inadvisable as the problem may simply reappear in the new setting, although if there are overriding school factors then transfer to another school may be necessary. The success rate for return to regular school attendance is high, about 70 per cent, particularly where the child is young, the condition is mild and there is early intervention.

Carr, A. (1999) *The Handbook of Child and Adolescent Clinical Psychology: A Contextual Approach.* London, Routledge.

Wenar, C. (1994) *Developmental Psychopathology: From Infancy through Adolescence,* 3rd edn. New York, McGraw-Hill Inc.

Seasonal affective disorder (SAD)

Seasonal affective disorder is an emotional disorder that is characterised by depression or mania during particular seasons. Depressive episodes include excessive sleeping, lack of energy and weight gain. Normal moods occur in the spring and summer months but depression appears in the autumn-winter months. The disorder can be treated through the application of phototherapy, bright artificial light of 10,000 lux. Various hypotheses have been suggested to explain the disorder including the melatonin hypothesis, the phase delay of circadian rhythms and the photon-counting hypothesis but none appear to explain the disorder fully nor why phototherapy works.

Contact

Seasonal Affective Disorder Association: Helpline 020 7969 7028

Self-esteem

The term self-esteem refers to the evaluations children make about themselves and their competence in a range of settings. These self-evaluations and competencies influence attitudes, motivation and behaviour. Self-esteem is not a fixed entity as it can fluctuate over time and can be affected by changing circumstances. These changes tend to be small.

Generally, self-esteem is relatively stable. Children with high self-esteem think and feel positive about themselves in terms of character, worth, strengths, skills and competencies. Those children at particular risk of experiencing low self-esteem include rejected children, isolated children, overweight and abused children.

Children evaluate their selves in five different domains and integrate these into a global self-evaluation. The five domains are educational ability, athletic competence, behaviour, social acceptance and appearance. Self-esteem is not only composed of children's specific views about the self but also about what children hope to be, what children think is possible and what children fear they might become. A particular child's self-esteem is also related to other children's perceptions and reaction to that child's behaviour. Children with high self-esteem generally have positive feelings and a positive outlook towards life. High self-esteem is protective in terms of warding off or dealing with stress, anxiety and depression. Sometimes children can appear to have high self-esteem but underneath are anxious and insecure. However, others may have high self-esteem and engage in antisocial and disruptive behaviour.

Children low in self-esteem generally experience self-dissatisfaction and self-disparagement, are hypersensitive, blame others, fear new situations, are uncertain and have difficulty in forming and maintaining relationships. Children can experience a lowering of self-esteem at ties of transition, e.g. going to secondary school, at times of puberty and when moving to a new school or a new neighbourhood.

However, many children experience an increase in self-esteem during adolescence. Social comparison plays a role in increasing the self-esteem of children. Children make comparisons with other children and rank themselves in terms of attractiveness and competencies in relation to those children and as a consequence self-esteem may be raised or lowered. Children also experience high self-esteem when they think that future possibilities can be realised.

Boys tend to have higher self-evaluations in the domains of physical prowess, appearance, science and mathematics, whereas girls tend to have higher self-evaluations in the domains of verbal and reading ability. Girls may be at risk of low self-esteem if they feel they do not adhere to or subscribe to what are perceived as the dominant masculine traits of assertiveness, competitiveness and decisiveness.

Parents who are democratic, caring, warm and supportive help to increase their children's self-esteem.

Advice to parents and teachers in helping to raise children's self-esteem

- Self-esteem cannot be raised through simply telling children that they are good without connecting it to their actual performance and competence.
- Security and trust – help the child to feel secure and safe and develop a sense of belonging.
- Role model – help the child by being a positive role model that the child can imitate, internalise and follow.
- Communication – help the child by acknowledging effort as well as achievement, provide accurate and authentic positive feedback.
- Purpose or aim – help the child to develop aims and goals in life, a sense of purpose.
- Standards and expectations – help the child by setting high but realistic standards and expectations.
- Problem-solving and coping skills – help the child develop problem solving skills so that obstacles and barriers to success can be overcome.
- Opportunities – plan learning opportunities, activities and situations where the child can experience success.
- Beliefs – challenge the child's irrational beliefs about his or her self, e.g. about ability and attractiveness.
- Provide assertiveness training where children need to assert their rights.

Mruk, C. (1999) Self-Esteem: Research, Theory and Practice. London, Free Association Books.
O'Brien, T. and Guiney, D. (2001) Differentiation in Teaching and Learning. London, Continuum.

Self-injury (self-mutilation)

Self-injury is the deliberate infliction of pain and/or injury on one's body without the intention of suicide. The most frequent self-injury is skin mutilation or cutting, particularly of the arms and hands and less frequently the face, upper body, breasts and genitals. Injury can be inflicted through burning, scalding, scratching, picking, biting, scraping, pulling out hair, scrubbing and swallowing harmful objects and substances.

Self-injury is often private and is seen partly as a means of coping with psychological distress or tension through relieving feelings of guilt and shame, particularly in connection with childhood abuse. It can be understood as a way of gaining control, asserting independence, forming a self-identity and as a means of expressing anger, despair and as a form of protest. Self-injury also evokes feelings of self-loathing in the form of self-blame, low self-esteem and the feeling that one is bad or contaminated. The effects of self-injury provoke strong reactions from GPs, family members and friends. Self-injury often occurs in specific settings, e.g. prisons, special hospitals, secure institutions, children's homes and hostels. Self-injury is mostly carried out by males and females in their teens, 20s and 30s, rarely in their 50s and more women than men are involved. It occurs disproportionately among gay men and women, people with learning difficulties and prisoners. Physical and sexual abuse, emotional neglect, bereavement are frequently identified as triggers for self-injury. Many people who engage in self-injury come from violent and disorganised families.

Self-injury may serve a variety of functions:

- controlling and reducing stress and tension;
- coping with anger;
- distraction from distress;
- providing a sense of control over one's life and feelings of empowerment;
- elicit a sense of caring;
- pride in bearing the pain;
- atonement for supposed wrongdoings;
- purging or cleansing feelings of contamination or sexual arousal;
- communicating distress;
- punishing people who are seen as at fault or neglectful;
- seeking care and support from others.

People who engage in self-injury are often secretive, feel ashamed and fear criticism. Many seek the opportunity to talk through their problem in a non-threatening context with an empathic listener.

Babiker, G. and Arnold, L. (1997) The Language of Injury: Comprehending Self-Mutilation. Leicester, British Psychological Society.
Strong, M. (1999) A Bright Red Scream: Self-mutilation and the Language of Pain. London, Penguin Books.

Separation anxiety disorder

Separation anxiety disorder is characterised by an intense separation anxiety that is developmentally inappropriate and that affects social interactions as for example in school refusal. The disorder is more frequent in prepubertal children than in adolescents. Children affected by the disorder are very concerned that harm will befall their parents or that their parents will leave them. They also fear that they themselves will be separated from their parent in some way. The affected children cling to their parents, avoiding even temporary separation. They may refuse to go to school or to sleep alone due to nightmares. Any separation or threat of separation may lead to temper tantrums, tearfulness and physical complaints such as headaches and stomach-aches. These behaviours may lead to or enable the child to stay at home thereby negatively reinforcing those behaviours.

Behavioural methods, in particular operant techniques, are used to treat the disorder, and include positive reinforcement to encourage separation behaviours and sanctions for clinging behaviours. Systematic desensitisation or gradual exposure may be used to increase separation behaviours. Cognitive approaches can also be helpful in encouraging the child to replace negative coping self-statements with positive coping self-statements. A family therapy approach may be necessary where parents are increasing their child's clinging behaviour because of their own needs or anxieties or because they are overprotective.

Graham, P. (ed.) (1998) *Cognitive-Behaviour Therapy for Children and Families.* Cambridge, Cambridge University Press.

Sexual abuse

Sexual abuse can be defined as the enforced involvement of children and adolescents in any sexual activity that is unwanted, not understood and to which they are unable to give consent and that violates legal constraints, social conventions and family roles.

There is a range of sexual activities including contact and non-contact abuse. Contact abuse can range from touching to penetration. Penetrative abuse is less common than non-penetrative abuse. Non-contact abuse takes the form of exhibitionism.

Prevalence figures for sexual abuse depend on the definitions of abuse and the types of abuse and are generally imprecise. It appears that females are more often sexually abused than males and cases of sexual abuse come from all social classes. Sexual abuse is disclosed by children and adolescents to other children, to an adult or to a helpline. The main sexual abusers are men although women can become involved by co-abusing with men or on their own initiative, however they constitute a small minority. A substantial number of sexual abuse cases occur within the home where fathers are the main sexual abusers but siblings can also be abusers. Stepfathers are disproportionately involved. Outside the home the sexually abused child or adolescent often knows the abuser in the form of a neighbour, family friend or babysitter. Sexual abuse by a complete stranger is relatively uncommon.

Sexual abuse is facilitated where there is a lack or absence of non-abusing parental supervision or where the child is socially isolated. Sexual abusers are often in denial, make attempts to justify their behaviour and deny that their behaviour has a negative impact on the child. They may use rewards to encourage compliance to engage in sexual activities and punishment for non-compliance. On disclosure of the abuse other family members may collude in suppressing knowledge about the abuse or blame the abused child. Sexual abusers themselves may have been abused.

Symptoms of sexual abuse include physical manifestations resulting from penetration (not always or often present), precocious sexualised behaviour, sullen and withdrawn behaviour, unprovoked irritability and aggressive behaviour, educational underachievement and loss of personal and social relationships. Adolescent symptoms include taking drug overdoses, running away from home or abusing other children.

The effects of sexual abuse include emotional blunting, depression, abrupt changes in mood, anger in response to slight frustrations, abnormal attachment behaviour, low self-esteem, poor social relationships and emotional and behavioural difficulties. Emotional and behavioural problems when extreme take the form of violent, antisocial and self-harming behaviour. However a specific group of behaviours that are linked with the experience of sexual abuse have not yet been identified.

The sexually abused can feel guilty and responsible for being abused, feel powerless and helpless, lack trust in others and experience insomnia, nightmares, physical complaints, intrusive thoughts, manifest sexualised behaviour, develop confusion over their sexual orientation and engage in self-destructive behaviours such as substance abuse, self-injury and suicide. Risk factors for being repeatedly sexually abused include low self-esteem, low self-efficacy, negative coping strategies, physical disabilities, learning difficulties, physical weakness and an absolute conformity to adult demands.

The risk factors for perpetrating sexual abuse include being highly motivated to engage in sexual abuse, experiencing children and adolescents as sexually arousing and unavailable access to adult sexual relationships. Family risk factors include disorganisation where family life is chaotic and there are few inhibitions restraining sexual abuse and over-organisation where family life is secretive and abuse is unacknowledged.

Sexual abuse is dealt with through a paediatric assessment in conjunction with social services, child mental health, the family GP and the police. A full family assessment is also undertaken. A negative result from a physical examination does not exclude the existence of sexual abuse. The only definite physical effects are the presence of semen or a sexually transmitted disease. Controversy surrounds the use of anatomically correct dolls. Sexually abused children and adolescents are treated though psychotherapy and cognitive-behavioural therapy. Psychotherapy requires talking to the child about the abuse in order for the effects of repeated exposure to memories and stimuli to be decreased. Fears and anxieties need to be managed through behavioural (relaxation techniques) and cognitive approaches (thought stopping and positive self-statements).

Corby, B. (2000) Child Abuse, 2nd edn. Buckingham, Open University Press.
Draucker Burke, C. (2000) Counselling Survivors of Childhood Sexual Abuse, 2nd edn. London, SAGE
  Publications.

Sexual disorders

There exist a number of disorders termed paraphilias. Paraphilia is defined by DSM-IV as sexual attraction to uncommon objects or activities over a period of six months or more resulting in psychological distress or impairment. However some people do not experience distress or impairment as a consequence of having a paraphilia but others do as a consequence of being victims of some sexual disorders, e.g. paedophilia. Some of these disorders can have legal implications as they involve non-consenting victims, e.g. paedophilia and are therefore sexual offences. Most people who have a paraphilia or sexual disorder are male but the prevalence of such disorders is difficult to determine.

Paraphilias include:

- Fetishism: Described as a dependency on an object in order for sexual arousal to occur, e.g. underwear, rubber clothing and shoes. Fetishism can be a private act using the object for masturbatory purposes or another person may be required to wear an object in order for sexual intercourse to occur. On occasion a person collects or steals articles of clothing for fetishistic purposes. The attraction to particular objects is experienced as compelling and irresistible and the object is required as an indispensable means for sexual arousal.
- Transvestism: Described as an activity whereby heterosexual men achieve sexual arousal through wearing women's clothing in part or fully. This cross-dressing often occurs in private and in secret but is known to some members of the family. Many of these men are married and are masculine in appearance. Transvestism may co-occur with masochism.
- Paedophilia and incest: Paedophilia is where adults are sexually attracted to children unrelated to them and who also derive sexual gratification by involving children in sexual activities. Paedophilia is more common among men than women and can co-occur along with mood disorders, substance abuse and other paraphilias. It can be heterosexual or homosexual. It may or may not involve violence or threats of violence. Self-report and penile plethysmographic studies have recorded evidence of some ordinary men being sexually aroused by paedophilic material. Specific paedophilic material is not necessarily required to arouse paedophiles' sexual interest in children as media images involving children are often sufficient to arouse sexual desire. Paedophiles are often known as friends or neighbours of families. Most paedophiles are in the age range from 20 to 50 years and are often married with children of their own. They often have a profile that is one of low self-esteem, poor impulse control and inadequate social skills. A significant proportion of sexual molestations occurring within and

outside the family are committed by adolescent males, many of whom were themselves sexually abused as children. These adolescent males are often described as having conduct disorders but as also experiencing anxiety and depression.

Risk factors for paedophilia include delayed psychological development, social isolation and sexual abuse. Sexually abused children suffer from sleep and eating disorders, fears and phobias, school problems and sexualising of behaviour.

Incest describes sexual relations between close relatives and is most common between brothers and sisters and fathers and daughters. It tends to occur in patriarchal families and in families where parents emotionally neglect their children and where the mother is absent or disabled. It can also occur in families where fathers are moralistic and fundamentalist with regard to religious beliefs. Victims of incest are at a higher risk of low self-esteem, self-blame and negative feelings about physical contact. They are also at risk for depression, anxiety, suicide and substance abuse.

- Voyeurism: Is mainly a male preference for obtaining sexual gratification by illicitly observing others undressed, partially clothed or having sexual relations. Voyeuristic observations or memories of observations are used for masturbatory practices. Voyeurs are frequently anxious and inhibited males who lack social skills, many are harmless but some do end up raping women whom they are observing.
- Exhibitionism: Is mainly a male preference for obtaining sexual gratification through exposing one's genitalia to other adults or children. Along with exposure goes masturbation. The aim is to shock or embarrass the unwilling recipient. The urge to expose is often experienced as compelling and irresistible and can be triggered by anxiety. Many are married but have unsatisfactory sexual relationships. Men are arrested for indecent exposure when found engaging in exhibitionism.

The main theories regarding paraphilias are behavioural, cognitive, biological, psychodynamic and feminist. The behavioural perspective sees paraphilias as resulting from either classical conditioning whereby sexual arousal becomes conditioned to socially inappropriate stimuli or operant conditioning where reinforcement of sexually deviant responses has inadvertently occurred. The cognitive perspective regards cognitive distortions or irrational beliefs and expectations as leading to paraphilias.

Alloy, L.B., Jacobson, N.S. and Acocella, J. (1999) Abnormal Psychology: Current Perspectives, 8th edn. Boston, MA, McGraw-Hill College.

Shyness

Shyness is a vague term but can include the following:

- being easily embarrassed;
- being apprehensive and reluctant in communicating to and with others;
- fearing negative self-evaluation;
- fearing rejection;
- being reticent;
- being self-conscious;
- avoiding social situations and social interactions;
- being socially anxious or phobic;
- lacking social skills.

Shyness can be seen as having behavioural, cognitive, emotional and physiological components.

Many people report being shy but shyness varies according to social situations. Inhibited behaviour is triggered by fear of new situations, new people or of being negatively evaluated. People may fear that they will not have the social competence to cope with new situations or new people and as a consequence become anxious.

Some people are termed privately shy and are preoccupied with their internal state of discomfort while others who are publicly shy focus on their socially awkward behaviour. Shyness is often due to people pondering on the possibility of negative eventualities and the worst possible scenarios or catastrophes.

Physiological components of shyness can include high pulse rate, heart palpitations, blushing and perspiration. Shy people employ various coping strategies including avoidance and withdrawal. People may avoid asking questions or responding to questions, may only provide short answers, avoid asserting themselves or expressing opinions.

Shyness can be characterised as self-consciousness or a high degree of self-awareness and self-reflection. Self-consciousness or self-focused attention can lead to negative feelings and a lack of self-confidence. Adolescents often experience self-consciousness. Shy people often refer to themselves negatively more than people who are not shy. They underestimate their social competence and expect rejection and negative evaluation. Children's self-awareness and self-evaluation develops rapidly from the second year and they begin to display self-efficacy beliefs. Shame and embarrassment may also emerge at this time. Embarrassment arises when people feel that their self-image is adversely affected, when they are shown up in public, when they do not know what to do or when their roles are not recognised. Children often model themselves on their parents and may be influenced by their parents' shyness or low self-confidence. They may also be influenced by their parents' lack of confidence in them or by the way their parents' label them. At first in early appearing shyness children may display fearful shyness, feel uncomfortable in new situations or with new people, in later appearing shyness they may feel self-conscious.

Shyness can be seen as being caused by learning (classical conditioning) or by cognitive processes (self-focused thinking), social learning (modelling and low self-efficacy) or as being biologically based (suggested neurotransmitters, serotonin and catecholamines).

Shyness can have unwelcome effects restricting social interactions, avoiding public places and being unable to take advantage of educational and occupational opportunities. Where shyness is unwelcome and restricts opportunities, interventions include those based on behavioural, cognitive and biological approaches. Behavioural interventions include relaxation training, systematic desensitisation and social skills training. Cognitive interventions include identifying, challenging and replacing safety behaviours, e.g. avoidance and withdrawal from social interactions and social situations and also challenging cognitive distortions. The biological approach has used drug therapy in the form of anxiolytics (beta-blockers and benzodiazepines) and antidepressants (MAOIs, monoamine oxidase inhibitor and SSRIs, selective serotonin reuptake inhibitors) to treat social phobia.

Crozier, W.R. (2001) Understanding Shyness: Psychological Perspectives. Basingstoke, Palgrave Publishers.

Sleep disorders

Sleep disorders are disrupted patterns of sleep that may include difficulties falling or staying asleep, unusual behaviours associated with sleep, excessive sleep or falling asleep at inappropriate times. Sleep disorders are experienced more frequently by individuals who work irregular and long hours and by those with psychiatric disorders such as depression.

- Insomnia is a chronic inability to sleep. It includes difficulties initiating sleep, frequent waking during the night, a short sleep time and sleep that is experienced as non-restorative. The effects in daytime are tiredness, sleepiness, impaired functioning, anxiety, depression and other changes of mood. It is estimated that insomnia affects 20 to 33 per cent of the population. Women and older individuals are at greater risk than men and younger individuals. The causes of insomnia are many and varied. They include noise, stress, anxiety, pain, medication, sleeping in an unfamiliar environment, being too hot or too cold, poor sleeping habits. Many individuals who experience insomnia take a variety of medications and prescription drugs. It is now generally agreed that sleeping drugs, apart from having side effects, are not an effective intervention in the longer term. The most effective intervention is to eliminate any possible environmental cause and to learn good sleeping habits.
- Excessive daytime sleepiness refers to the inability to stay alert during the day or frequent sleep attacks during the day. It has been estimated to affect between 0.5 to 5 per cent of the general population. Young adults, the elderly and shift workers have a higher than usual rate of excessive sleepiness.

- Sleep apnea is a respiratory disorder in which breathing stops for ten seconds or more throughout the night. The incidence of sleep apnea increases with age and can be associated with snoring, the incidence of which also increases with age. A diagnosis of sleep apnea requires the individual to spend the night in a sleep laboratory. The usual intervention is the wearing of a nasal mask attached to a mechanism that increases airflow and relieves the obstruction at the back of the throat. In some cases, surgery may be undertaken.

There are a number of sleep disorders that are much more common in children:

- Nightmares are unpleasant dreams and are quite common. Estimates of between 10 and 50 per cent of children aged three to five are reported to experience nightmares.
- Night terrors are characterised by severe agitation such that the individual wakes screaming in terror and can be inconsolable for several minutes. Night terrors can be differentiated from nightmares as the individual is not able to recall what has happened.
- Sleepwalking is quite a common occurrence in children compared to adults. It has been estimated that between 15 to 30 per cent of children has at least one incidence of sleepwalking compared to less that one per cent in adults. Sleepwalking usually takes place a few hours after the child has fallen to sleep. The child walks with their eyes open, usually not bumping into anything. General advice for parents of children who sleepwalk is not be too concerned as sleepwalking is seldom a major problem. There are mixed views regarding whether to waken the child or not with some advising that it is essential not to wake a child and others advising that waking a child is not harmful and should be done. The causes of sleepwalking are not known.

Social cognition and behaviour

Social cognition is an approach that is concerned with social perception, i.e. how people make sense of themselves and other people. It focuses on attributions or causal explanations, schemas or cognitive structures or representations, self-concepts, social information-processing and inferential processes.

Attribution theory is concerned with whether the locus for causality of behaviour is internal, i.e. personal, or external, i.e. environmental or situational. Internal factors include motivation and ability whereas external factors include the actual situation and other people's actions. Attribution theory is also concerned with the process of misattribution, people making errors, displaying bias (i.e. misattributing causes to themselves, other people or the situation). The fundamental attribution error occurs when a person attributes another's behaviour to that person's disposition or qualities rather than to their situation or environment. The actor-observer effect occurs when a person tends to explain others' behaviour as due to their disposition and their own behaviour as to situational constraints. The false-consensus effect occurs when a person sees their behaviour as typical, normal or usual and that in a given situation others would behave in the same way. The self-serving bias is when a person takes credit for successes and denies responsibility for failures. The self-centred bias is where a person claims more credit for a jointly produced success than is due to that person. Attributional style is where people make particular types of causal inferences rather than others. A pessimistic attributional style regards negative events as caused by internal, stable and global factors. The aim of reattribution training is to enable people to make more positive attributions.

Schemas are cognitive or conceptual frameworks that are applied to the external world. They influence the interpreting and assimilation of new information. Person schemas are those used to categorise other people usually in terms of their traits, e.g. extraversion or introversion. Self-schemas are those we apply to ourselves. Individuals at risk of depression may possess negative self-schemas that are activated by certain events. People may think of themselves in terms of an actual and an ideal self and any unresolved discrepancy between the two could result in unhappiness. Self-regulation refers to the ways in which people attempt to control their behaviour. Self-efficacy beliefs, expectations that one can achieve chosen goals also influence self-regulation. Self-control is also influenced by how positive people feel about themselves, their level of self-esteem. In order to account for a poor impression or failure people may resort to self-handicapping, attributing one's failures to other less damaging factors than low ability or bad character, e.g. low effort, a bad mood, depression, unrealistic goals and drugs. Other schemas are role schemas, our expectations of others and event schemas, expectations of what things should happen in specific situations.

Fiske, S.T. and Taylor, S.E. (1991) Social Cognition, 2nd edn. New York, McGraw-Hill.

Social constructionist perspective

This perspective sees all knowledge, theories and concepts as being provisional and subject to change and as socially constructed, in other words socially and culturally determined. Knowledge, theories and concepts are based on particular perspectives, consequently their acceptability depends on the perspective chosen. This perspective tends to be anti-positivist, rejecting the idea of objective measurement and definitive empirical research. All theories and concepts are seen as open to modification or refutation depending on the chosen epistemology. Instead, the idea of people's experience as valid evidence is prominent. This means that people's experiences and their interpretations of those experiences are valid explanations.

From this perspective symptoms are seen as social constructs, i.e. interpretations of current experiences and these symptoms are not seen as objective independently of those interpretations. The interpretations of professionals, diagnoses or assessments are simply seen as taking precedence over the interpretations of lay people. Diagnoses and assessments are themselves predetermined by particular perspectives. The meanings attributed to experience are social constructs in that they are constructed through social dialogue and through social interactions. This perspective focuses on subjectivity, i.e. the particular thoughts and feelings people have about their experiences. It also focuses on people's sense of personal identity that is also formed through language and social interaction. The categorisation and labelling of behaviour, assessments and explanations are all seen as socially constructed. For instance, concepts such as 'masculinity' and 'femininity' are seen as socially and culturally determined, their meaning dependent on the conceptions of masculinity and femininity current in a given society. Boys and girls, women and men internalise those conceptions as norms or ideals that influence their social behaviour. Those who deviate from these norms or ideals of masculinity or femininity are considered as deviant or abnormal.

Burr, V. (1995) An Introduction to Social Constructionism. London, Routledge.
McGhee, P. (2001) Thinking Psychologically. Basingstoke, Palgrave.

Social learning theory

Social learning theory is based on the work of A. Bandura (1925–) and W. Mischel (1930–). This approach is based on reciprocal determinism, the idea that people influence their environment as well as being influenced by it. Learning is seen as occurring in the absence of operant conditioning processes like reinforcement and focuses on cognitive processes. People are seen as active in information processing their external world. People are influenced by external events but can also influence external events. There is an emphasis on the variability of behaviour and the influence of situations on behaviour. Trait descriptions and global self-concepts are avoided. People have self-concepts and self-regulatory or self-control processes that may vary with situations and times. A core concept is that of perceived self-efficacy, a person's belief that they have the ability to influence or control their behaviour or outcomes. Self-efficacy can influence behaviour, thinking, motivation, performance and feelings. Judgements about levels of self-efficacy are made on the basis of behaviours in specific situations.

Social learning theory emphasises observational learning and self-regulation. Observational learning involves learning behaviour through observing others' behaviour, how others behave. Self-regulation involves controlling one's own behaviour without reacting automatically to the external environment. People regulate their behaviour through self-reinforcement and self-punishment in relation to standards they set themselves. Through observational learning people can learn by observing others, the people observed are called models and the process of demonstrating behaviours is called modelling. This form of learning depends on four cognitive processes, attention, retention, reproduction and motivation. The learner must pay attention to the model and this will depend on the status and influence of the model. What is learned needs to be retained and this depends on task complexity and learning ability. Learners need to reproduce what is learned and finally learners need to be motivated to perform the modelled behaviour. Observational learning explains how new and complex behaviour is acquired independent of reinforcement. Emotional as well as behavioural responses can be acquired through observational learning. Behaviour is maintained through self-regulation or through expectancies or anticipated consequences. People can experience consequences directly, vicariously and through their own actions.

Social learning regards learning as dependent on individuality rather than as necessarily proceeding through stages. Aggression is learned through observation of family models, peer models and media models. Whether aggressive behaviour occurs depends on cognitive appraisal of the arousal stimuli and expectations of the consequences of aggression. Aggression is maintained by its consequences whether direct, vicarious or self-produced.

Emotional and behavioural difficulties are learned through direct experience or through exposure to negative models. Parents are seen as a significant source of modelling inappropriate behaviour. People are seen as having negative expectancies and negative self-concepts that activate maladaptive behaviour. Anxiety is the consequence of perceived self-inefficacy, expecting and believing that one is unable to cope with damaging situations or events. Depression is the consequence of expecting and believing that one is unable to acquire desired outcomes.

Social learning interventions include modelling and guided participation. Models demonstrate desirable behaviours, these being broken down into subskills or subtasks. In guided participation a person is actively and directly guided in learning behaviour. Modelling can be live or symbolic (through a video). The process of modelling is seen as increasing a person's level of perceived self-efficacy. Modelling can be assisted through behaviour rehearsal where the learner practises the modelled behaviour.

Bandura, A. (1977) Social Learning Theory. Englewood Cliffs, NJ, Prentice-Hall.
Mischel, W. (1968) Personality and Assessment. New York, Wiley.

Social skills training

Social skills training aims to address identified people's social skills deficits. These deficits are defined as a lack or absence of the necessary skills for engaging appropriately in interpersonal and social interactions. The absence or inadequacy of social skills is associated with emotional and behavioural difficulties. In order to perform a social skill people must be able to know how and when to perform the skill, be competent at the skill and be motivated to perform the skill. It should be noted that some people who have the skill in their repertoire for various reasons choose not to perform it.

Social skills training approaches can include instruction, prompting, shaping, reinforcement, rehearsal, role-play, feedback and modelling. People often need to see the skill demonstrated or performed and will require time to practise or rehearse the skill. Modelling can be video or live modelling. Peer modelling is seen as being more effective than adult modelling. Self-modelling is a process whereby people model successful performances, these are videoed and people then view their own performance.

Social skills can be broken down into micro-skills including listening, engaging in conversation, asking, following instructions, expressing feelings, sharing, helping, negotiating, asserting one's rights, dealing with teasing, avoiding fights, complaining, criticising, dealing with criticism, coping with failure, resisting group pressure and planning.

Procedures for social skills training include assessment (interview, self-report, checklist, rating scale, observation) to determine if a deficit exists, social skills intervention (instruction, modelling, rehearsal, shaping, reinforcement, role-playing, practice) and post-intervention evaluation to see if skills are acquired.

Social skills training has been used to help change the disruptive behaviour of children and adolescents. It has also been used to reduce anxiety and social isolation among children and adolescents. Social skills training is also used with the elderly and schizophrenics to help them to avoid social isolation and engage in positive social interactions.

Hargie, O., Saunders, C. and Dickson, D. (1994) Social Skills in Interpersonal Communication, 3rd edn. London, Routledge.

Sociometry

A theory and practical approach developed mainly by Jacob Moreno in order to discover or reveal the social interactions or social dynamics within a given group. Group members are given a sociometric test that enables a sociogram to be constructed. A sociometric test is a rating scale where every member of the given group is asked to express their preferences in terms of likes and dislikes for other members of the group. Other questions can be asked such as who members would work with and who they would socialise with. A sociogram represents in visual terms through interconnecting arrows the expressed preferences of group members. Sociometry can be used to identify factors such as hostility and social isolation occurring within groups.

Somatoform disorders

Somatoform disorders are those mental disorders where there are physical symptoms that indicate a somatic disorder without any detectable physical damage or malfunction that explains the symptoms. The symptoms are therefore believed to be associated with psychological processes.

Somatoform disorders include pain disorder, body dysmorphic disorder, hypochondriasis, conversion disorder and somatisation disorder.

Pain disorder occurs where a person complains of pain but there appears to be no underlying physical cause but complaints often appear associated with conflict, stress or attention-seeking behaviour.

Body dysmorphic disorder is where a person is preoccupied with an imagined or actual physical defect, particularly of the face but also with skin, hips, breasts, legs, penis and body hair. Constant checking of the defect may occur and attempts may be made to disguise the defect or to eliminate it through cosmetic surgery. This type of disorder occurs mainly among women, beginning in late adolescence and is often associated with social phobia and depression. Preoccupation with a physical defect can be a symptom of other disorders such as obsessive-compulsive disorder.

Hypochondriasis is a disorder where people are preoccupied with fears of being seriously ill even though they have been medically examined and found to be healthy. People overreact to insignificant physical sensations and attribute them to serious underlying illnesses.

Conversion disorder is where people develop a sudden paralysis, blindness, loss of voice, loss of smell that have no apparent physical cause. People can also develop anaesthesias, loss of sensation and insensitivity to pain. The symptoms often appear suddenly in stressful situations and enable the people affected to escape criticism, to avoid responsibility or enable them to gain attention. Some people affected appear calm and indifferent to their symptoms. Conversion disorders usually develop in late adolescence or early adulthood due to stress and more women than men are diagnosed. However during the first and second world wars some men experiencing combat developed the disorder. Misdiagnosis of neurological disorders as conversion disorders do occur, thus it is necessary to ensure that diagnosis of conversion disorder is thorough and accurate. It may be difficult to distinguish a conversion disorder from malingering, i.e. pretending that one is physically incapable in order to avoid responsibility or duties. In some cases such as factitious disorders people deliberately produce physical or psychological symptoms in order to take on the role of patient.

Somatisation disorder refers to multiple, recurrent physical complaints that do not appear to have a physical basis. It tends to begin in early adulthood, affects women more than men and runs in families. A person suffering from this disorder must experience pain in different bodily areas, have gastrointestinal symptoms, a sexual problem and a conversion or similar disorder. The symptoms can show cultural variations. People who experience this disorder visit doctors and hospitals regularly and frequently take medication. They often exaggerate their symptoms in the context of a complex medical history. It can occur along with anxiety, personality and mood disorders. It has been suggested that people with this disorder are hypersensitive to physical sensations or misinterpret them as serious illnesses. The symptoms can be seen as enabling people to avoid responsibility or to gain attention.

The psychoanalytic perspective sees conversion disorder as being caused by a past traumatic event that has been repressed but that re-emerges in the form of physical symptoms. It is also seen as providing primary gains (initial relief from anxiety and conflict) and secondary gains (avoiding responsibility or manipulating others). The behavioural perspective also sees conversion disorder as securing a desirable end. Over the years the prevalence of conversion order appears to have decreased in developed countries but remains more prevalent in underdeveloped, rural countries. Cognitive-behavioural interventions have focused on changing people's misinterpretations of physical sensations, using reinforcement or incentives for improvement and relaxation training.

Davison, G. and Neale, J.M. (2001) Abnormal Psychology, 8th edn. Chichester, Wiley.

Stereotypes and stereotyping

Stereotyping is the cognitive process of creating or forming stereotypes through categorising people as members of a group rather than as individuals. It consists of regarding all members of a social group as having the same characteristics regardless of variations within the group.

Stereotypes are used as explanatory concepts by social groups to explain the actions of other groups and to justify their own beliefs and behaviour. A group of people are seen as having a defining characteristic and thereby separated from other people, e.g. on grounds of nationality, ethnicity, gender, age, occupation or appearance. Once defined and separated people are ascribed another attribute, usually a personality or dispositional attribute. These attributes in turn are ascribed to all the group members. Stereotypes therefore are generalisations from the particular to the general, they can be positive as well as negative.

Stereotyping can be seen as having a variety of purposes of functions and as arising from limitations on cognitive processes, as culturally determined, as inaccurate, negative and inflexible. Stereotypes are often ethnocentrically and culturally determined and believed to be the only valid way of perceiving and understanding other groups. Particular characteristics are seen as inherent or innate in the stereotyped group. Stereotypes are seen as being held in order to provide scapegoats, in order to redirect aggression, to provide rationalisations for behaviour, as a means of maintaining a particular social identity and as the result of an authoritarian personality and as arising from inter-group competition. Other reasons are cognitive distortions in the form of inflexible and incorrect generalisations about other groups.

Categorisation of people, although often giving greater weight to negative rather than positive information, is found useful in social interactions through avoiding cognitive overload. People are seen as cognitive misers avoiding too much thought by taking short-cuts and as a result being more likely to stereotype other people. At times people display various attributional biases such as the fundamental attribution error, the actor-observer effect, the self-serving bias, the false-consensus effect, the Just World Hypothesis and the hindsight bias. These biases show that frequently people do not bother to use logical or statistical reasoning about people and groups but use heuristics or shortcuts based on assumptions about the causes of people's behaviours.

Stereotypes are very resistant to change for a number of reasons that include self-fulfilling prophesies, behaving in a way that actually brings about stereotypical outcomes, seeking out confirming rather than disconfirming instances of stereotypes, subtyping or classifying people as exceptions to the rule when confronted with people who do not fit the stereotype.

Hinton, P.R. (2000) Stereotypes, Cognition and Culture. Hove, Psychology Press.

Strategic family therapy

The main exponents of the strategic approach are C. Madanes and J. Haley who developed a directive, goal and task setting action planning approach to family therapy that concentrates on current family problems.

This approach to family therapy focuses on family dynamics and the strategic actions of others, i.e. the way people predict the behaviour of family members and how decisions are made about those members. Family problems or symptoms are seen as resulting from repetitive and cyclical interactions. Symptoms or problems are seen as strategies for controlling a particular family relationship. The behaviour of individual family members is maintained by the actions of others. Every family member is seen as attempting to influence each other by defining or redefining the relationship. These attempts frequently result in conflict or power struggles between family members and if present attempts will be made to involve the therapist in these conflicts. Family members either exaggerate minor difficulties or minimise serious problems. Strategic therapy focuses on the main family problems, maintaining factors and attempts at solving those problems. Strategic interventions aim to disrupt negative interactions through enabling the family to perform particular tasks that change the negative cycles. These tasks can be directive or paradoxical. Family members are directed to do something unexpected for each other in order to disrupt a cycle of negative interaction. Paradoxical tasks can take the form of symptom prescription, i.e. asking a family member to perform the undesirable behaviour or through positive connotation relabelling a negative action as positive. The aim is to provoke a change in behaviour through family members recognising and acknowledging that the power exists to control the symptoms.

Dallos, R. and Draper, R. (2000) An Introduction to Family Therapy: Systemic Theory and Practice. Buckingham, Open University Press.

Stress

Stress can be defined in various ways. It can be an environmental or external demand called a stressor, e.g. occupational, relational, financial and familial demands. There are a variety of responses to these demands, e.g. physical (insomnia, headaches, indigestion) and psychological (anxiety and depression) and behavioural (avoidance and escape). Stress can also be seen in interactional terms as being the result of an interaction between environmental demands and the level of individual coping skills. It appears difficult to objectively define or measure stress given there exists a cognitive component or individual differences in responses to stress. The experience of stress depends on how people perceive and interpret their environment, the process of cognitive appraisal.

Stress is believed to have an influence on biological processes as in the fight/flight response. In the case of psychoneuroimmunology, studies of the influence of psychology on immune systems have provided evidence that stress affects immune function, e.g. as in the case of clinically depressed people and stressed people's susceptibility to viral infections. Social support can help in relieving stress and thereby improve the functioning of the immune system.

Stressors in the external environment include bereavement, work, unemployment, family and disasters.

- Bereavement is associated with a process of shock, denial, depression, guilt, anxiety anger and acceptance and can have a significant influence on physical and mental health.
- Work stressors include the physical environment (noise, lighting and heating), lack of job satisfaction, lack of control in the work situation, open plan offices and negative working relationships.
- Unemployment is associated with the loss of self-respect and lowered self-esteem, poorer mental and physical health.
- Family stressors include parental conflict, parental mental illness, parental alcoholism, parental criminality, absence of a parent, physical abuse, poverty and overcrowding.
- The influence of stressors depends on factors such as type, severity, duration, the perceived threat, loss and controllability.

Stress is also believed to have an impact on blood pressure, heart disease and asthma. Essential hypertension or high blood pressure has been linked to both positive and negative emotional states, of the negative states anger and defensiveness appear to be the main factors. However genetic predisposition also plays a significant part in causing high blood pressure. Anger, hostility and cynicism have also been connected to coronary heart disease. A Type D personality has been proposed that is characterised by negative affectivity, high levels of anger, depression and anxiety. As regards asthma psychological stress can trigger attacks. However, people who are stressed are likely to engage in unhealthy behaviours such as heavy smoking, drinking, substance abuse, inadequate sleep and exercise. Thus the effect of stress may be indirect as a cause of illness.

The experience of stress is mediated through cognitive appraisal. Cognitive appraisal mediates between environmental demands, resources and individual belief systems. Primary appraisal decides whether there is a problem and secondary appraisal looks at the coping skills available to address that problem. There exist a number of factors that mediate environmental demands including perceived levels of control, perceived levels of social support and cognitive styles such as attributional and problem solving styles. Those who experience learned helplessness feel they have been unable to exert control over their behaviour and thus are at risk of feeling stressed.

Those who have an attributional style that responds to stressors by making external, stable and global attributions are also at risk of being stressed. Those who have an external locus of control who feel their behaviour is under the control of external factors are likely to feel stressed. Pessimistic attributions are also likely to lead to stress.

Coping strategies for stress include attribution retraining, problem solving interventions and increasing perceived levels of social support. Avoidance or escape as a coping strategy for stress is likely to increase rather than decrease stress. Other ways of reducing stress include biofeedback training, relaxation training, cognitive restructuring and stress-inoculation training.

Cassidy, T. (1999) *Stress, Cognition and Health*. London, Routledge.
Ellis, A., Gordon, J., Neenan, M., and Palmer, S. (1997) *Stress Counselling: A Rational Emotive Behaviour Approach*. London, Cassell.

Substance dependence and abuse

Substance dependence refers to tolerance whereby larger doses of the substance are required in order for the desired effect to be experienced. Withdrawal symptoms occur when the substance is no longer taken or when the amount is reduced. These symptoms are physical and psychological. Substances are then taken to avoid or relieve the withdrawal symptoms. The user takes more of the substance, for longer periods, spends more time seeking out the substance, takes longer time recovering from its effects, ignores harmful effects and abandons social activities. Substance abuse is defined as a lesser problem that includes failure to perform social and work roles, substance use in perilous situations, legal offences and substance use regardless of interpersonal difficulties.

Substance dependency is seen as being influenced by:

- social and cultural attitudes to consumption of substances;
- family influences (parental and sibling tolerance and use of substances, negative parenting practices – low behavioural expectations, inadequate supervision, punitive discipline and family conflict);
- peer groups (maintaining the use of substances);
- delinquency (prior to substance use);
- difficult temperament (need for novel sensations, risk-taking);
- social identity needs (need to feel part of a subculture);
- cue reactivity (cues associated with substances elicit substance taking);
- psychological stress reduction through self-medication;
- educational failure (lack of success at school);
- availability and cost of substances;
- coping skills (perceived self-efficacy);
- biological factors (genetic predisposition);
- classical conditioning (specific stimuli paired with substance use and generalisation to other contexts);
- operant conditioning (positive reinforcement through experiencing euphoria and negative reinforcement, escaping withdrawal symptoms);
- social learning (modelling the behaviour of other users and experiencing low self-efficacy);

- outcome expectancy beliefs (expecting that a substance will have an effect produces the behaviour).

Experimentation with substances is common among adolescents, particularly alcohol, cigarettes and cannabis. Risk factors for adolescent substance abuse include learning difficulties, emotional and behavioural difficulties, insecure attachment, child abuse, parental and family problems, school failure and membership of a deviant peer group.

Different types of substance dependence include alcohol, nicotine, marijuana, heroin, amphetamines, cocaine and hallucinogens. All substances have positive as well as negative effects depending on the substance, the individual, the dose, the purity and habitual use.

- Alcohol in large quantities interferes with thinking processes, with motor coordination, balance, speech and vision. In large amounts it can also lead to sedation, sleep and death. Long-term effects can include malnutrition, amnestic syndrome (severe memory loss), cirrhosis of the liver, heart problems and foetal alcohol syndrome. Alcohol dependence can have the following symptoms: anxiety, depression, restlessness, sleep problems and in rare cases delirium tremens, visual and tactile hallucinations. It is also associated with polydrug use where more than one substance is taken in a cocktail or separately. The alcohol dependent are likely to drink daily, are unable to abstain, go on binges, suffer blackouts, quarrel with friends and family, have days off work and become involved in accidents. Alcohol use is implicated in suicide, traffic accidents and murder.
- Marijuana is made from the dried leaves of the hemp plant and contains THC (delta 9, tetrahydocannabinol). Its effects include bloodshot eyes, dry mouth and an increased appetite as well as euphoria. The long-term effects can include lung damage. It has medical uses in reducing some side effects of chemotherapy and in relieving pain. However it adversely affects driving skills and at high levels can lead to sensory disturbances. Heavy adolescent users of marijuana are at risk of cocaine use in adult life but generally use of marijuana is not a stage on the way to hard drug use.
- Heroin produces euphoria, relieves anxiety and boosts self-confidence. Withdrawal leads to muscle pains, sneezing, sweating, tearfulness and yawning and finally to cramps, chills, flushing, sweating, rapid heartbeat and high blood pressure. Abusers are at risk of an early death through murder, suicide, accident or an overdose. They may also need to resort to deviant or illegal activities in order to finance the habit, e.g. prostitution, drug dealing, theft and robbery.
- Amphetamines are synthetic stimulants. Amphetamines increase alertness, reduce appetite and inhibit sleepiness. However, prolonged and heavy use can lead to irritability, even paranoid and violent behaviour resulting in an amphetamine psychosis.
- Cocaine is an alkaloid extracted from leaves of the coca plant. It blocks the reuptake of dopamine and increases neural transmission. Cocaine produces euphoric feelings, increases sexual desire and feelings of self-confidence. It also increases blood pressure

and heart rate. An overdose may lead to nausea, insomnia, paranoia and tactile hallucinations. Prolonged use can lead to irritability, paranoid thinking, sleeping and eating problems.

• Hallucinogens include mescaline (peyote cactus), psilocybin (Mexican mushroom), PCP (phencyclidine), and LSD (lysergic acid diethylamide). They produce distortions in sensory perceptions, changes in visual perception and time and space perception. Users can experience 'bad trips' or panic attacks and flashbacks.

Factors related to substance dependence and abuse include:

• positive attitudes towards taking substances;
• parental influence and parental problems;
• peer influence;
• media influence;
• social and subcultural acceptability;
• substance availability;
• positive effects – enhancing positive mood or reducing negative moods;
• positive expectancies about the effect of a substance;
• perceived prevalence of use by others;
• an antisocial personality disorder and ADHD;
• rebelliousness and aggressiveness;
• a genetic predisposition.

There are a variety of interventions aimed at reducing or eliminating substance dependence and abuse. However a number of people change from uncontrolled use to moderate use or even abstention. This unassisted change can occur through experiencing an illness, an accident, seeing the negative effects on other users, religious conversion, obtaining a new job or meeting a new partner, influence of friends or family and legal problems. Unassisted change requires the user to be motivated to change, to make a public commitment to change and to form a new self-identity free of substance abuse. Change can proceed through a five-stage model of precontemplation, contemplation, preparation, action and maintenance. On the basis of this model substance abusers go from no intention of changing their behaviour, to contemplation of change, to preparing for change and finally to implementing and consolidating change. The main problem with this model is the likelihood of relapse.

Regarding intervention, motivation to change is a significant problem and motivational interviewing is a technique used to encourage motivation to change behaviour. The techniques of motivational interviewing include:

• the avoidance of labelling users as 'addicts';
• assuming that the user wants to change and the asking of evocative questions;

- listing advantages and disadvantages of changing behaviour;
- acknowledging the positive effects of substance use while drawing out 'Yes, but...' responses;
- expressing the user's doubts after a paradoxical challenge to a user's defence for using substances;
- asking the user to make the case for changing behaviour.

Interventions

The main interventions for alcohol abuse include:

- biological treatments (taking the drug disulfiram or Antabuse to induce vomiting when alcohol is drunk but this approach assumes commitment and compliance and has a high drop-out rate; other drugs also depend on compliance);
- self-help support groups (Alcoholics Anonymous – provides support, counselling and companionship through Twelve-step Programmes, a spiritually based approach);
- cognitive and behavioural approaches (aversion therapy, covert sensitisation, reinforcement programmes, social and assertiveness skills training, problem solving training, behavioural self-control training, motivation enhancement therapy, controlled drinking programmes and stress-management counselling).

The main interventions for illegal substance use include:

- detoxification – substance withdrawal;
- biological treatments (methadone – a heroin substitute treatment, however users can become addicted to methadone, many return to heroin or drop-out due to side-effects);
- cognitive-behavioural approaches (avoiding high-risk contexts, relapse prevention training, token economy programme using vouchers);
- self-help residential rehabilitation homes and therapeutic communities.

The main preventative interventions include:

- controlling or regulating the availability of the substance;
- changing acceptability through health education (non-threatening, guidelines for sensible use, coping skills for peer pressure, peer counselling);
- family support programmes (parenting skills);
- media campaigns (targeted messages, appropriate media channels, credible speakers, focus on advantages of abstention or moderate use and disadvantages of excessive use);
- workplace and occupational policies;
- youth club and other community related activities;

- harm minimisation (urban planning, training staff of licensed premises, changing drinking times, needle-exchange programmes).

McKim, W.A. (2000) *Drugs and Behavior: An Introduction to Behavioral Pharmacology*, 4th edn. Upper Saddle River, NJ, Prentice Hall.

Robson, P. (1999) *Forbidden Drugs*, 2nd edn. Oxford, Oxford University Press.

Royal College of Psychiatrists (2000) *Drugs: Dilemmas and Choices.* London, Gaskell.

Advice on substance abuse

Alcohol abuse:

- Identification of extent, effects and probable consequences of excessive drinking. Use of motivational interviewing to assess motivation of user to change to behaviour.
- Set short-term and long-term achievable targets.
- Identify potential obstacles to reducing or eliminating excessive drinking. Ask person to keep a diary of substance consumption and relapses.
- Detoxification at home or in hospital. Medication: use of Antabuse.
- Self-help groups: Alcoholics Anonymous, Al-Anon and Al-Teen.

Psychoactive substance abuse:

- Identification of the kind, dose and the dependency.
- Psychoeducation about the effects of continued use.
- Use of motivational interviewing to assess motivation of user to change behaviour.
- Detoxification in hospital.
- Self-help groups.

Suicide and attempted suicide

Suicide or self-intentioned death is no longer a criminal offence in the UK although it was up to 1961. Many people who commit or who attempt suicide are depressed at the time, however some people who are not depressed also commit suicide as with some alcoholics and some schizophrenics. Physical illness is a significant factor in many suicides. Suicide is rare before age 14, increases during adolescence and rises in old age. There are many more attempted suicides than suicides.

Men are more likely to commit suicide than women are but women are more likely to attempt suicide than men. Single, divorced and widowed people are at a greater risk of suicide. Suicide is higher among semi-skilled and manual workers. Unemployment is also a risk factor. Suicide is higher among certain occupational groups, e.g. doctors, nurses, farmers and dentists. Relatives of suicides often feel shame, guilt, bewilderment and distress. The suicide rates for adolescents are increasing, particularly for working-class males in the 15–24 age group and suicidal ideation is also high among adolescents. Gay adolescents are at particular risk. Adolescent suicide is influenced by lack of emotional self-control, poor problem solving skills, substance abuse, school and family problems.

Factors influencing suicide include:

- depression (feelings of hopelessness and entrapment);
- alcoholic abuse;
- substance abuse;
- schizophrenia;
- borderline personality and antisocial personality disorders;
- suicidal ideation (cognitive distortions);
- child abuse (abusers and abused);
- communicating an intention;
- social isolation (rural areas, lack of social support networks, living alone);
- imprisonment (male prisoners on remand, murderers and arsonists);
- unemployment;
- media reports of suicides (contagious effect);
- relationship crisis;
- bereavement;
- cognitive rigidity (failure to engage in alternative-thinking);
- depressogenic attributional style – internal, stable and global (depressed people blame themselves and think causes of negative events will always exist and will inevitably affect their future);
- perfectionism (unrealistic goals, highly self-critical, fear of failure).

Factors influencing repeated suicide attempts include:

- unemployment;
- occupational stress;
- divorce, separation or living alone;
- financial problems;
- marital breakdown (arguments with spouse or partner);
- relationship problems (boyfriend/girlfriend problems);
- child abuse (sexual abuse);
- contact with psychiatric in- and out-patient service;
- contact with the criminal justice system;
- violent behaviour (anger, hostility and irritability);
- substance abuse (alcohol abuse);
- history of self-injury;
- psychological sense of isolation.

Personal reasons suggested for suicide include self-directed aggression, hostility towards others, efforts to manipulate others, attempts to make amends, to escape unbearable or unacceptable feelings, in response to emotional and physical pain. People are often ambivalent about committing suicide, focusing on a narrow range of alternatives, frequently communicating their intention occasionally as a cry for help but also as a means of withdrawal.

Perspectives on suicidal behaviour include:

- Psychodynamic: Suicide is seen as either an attack on a lost love-object that has been internalised or an expression of the death instinct. It is hatred redirected towards the self. Similar approaches see suicide as the act of eliminating bad internal objects from the self or as a way of seeking help or signalling distress resulting from anxious or insecure attachment in the past.
- Biological: Low levels of serotonin's main metabolite 5-HIAA in cerobrospinal fluid have been linked particularly to impulsive and violent suicide.
- Behavioural: Depression is the result of extinction, behaviours no longer receive reinforcement. Reinforcement may be reduced or lost due to negative changes in the environment (unemployment) or a lack of skill in obtaining reinforcement (social skills or interpersonal skills deficits). Depressed people tend to elicit negative reactions from other people rather than reinforcement.
- Cognitive: Depression is the result of irrational thinking or cognitive distortions.

Prevention and interventions for suicidal risk:

- Reducing or eliminating the available means of committing suicide (domestic gas, guns, medication).
- Setting up suicide prevention centres, e.g. the Samaritans staffed by trained volunteers using 24-hour telephone call lines.
- School-based interventions raise awareness of suicide, provide information and help and encourage suicidal children and adolescents to make contact with the programme.
- Cognitive-behavioural interventions include rational-emotive therapy (challenging irrational thinking), cognitive therapy (disputing cognitive distortions) and problem solving skills training (thinking in terms of alternative solutions).
- Dialectical behaviour therapy is an eclectic approach using behavioural, cognitive and supportive approaches. It includes skills training, contingency management, cognitive-behavioural modification, validation (acceptance) fostering techniques, reflection and empathy.

Hill, K. (1995) The Long Sleep: Young People and Suicide. London, Virago.
O'Connor, R. and Sheehy, N. (2000) Understanding Suicidal Behaviour. Leicester, British Psychological Society.
Williams, M. (1997) Cry of Pain: Understanding Suicide and Self-Harm. London, Penguin Books.

Contact

Samaritans, 24-hour national helpline 0845 909090.

Superego

The superego is a Freudian psychoanalytic term referring to the part of the ego that engages in critical self-evaluation. It also mediates between conflicting desires or wishes. Most of the superego is unconscious. It is where parental introjects or internal objects reside. In other words our superego originates from our parents, particularly the father, between the ages of three and five and is the result of the Oedipus complex. The father's commands are introjected or become part of one's self and the father's injunctions are then experienced as coming from within, the superego. The image of the father and his injunctions are also influenced by the child's feelings, the introjected father being as the child imagines him to be.

The superego is not synonymous with the term 'conscience'. The superego can be punitive or harsh where there is no actual transgression. It can produce unconscious guilt. The superego can be healthy or unhealthy. It is healthy if it recognises and criticises actual transgressions and leads to reparation or a wish to rectify those transgressions. An unhealthy, harsh and unforgiving superego can lead to endless self-reproach and self-punishment even terminating in suicide or murder. If the superego is extremely harsh and the guilt unbearable people may unconsciously project their unconscious guilt on to others in order to escape those feelings of guilt. Alternatively they may escape unconscious guilt by provoking a punitive reaction from other people through actually committing a transgression. By committing a transgression it serves to rationalise guilty feelings and the punishment provoked serves to relieve those guilty feelings. People can turn their superego outwards and direct it at others, persecuting them instead of persecuting themselves.

Suppression

Suppression occurs when people intentionally and deliberately exclude from consciousness thoughts, feelings, desires and memories. In psychoanalytic terms it is a conscious defence mechanism used to cope with emotional conflicts, unacceptable thoughts and desires and unpleasant memories.

Symptoms

Symptoms are any observable physiological, neurological or psychological indicators of a state or change of a state linked to particular problem or disorder. Symptoms when occurring in a pattern or when clustered together to form a specific disease or disorder are called syndromes, e.g. Asperger's syndrome.

The sources of information regarding the symptoms of emotional and behavioural difficulties and disorders are acquired through observation, interview, reports and tests. People may have symptoms from more than one domain, e.g. emotional as well as behavioural symptoms. Symptoms need to be at a certain level of severity, frequency or duration before they can be considered as constituting a problem or disorder. The impact of symptoms on family life, work, school, relationships and social life need to be assessed, in particular the impact of symptoms on the individual and other people.

Symptom formation is a psychoanalytic term referring to the appearance of a symptom as a symbolic expression of an underlying emotional conflict brought about through the return of the repressed.

Systematic desensitisation

This is a form of behaviour therapy formally developed by Joseph Wolpe for anxiety and fears. Various theories have been suggested to explain systematic desensitisation including counter-conditioning, reciprocal inhibition, extinction, realistic thinking, changing expectations about fearfulness and strengthening beliefs about coping. The sufferer imagines successively more anxiety-producing situations while simultaneously engaging in behaviours that reduce that anxiety, e.g. relaxation. The sufferer gradually or systematically becomes less sensitive to the anxiety-producing situations. There is a three-stage procedure. Firstly a sufferer is taught to perform a behaviour that reduces anxiety, e.g. to relax. The particular situations that cause anxiety are then ordered in terms of an anxiety-producing hierarchy. Finally the sufferer imagines the anxiety-producing situations in order of increasing anxiety while at the same time performing an anxiety-reducing behaviour such as relaxation. Deep muscle relaxation is used as a preliminary procedure to systematic desensitisation as well as a competing behaviour to anxiety. An anxiety hierarchy is a list of stimuli and situations that evoke anxiety. The stimuli and situations are ranked from least to most anxiety producing. After relaxing the sufferer imagines each successive anxiety-producing situation until no anxiety is experienced. This therapeutic approach depends on gradual, repeated and safe exposure to anxiety-producing situations. However the main element is being repeatedly exposed to anxiety-producing situations without experiencing negative thoughts and feelings. Coping sensitisation is another procedure. This time sufferers reduce their anxiety by imagining that they are coping with the anxiety-producing situation and their associated feelings. The sufferers also learn to use anxious feelings as triggers for employing coping skills. Systematic desensitisation is not recommended for young children or for people who have a skills deficit. This intervention is effective for many anxiety and phobic conditions.

Spiegler, M.D. and Guivrement, D.C. (1998) Contemporary Behavior Therapy, 3rd edn. Pacific Grove, CA, Brooks/Cole Publishing.

T

Targets

Targets are the goals or aims of an intervention. From the behavioural perspective they are usually defined in SMART terms: Specific, Measurable, Achievable, Relevant and Time-related.

There should be a minimal number of targets, three or four to avoid overloading the client and to facilitate monitoring. Target setting needs to consider whether clients are committed or motivated to achieve the targets and that they have the capability to achieve those targets. Therefore intervention targets should be discussed, understood and agreed between all participants, particularly the client. Success criteria should be established in order to determine whether clients have reached their targets.

Vague, imprecise and unrealistic targets are unlikely to be achieved. How targets are to be monitored is also another important consideration.

Teenage pregnancy

Teenage pregnancy is recorded as higher in Britain than in any other Western European country. It is generally geographically concentrated in the most deprived areas of the UK.

The risk factors for unwanted pregnancy include socio-economic deprivation, experiencing emotional difficulties, being in care or leaving care, being a child of a teenage mother, having educational difficulties, being a truant, having been sexually abused, having a psychiatric disorder, particularly a conduct disorder, and being engaged in criminal behaviour. Some ethnic minority groups are over-represented in teenage pregnancy statistics, including Bangladeshi, Pakistani and African-Caribbean parents.

The reasons teenagers have babies include being ignorant or misinformed about sex, not using contraception, ineffective use of contraception, peer pressure or pressure from partners to have sex, forced sex, poor interpersonal skills in discussing sex and contraception with partners. The consequences of having babies when a teenager can include disrupted or broken relationships, disengagement from education, high reliance on social security benefits, frequent moves of home, post-natal depression and health problems.

Approaches to reducing unwanted teenage pregnancy include sex education policies in schools focusing on boys' responsibilities as well as girls', school-based sex education linked with contraceptive availability, using peer educators to disseminate information and advice to teenagers, improving access to contraception and providing helplines.

Advice for parents to help their children to avoid teenage pregnancy:

- Both parents should involve themselves in providing advice and guidance to their children. Parents should have a point of view based on beliefs, reason and experience.

- Be clear and certain about your own attitudes and values with regard to sex and early pregnancy. Avoid hypocrisy.
- Provide factual information or books that give detailed information on sex, sexually transmitted diseases, contraception and teenage pregnancy.
- Encourage your children to avoid alcohol and substance abuse that may inadvertently lead to unwanted pregnancies.
- Discuss sex and love and sexual and loving relationships clearly, appropriately, honestly and openly. Outline the possible consequences of early and unsupported pregnancy.
- Ensure that your children are adequately supervised and monitored and that they associate with responsible and emotionally mature friends. Make sure they keep reasonable times and maintain acceptable standards of behaviour.
- Be aware of the kind of friends or families they mix with. Welcome friends into your home so that you get to know them and possibly their parents too.
- Encourage group rather than couple type activities and discourage early dating and relationships with boys or girls much older or much younger than your teenagers.
- Discuss the value of educational and occupational options and opportunities with your children that encourage them to become involved in long-term planning for the future. Explain how teenage pregnancy can obstruct long-term plans in terms of financial and other constraints and how it can lead to unhappiness and even depression.
- Challenge attitudes and values that may lead to teenage pregnancy.
- Ensure that you have a warm and close relationship with your children, based on firm and consistent discipline. Try to set time apart to be together as a family. Be attentive and listening. Praise effort as well as achievement. Show interest in and engage with their leisure time activities. Be polite and respectful towards them and ask for it in return.

Social Exclusion Unit (1999) Report on Teenage Pregnancy. London, The Stationery Office.

Contacts

Brook Advisory Helplines:
Emergency contraception 020 7617 0801
Pregnant and unsure 020 7617 0850
Abortion 020 7617 0803
Sexually Transmitted Diseases (STDs) 020 7617 0807
Department of Health Sexwise. Telephone Advice Helpline 0800 282 930 (7 a.m. – midnight)

Temperament

The term temperament refers to a collection or group of personal characteristics, dispositions or reactions. These dispositions are regarded as characteristic of an individual child, adolescent or adult.

Infants have been described as having certain kinds of characteristics such as motor activity, regularity of behaviour, distractability, particular responses to new stimuli, adaptability, attention levels, persistence, energy, responsiveness and mood.

A difficult temperament is one characterised by irregularity, irritability, withdrawal, slow adaptability, intensity, negative mood and a vigorous reaction to changes. A slow-to-warm-up temperament is one characterised by inactivity, moodiness, slowness to adapt to new people and situations and passive rather than active resistance to new situations or changes. An easy temperament is characterised by a positive mood and adaptability to new people and situations.

Children with difficult temperaments are likely to find it difficult to adjust to school and are frequently aggressive towards siblings and peers. By contrast children who are slow to warm up are likely to be ignored or rejected by peers.

There is believed to be a moderate hereditary influence on temperament. However, early temperamental characteristics do not necessarily continue to exert an influence in later life, consequently temperament can change. 'Goodness of fit' plays a part in determining whether change in temperament will occur. If a carer remains calm, patient and sensitive then a child with a difficult temperament is likely to change to be less difficult. But if the carer is impatient, demanding and punitive the difficult child is likely to become more resistant.

Shaffer, D.R. (1996) Developmental Psychology: Childhood and Adolescence, 4th edn. Pacific Grove, CA, Brooks/Cole Publishing.

Theory of mind

The theory of mind is people's understanding of their own and other people's cognitive and emotional processes.

By the age of three children usually have a theory of mind. Children have ideas about other people's beliefs, attitudes, desires and feelings. This notion is based on the idea that other people possess different belief systems and their behaviour may differ from what is simply observed in the past. Children also develop metacognition, the ability to think about thinking itself.

The theory of mind has been put forward as an explanation for autism. The theory of mind conceptualises children as being able to perceive that other people share the same interests, see things as they do and understand other people's intentions. From the theory of mind perspective autistic children lack a theory of mind and therefore fail to understand other people's intentions and as a consequence fail to relate socially and interpersonally.

Interventions based on the theory of mind have aimed to teach children to understand minds, including beliefs and emotions. Children have been taught the principles that underlie concepts through the use of puppets, role-play and stories. They have also been taught to understand feelings through identifying emotions in photographs.

Theory of planned behaviour

This theory is an extension of the theory of reasoned action (see below) and relates people's perceived control over their own behaviour to their beliefs about the level of resources and opportunities they need to perform the behaviour. People who think that they do not have the resources or the opportunities are unlikely to form a strong intention to perform a desirable behaviour even if they look favourably on performing that behaviour.

Ajzen, I. (1991) 'The theory of planned behaviour', Organizational Behavior and Human Decision Processes, 50.

Theory of reasoned action

This theory regards people's behaviour as being influenced by their intentions, those intentions in turn being influenced by their attitudes towards those behaviours and by perceived social norms.

Ajzen, I. and Fishbein, M. (1980) Understanding Attitudes and Predicting Social Behaviour. Englewood Cliffs, NJ, Prentice-Hall.

Therapeutic relationship

The therapeutic relationship or therapeutic alliance is at the heart of counselling and psychotherapy approaches. The kind of therapeutic relationship depends on the perspective. The core conditions in the counselling relationship in person-centred or client-centred counselling comprise:

- acceptance or unconditional positive regard;
- empathy;
- genuineness or authenticity;
- trust.

However the therapeutic relationship in psychoanalytic and cognitive-behavioural approaches is different. In psychodynamic approaches the relationship focuses on transference, counter-transference, resistance and defence mechanisms. The aim of psychodynamic approaches is to enable the client to develop insight into their problems through interpretations. In cognitive-behavioural approaches the relationship is active-directive and psychoeducational. The aim is to teach clients cognitive and behavioural techniques that they will be able to practice in order to alleviate or solve their problems.

Factors influencing the counselling relationship include the counsellor's perceived level of expertise, credibility, trustworthiness and attractiveness. Attractiveness includes appearance, similarity and warmth. Other factors include the counselling setting, counsellor status and client expectations. Prolonged counselling relationships can lead to client dependency, to treating the counsellor as a guru or seeing the councillor as having magical solutions to problems.

In terms of the effectiveness of different therapeutic approaches one finding is that the therapeutic relationship is the common factor in all approaches and is correlated with positive outcomes. The quality of the relationship itself may be the determining factor for positive outcomes or alternatively it is a precondition for positive outcomes. The relationship can also been seen as an indicator of progress or effectiveness of a particular therapeutic approach. However, disagreements can exist between clients, counsellors and external assessors over the effectiveness of a counselling relationship.

The quality of a client's relationship prior to counselling can affect the development of a counselling relationship as can a client's low expectation. The quality of the first few sessions of a counselling relationship can also influence the course of a relationship. Negative client experiences of the relationship in the initial sessions can lead to dropping-out or adversely affect the likelihood of a positive outcome.

For a counselling relationship to be successful there are a number of points worth considering:

- the quality of the counsellor-client relationship regardless of the approach;
- exploring the quality of the client's past relationships;
- exploring early on the client's expectations of the counsellor and the counselling relationship;
- agreement on counselling goals and tasks;
- concentrating on the initial sessions to prevent dropping-out.

Feltham, C. (ed.) (1999) Understanding the Counselling Relationship. London, SAGE Publications.

Tics

Tics are abnormal, short-lived, involuntary and stereotyped motor or phonic movements. Motor tics include grimacing and shrugging, stamping and imitating other people's movements. Vocal tics include barking, grunting and throat clearing. They can vary in intensity on an hourly or daily basis.

Tics are often transient but can be chronic. Tics are usually worse when the sufferer is stressed or relaxed. They are often reduced when the sufferer is absorbed in an activity like reading.

Onset often occurs at seven years of age and is rare before two years or after 15.

Motor tics involve the face, head or neck. Vocal tics start at a later age between eight years and 15. Obscene speech, gestures and actions and echoed speech and actions are also possible. Tics are relatively common but tic disorders are rare. Severe and chronic motor and vocal tics are a symptom of Tourette's syndrome.

Tics often run in families and and are thought to have a genetic basis. Drug therapy with haloperidol, pimozide and clonidine can reduce the severity of chronic tics but have side-effects. Tics can be suppressed but only for a short period after a great exertion. Punishment, ostracism and criticism make tics worse. Habit reversal is another form of treatment for tics. This involves psychoeducation-instruction about the nature of tics, teaching incompatible or competing responses for when tics are about to take place, relaxation training, a reinforcement programme for compliance and contingent negative practice, i.e. performing the tics and allowing them to happen.

Goodman, R. and Scott, S. (1997) Child Psychiatry. Oxford, Blackwell Science.

Kaplan, H.I. and Sadock, B.J. (1996) Concise Textbook of Clinical Psychiatry. Baltimore, MA, Williams & Wilkins.

Time out

Time out or time out from generalised reinforcers is a behavioural intervention that requires an individual who is misbehaving to be temporarily withdrawn or moved from a particular setting and placed in another setting where the individual no longer receives generalised reinforcement for undesirable behaviour. Normally the individual is moved to a time out room or area where there is no possibility of receiving generalised reinforcers or being reinforced for undesirable behaviour.

To be effective time out requires that the individual should be given a warning and be told of the reasons for time out and also be aware of the length of time to be spent in time out. Reinforcers must be absent from the time out setting and the time spent on time out should be brief and strictly adhered to and not permit the individual to escape or avoid disliked situations or tasks.

Time out is particularly applicable to children who act out and who wish to stay in the classroom. It must be consistently applied according to the rules, especially given that time out is frequently misapplied in school settings.

Another consequence of time out is that it provides a teacher or parent with relief from the negative effects of an individual's behaviour that may serve to calm the teacher or parent. However time out may also become addictive for the parent or teacher and if resorted to at the slightest pretext its effectiveness is reduced.

A time out log should be maintained recording the nature of the offence, the activity engaged in, the time sent out, the time returned, any offences committed while in time out and the activity returned to.

Token economy

A token economy is a behavioural system that aims to motivate people to perform appropriate behaviours and to prevent them performing inappropriate behaviours. It originated as a psychiatric programme for hospital patients developed by T. Ayllon and N. Azrin in 1961. It is primarily used for groups of people in particular settings. People earn token reinforcers for desirable behaviours. These tokens can take the form of points or credits for appropriate behaviours and the loss of points for inappropriate behaviours. The tokens can be exchanged for primary or secondary reinforcers.

A token economy comprises a list of appropriate and inappropriate target behaviours, a list of reinforcers, types of tokens and procedures and rules for running the token economy. Token economies have been implemented in psychiatric hospitals, in juvenile offender institutions and in schools. In classrooms children are rewarded with tokens for desirable behaviour and lose tokens for undesirable behaviours (response cost). Actual reinforcers have included material objects and preferred activities in the classroom or at home. School trips have also been used as reinforcers. Token economies have been used to reinforce learning skills as well as adaptive behaviour and they have also been used to reinforce individual and small group behaviours.

Token economies have been used to treat a range of target behaviours in a variety of diverse settings with people of all age groups. However a serious limitation of the effectiveness of token economies is that gains tend to diminish when people leave the token economy system and return to the home setting. This is because people are being reinforced for inappropriate behaviours at home. Thus for changes to be maintained, the home environment needs to change in order to reinforce the behaviours learned in the token economy, e.g. through parent training or through foster carers.

Spiegler, M.D. and Guivrement, D.C. (1998) *Contemporary Behavior Therapy*, 3rd edn. Pacific Grove, CA, Brooks/Cole Publishing.

Tourette's syndrome

Gilles de la Tourette syndrome is a severe and chronic tic disorder. The disorder affects males more than females. It usually begins in early childhood with motor tics and gradually progresses to motor and vocal tics that can include in a minority of cases coprolalia (repetitive verbal obscenities), copropraxia (repetitive obscene gestures), echolalia (repetition of overheard words) and echopraxia (repetitive imitation of others' movements). The tics can wax and wane but the tics can become severe enough to lead to self-injury. Obsessive-compulsive disorder or ADHD frequently accompanies the disorder.

Those affected often display emotional and behavioural difficulties that along with the other symptoms often lead to peer rejection. The worst symptoms tend to occur during adulthood. Biological and genetic causes are seen as underlying the disorder, e.g. abnormalities of the basal ganglia. The onset of the disorder and its course are influenced by psychological factors, e.g. stress and coping skills. Interventions include psychoeducation for all those involved, habit reversal training (relaxation techniques), contingent negative practice and drug therapy (haloperidol and pimozide).

Goodman, R. and Scott, S. (1997) *Child Psychiatry*. Oxford, Blackwell Science.
Kaplan, H.I. and Sadock, B.J. (1996) *Concise Textbook of Clinical Psychiatry*. Baltimore, MA, Williams & Wilkins.

Trait

A trait is an inferred predisposition, a relatively enduring or stable characteristic or attribute of a person, particularly a pattern of behaviour, a consistency that manifests itself in particular contexts or settings, e.g. aggressiveness or shyness. Trait theorists adopt a nomothetic approach to personality believing that general hypotheses can be developed to explain personality differences. However there is no generally accepted scientific basis for traits.

Trait factors are used to explain the regular and consistent behaviour of people in particular situations. Trait theories see behaviour as being determined by particular characteristics of people rather than always by the situation they find themselves in. These trait theories also regard traits as having a genetic or biological basis. Traits can be used in a circular way to explain behaviour, i.e. as simply descriptions rather than explanations of behaviour. This circularity is avoided by referring to broad dispositions that influence people's behaviour.

Trait theories have been criticised for ignoring the influence of situations or reinforcement on behaviour. Situationists have contended that there is little cross-consistency to behaviour. Trait theorists have disagreed on the definition and measurement of traits but do agree that there are broad behavioural consistencies. Trait theorists also agree that situations do influence behaviour but would also state that there is sufficient consistency for traits to be identified. People therefore are seen as manifesting a trait or a pattern of behaviour over a range of situations. Traits will be prominent in situations where people are experiencing fewer constraints on their behaviour and when people are freer to select situations. Some traits appear to be stable over time, e.g. extraversion and neuroticism. Interactionism is the dominant paradigm or perspective in personality research looking at both traits and situations in terms of explaining personality and behaviour. Personality factors and behaviours are seen as the consequence of interactions between traits and situations.

With regard to emotional and behavioural problems trait theorists focus on maladaptive learning and its underlying biological, genetic and physiological factors, e.g. H. Eysenck's traits of Neuroticism, Extraversion and Psychoticism.

Trait negativity bias refers to the tendency to focus on the negative rather than positive behaviours of a person. A single instance of a person's misbehaviour in an otherwise positive report evokes a negative reaction and results in an overriding negative impression of that person.

Trait anxiety refers to a general characteristic of anxiety displayed across a range of settings and situations. It is contrasted with state anxiety, anxiety in response to a particular setting or situation at a particular time.

Matthews, G. and Deary, I.J. (1998) Personality Traits. Cambridge, Cambridge University Press.
Mischel, W. (1968) Personality and Assessment. New York, Wiley.

Transference

Transference is a psychodynamic term that refers to strong feelings, particularly of love and hatred, that were originally directed towards others but that have been transferred to an analyst or therapist during analysis or therapy. Clients act out childhood emotions through the therapeutic relationship or alliance. Unconscious emotional conflicts emerge into conscious awareness. The transference is a means through which the analyst understands the client's unconscious conflicts and also a means by which the client works through those conflicts.

Transference possibilities can be said to be present in all relationships. In the therapeutic and counselling relationships the therapist focuses on the transference to enable the client to understand how current feelings are related to past relationships and their attached feelings. The client's negative relationships with his or her parents are manifested in the relationship with the therapist. Clients treat therapists as if or as though they were parents, as a father or mother figure or even as a lover. The therapist enables the client to understand the nature of the transference and the emotions connected to the transference. The client through understanding the transference is more able to cope with the emotions by either controlling them or by expressing them more appropriately. Clients are able to express strong emotions in a safe setting without threatening or ruining the therapeutic relationship. The transference can be of positive as well as negative feelings. In some therapist-client relationships an erotic transference may develop, i.e. intense sexual feelings or infantile needs are expressed.

The therapist may also develop the counter-transference in the therapeutic relationship with the client. Transference resistance may also develop, the client resisting past memories and resisting the termination of the client-therapist relationship.

Jacobs, M. (1999) Psychodynamic Counselling in Action, 2nd edn. London, SAGE Publications.

Transitional object

A psychoanalytical (Winnicottian) term referring to a familiar object such as a toy or blanket that a child finds comforting. The object is usually invested with strong emotional attachment and is seen as a means by which a child can move from infantile narcissism or self-love to object-love or love of another person. It is also a means of moving from dependency to independence.

Jacobs, M. (1995) D.W. Winnicott. London, Sage Publications.

Truancy

Truancy or external truancy refers to unauthorised absence from school. It is a common phenomenon particularly among secondary children in National Curriculum Years 10 and 11. Many of these children engage in post-registration truancy, leaving the school after morning and afternoon tutor registrations.

In the main truants are older pupils from unskilled or semi-skilled, working-class backgrounds who live on inner city council estates. Risk factors include being a poor reader, being bullied at school, being brought up in a single parent family or a large family, or being a member of a traveller family. Parental factors include parental criminality, inadequate parental supervision, inconsistent parental discipline, a lack of parental commitment to education and parental collusion (using children for errands, for helping with housework, to look after other family members, for accompanying parents on shopping trips and visits to hospitals, etc.).

Truants frequently complain that they dislike a particular teacher or subject or see school and certain subjects as irrelevant. The effects of truancy include poor educational achievement, delinquency (shoplifting, vandalism and theft), unemployment. Truancy is associated with conduct disorders. Truancy rates vary between different schools even where there are similarities in intakes. However, due to recording discrepancies recorded truancy rates may not reflect the true extent of actual truancy.

Truants tend to congregate together in certain spaces such as parks, open spaces, streets, empty garages, stairwells and even in the homes of parents who are out during the day. Internal truancy also occurs when children absent themselves from lessons but remain on the school premises. During internal truancy, truants may commit acts of vandalism and graffiti, disrupt lessons and set off fire alarms.

Interventions include:

- contacting parents immediately by phone to report absences;
- drawing up home-school agreements with parents;
- home-school liaison staff;
- imposing fines and Parenting Orders on parents who fail to send their children to school;
- joint truancy patrols combining the Educational Social Work Service (ESWS) and the police;
- shopkeeper watch, challenging children and refusing to serve them;
- anti-bullying policies;
- computerised tutor registration;
- subject registration;
- addressing learning difficulties, particularly reading problems;
- addressing emotional and behavioural difficulties;
- providing mentors for at risk children;
- providing work experience;
- providing after-school activities.

Carlen, P., Gleeson, D. and Wardhaugh, J. (1992) Truancy: The Politics of Compulsory Schooling. Buckingham, Open University Press.

Social Exclusion Unit (1998) Truancy and School Exclusion Report.

US Department of Education (1996) Manual to Combat Truancy.

U

Unconditional positive regard

Unconditional positive regard or acceptance is a Rogerian or person-centred counselling term referring to the belief that the client should be valued as a person regardless of whatever feelings are being manifested at the time. The counsellor continues to accept or value the client throughout the counselling relationship regardless of how the client values him or herself. However acceptance does not equate with liking. The person-centred counsellor is not required to like the client or to be on their side in the sense of validating their beliefs or feelings unconditionally.

The aim of the counsellor through acceptance is to challenge the client's conditions of worth and the defences that have arisen through negative and restrictive relationships with significant others. The worth of the client is not dependent on conditions of worth, behaving and conforming according to other's expectations. Clients who have experienced rejection may be reluctant to trust the counsellor and may seek to test out the counsellor. The counsellor needs to communicate acceptance to the client through warmth. Warmth can be displayed in a number of ways, through verbal (using first name) and non-verbal communication (smiling, tone of voice and eye contact).

Unconditioned or unconditional response

An unconditioned response in classical conditioning is any response (salivation) that is elicited by a specific unconditioned stimulus (food). This connection or association may result from past learning or from an innate biological drive.

Unconditioned or unconditional stimulus

An unconditioned stimulus in classical conditioning is a stimulus (food) that elicits an unconditioned response (salivation).

Unconscious

A psychodynamic term that refers to processes occurring outside or below the level of conscious awareness, e.g. the Freudian unconscious and the Jungian collective unconscious.

A Freudian psychoanalytic term that refers to unacceptable or threatening repressed drives or conflicts (aggressive impulses and sexual desires) these being unconscious processes that exist outside conscious awareness. These repressed drives and conflicts influence thinking, feeling and behaviour. Unconscious drives and conflicts often find expression in disguised forms in dreams, failures of memory, slips of the tongue, pen and jokes. Alternatively the drives and conflicts may force their way into consciousness in the form of anxiety feelings. Dreaming is seen as a disguised form of wish fulfilment, as a means of protecting sleep.

The unconscious originates in infancy and its drives and conflicts are disguised by censorship. It is directed by a pleasure principle and it is also timeless, amoral and contradictory, opposed wishes and desires co-existing together. The unconscious does not adhere to the reality principle and therefore seeks gratification regardless of the demands and constraints imposed by the external world. At times, however, reality breaks through into consciousness in the form of the 'return of the repressed.'

The ego defends itself against unconscious drives and conflicts that threaten to engulf it through defence mechanisms. These defence mechanisms redirect the drives into safer areas. Defence mechanisms include repression, reaction formation, projection, introjection, rationalisation, denial and sublimation.

Adolescent and adult thinking and behaviour are seen as influenced by unresolved unconscious conflicts that have arisen in infancy. The aim of Freudian psychoanalysis is to reduce the influence of unconscious conflicts on thinking, feeling and behaviour by bringing them into conscious awareness, increasing insight and thereby expanding the area of rational choice and action.

Unconscious conflicts and drives are accessed through the interpretation of dreams, the transference and the counter-transference. They are also accessed through the use of projective techniques that rely on the interpretation of responses to ambiguous stimuli, e.g. the Rorschach Inkblot Test and the Thematic Apperception Test.

Easthope, A. (1999) The Unconscious. London, Routledge.
Mollon, P. (2000) The Unconscious. Duxford, Cambridge, Icon Books.

Undoing

Undoing is a psychoanalytic term referring to a defence mechanism whereby an attempt is made to resolve an unconscious conflict by making some act as though it had not occurred. The aim is to fend off unacceptable feelings through negating the act as well as its consequences by performing a specific act. It is thought to occur in obsessional and compulsive rituals.

V

Vandalism

Vandalism is not a legal term but refers to intentionally destroying, damaging or defacing public or private property. The act of vandalism may be perceived as being serious or not depending on those who are perpetrating the acts, their motives, the nature of the acts, the type and seriousness of the damage. The destruction of GM crops, damage to military property, damage by animal rights activists, the effects of football hooliganism, and the destruction of school property may be regarded as serious or not depending on beliefs and attitudes.

There are different types of vandalism:

- acquisitive vandalism where damage to property occurs in the effort to obtain money or goods, e.g. breaking a window to steal a computer;
- tactical vandalism occurs where damage to property has a political or non-pecuniary motive, e.g. writing political slogans or destroying GM crops;
- vindictive vandalism occurs where damage to property is caused for reasons of revenge against a particular individual or institution, e.g. scratching a teacher's car;
- play vandalism occurs where damage to property is motivated by the exercise of a skill or in competition with others, e.g. tag graffiti on tube trains;
- malicious vandalism is the apparently unmotivated and irrational random destruction or damage to property by individuals or groups, e.g. of public or private amenities (buses, trains, gardens and parks).

Municie, J. (1999) Youth and Crime: A Critical Introduction. London, SAGE Publications.

Variability of behaviour

Variability of behaviour is often related to different individuals, contexts, situations and times. In schools pupil behaviour may vary according to:

- teacher factors (being late to lessons, being out of the room, non-response to incidents, inconsistency in application of rules, loud reprimands and not listening to pupils' explanations);
- form or class composition (inter-group and inter-ethnic conflict and EBD pupils);
- the subject (lack of interest in the subject, perceived difficulty of the subject and perceived irrelevance of the subject);
- streaming (lower streams);
- unsupervised settings (public spaces and movement between lessons where supervi-

sion of pupils is inadequate or non-existent);

- time (inadequate time to communicate with pupils and other teachers), the time of day and related activities or transitions;
- timetable factors (inexperienced or supply teachers placed with the most difficult pupils).

Violence

Violence is aggressive behaviour that intends physical or psychological harm or damage. Instrumental aggression aims to achieve a goal whereas hostile aggression is performed solely to inflict physical or psychological harm. Violence that occurs during wartime, in cases of public disorder or in self-defence is seen as justifiable and commendable depending on one's ideological, political or ethical viewpoint. The use of violence can achieve individual, group, social and political objectives and because of this is often reinforced.

Individual perspectives relating to violence include

- Biological perspectives have suggested genetic causation, neurotransmitter imbalances (lower levels of serotonin), brain damage, frontal lobe malfunctions, male sex hormones (testosterone and adrenaline) and XYY (extra Y chromosome) syndrome as possible factors in violent behaviour.
- Biopsychosocial pespectives have suggested male biology (minimal brain dysfunction, androgens and monoamine oxidase), male socialisation (masculinity, dominance, competition, assertion and power), school behaviour (educational failure), alcohol abuse, gang membership, violent and punitive parenting, severe corporal punishment.
- Psychodynamic perspectives have suggested that frustration leads to violence, that under-controlled individuals with few inhibitions become involved in violence, and that a weak superego, poor or non-existent parent-child attachment also lead to violence. Other psychodynamic perspectives suggest that feelings of shame, experiences of being humiliated, being perceived as unworthy, feeling that others are disrespectful predispose people to violence. Individuals who fear or actually feel that they are 'losing face' or being shamed up are likely to become angry and resort to violence.
- Trait perspectives have suggested that extraversion is a trait factor that increases the risk of being violent.
- Developmental perspectives have suggested that the manifestation of certain behavioural disorders (conduct disorders, ADHD, attachment problems and learning disorders) in childhood increases the risk of being violent in adult life.
- Cognitive perspectives have suggested an hostile attribution bias tends to interpret ambiguous behaviour as hostile.
- Social learning perspectives have suggested that observational learning and modelling influence people in imitating or copying the violence of others.

Social psychological and sociological perspectives relating to violence

- Differential association theory suggests that violent behaviour is learned through association with violent people.
- Interactionist theory suggests that self-image and self-definition influence the resort to violence.
- Labelling theory suggests that being labelled a deviant transforms a minor offender into a significant or habitual offender.
- Strain theory suggests that strains such as neighbourhood problems, adverse life events, school or peer problems and poor relationships with adults put people at risk of being violent.
- Control theory suggests that individuals who lack self-control become violent.
- Deficient child rearing practices.

Interventions with violent offenders

- A psychodynamic approach suggests therapy that addresses displaced anger and hostility arising from early parent-child experiences, the focus being on loss and rejection.
- Cognitive-behavioural approaches suggest rational emotive behavioural therapy – challenging irrational beliefs, anger management, aggression replacement training, assertion and social skills training, relaxation training, self-instructional training, problem solving training.
- Therapeutic communities (Grendon Prison).
- Family system approaches such as parent training, family therapy.

Devine, J. (1996) Maximum Security: The Culture of Violence in Inner-City Schools. Chicago, The University of Chicago Press.

Englander, E.K. (1997) Understanding Violence. Mahwah, NJ, Lawrence Erlbaum Associates.

Gilligan, J. (2001) Preventing Violence. London, Thames and Hudson.

Jones, S. (2000) Understanding Violent Crime. Buckingham, Open University Press.

Monahan, J. and Steadman, H.J. (1994) Violence and Mental Disorder. Chicago, IL: The University of Chicago Press.

Prins, H. (1999) Will they do it again?: Risk Assessment and Management in Criminal Justice and Psychiatry. London, Routledge.

Varma, V. (ed.) (1997) Violence in Children and Adolescents. London, Jessica Kingsley Publishers.

Vulnerability

Certain children are vulnerable or at risk of manifesting emotional and behavioural difficulties. These include children and young people in public care, young carers, children with special educational needs and refugee and traveller children.

Children and young people in public care who have experienced child abuse and inse-cure attachment can be vulnerable to exclusion from school, homelessness and delin-quency. Young carers are vulnerable due to the heavy responsibilities they bear in looking after parents who may have physical, psychological or psychiatric problems. Children with special educational needs are vulnerable due to a range of difficulties connected to phys-ical and mental disabilities. Refugee children can be vulnerable to traumas and post-trau-matic stress disorder due to their experiences of torture, violence and war. Traveller children can be vulnerable due to their frequent changes of neighbourhood and school and the experience of social rejection.

W

Whole-school behaviour policies

The aim of a whole-school behaviour policy (WSBP) is to address behavioural problems from a whole-school perspective. Other policies such as anti-bullying, anti-racist and anti-sexist policies are usually incorporated into the WSBP.

By having a WSBP it is hoped that an effective and consistent approach to behaviour will permeate the school as an organisation. School governors, teaching and non-teaching staff should publicly agree to the underlying philosophy and principles of the behaviour policy and actually implement the principles in practice.

WSBPs usually consist of the principles, a statement of the rights and responsibilities of pupils as well as staff along with a code of conduct and the ways in which the WSBP will be implemented. There should be an assessment period or audit based on systematically collected data (referral and incident slips, detentions and exclusions) that describes current pupil behaviour in classrooms and public spaces. The information collected provides a baseline for comparing pupil behaviour with behaviour in the school after the WSBP has been implemented. Staff should agree to the code of conduct, the rewards for compliance and the sanctions for non-compliance.

The code of conduct once agreed should be implemented consistently by all members of staff. WSBPs founder on disagreements about the underlying principles as well as on failures in consistently adhering to and implementing the policy.

It is hoped that a WSBP will have a positive effect on pupils who will experience a consistent approach by staff to discipline and behaviour throughout the school.

Clarke, D. and Murray, A. (eds) (1996) Developing and Implementing a Whole School Behaviour Policy: A Practical Approach. London, David Fulton Publishers.

Wish fulfilment

A psychoanalytic term that refers to the satisfaction of an unconscious wish through a disguised form such as in a fantasy, dream or slips of the tongue or pen.

Withdrawal

Withdrawal refers to the symptoms arising from substance abuse when the substance is withdrawn or reduced. Depending on the type of drug, symptoms can include anxiety, delirium, agitation, insomnia, increased dysphoria, muscle pains, sweating, fever, diarrhoea, nausea, tremor and formication.

Withdrawal can also refer to a type of behaviour where an individual withdraws from social and interpersonal interactions and situations. Withdrawn or quiet children are often anxious children who are unable or unwilling to communicate with others in school, whether adults or peers. They may suffer from anxiety, isolation, a lack of friendship and non-participation in activities.

Collins, J. (1996) *The Quiet Child*. London, Cassell.
McKim, W. (2000) *Drugs and Behavior: An Introduction to Behavioral Pharmacology*, 4th edn. Upper Saddle River, NJ, Prentice-Hall.

Working through

Working through is a psychoanalytic term. It refers to the process whereby clients are given sufficient time to overcome resistances, understand analytical interpretations, gain insight into their unconscious conflicts and thereby reduce the emotional impact of those conflicts.

X

XYY syndrome

XYY syndrome refers to a chromosomal abnormality discovered in the 1960s, an extra Y chromosome that was thought to be associated with an increase in masculinity and a tendency towards violent behaviour. The extra chromosome is connected to minor cognitive difficulties, delayed language development and a height slightly above the population average. However there appears to be no more likelihood of men with an XYY complement of chromosomes being convicted of violent offences than a control group. The higher rate of imprisonment of such men appears to be connected to minor property crimes. Most violent men do not have an extra Y chromosome.

Rutter, M., Taylor, E. and Hersov, L. (1994) Child and Adolescent Psychiatry, 3rd edn. Oxford, Blackwell Science.

Wasserman, D. and Wachbroit, R. (eds) (2001) Genetics and Criminal Behavior. Cambridge, Cambridge University Press.

Y

YAVIS

YAVIS is an acronym that stands for young, attractive, verbal, intelligent and successful. It has been suggested that the combination of YAVIS qualities in people make ideal clients for therapists, particularly in terms of successful therapy.

Bibliography

Ayers, H., Clarke, D. and Ross, A. (1996) *Assessing Individual Needs: A Practical Approach*, 2nd edn. London: David Fulton Publishers.

Ayers, H., Clarke, D. and Murray, A. (2000) *Perspectives on Behaviour: A Practical Guide to Effective Interventions for Teachers*, 2nd edn. London: David Fulton Publishers.

Ayers, H. and Gray, F. (1998) *Classroom Management: A Practical Approach for Primary and Secondary Teachers*. London: David Fulton Publishers.

Bateman, A., Brown, D. and Pedder, J. (2000) *Introduction to Psychotherapy*, 3rd edn. London: Routledge.

Bateman, A. and Holmes, J. (1995) *Introduction to Psychoanalysis: Contemporary Theory and Practice*. London: Routledge.

Bergin, A.E. and Garfield, S.L. (eds) (1994) *Handbook of Psychotherapy and Behavior Change*, 4th edn. Chichester: Wiley.

Carr, A. (1999) *The Handbook of Child and Adolescent Clinical Psychology: A Contextual Approach*. London: Routledge.

Carr. A. (ed.) (2000) *What Works with Children and Adolescents*. London: Routledge.

Carr, A. (2001) *Abnormal Psychology*. Hove: Psychology Press.

Ceci, S.J. and Williams, W.M. (eds) (1999) *The Nature–Nurture Debate: The Essential Readings*. Oxford: Blackwell.

Clark, D.M. and Fairburn, C.G. (eds) (1997) *Science and Practice of Cognitive Behaviour Therapy*. Oxford: Oxford University Press.

Clark, W.R. and Grunstein, M. (2000) *Are We Hardwired? The Role of Genes in Human Behavior*. Oxford: Oxford University Press.

Clarke, D. and Murray, A. (eds) (1996) *Developing and Implementing a Whole-School Behaviour Policy: A Practical Approach*. London: David Fulton Publishers.

Cole, T., Visser, J. and Upton, G. (1998) *Effective Schooling for Pupils with Emotional Behavioural Difficulties*. London: David Fulton Publishers.

Cooper, P. (ed.) (1995) *Helping Them to Learn: Curriculum Entitlement for Children with EBD*. Stafford: NASEN.

Cooper, P. *et al.* (1994) *Emotional and Behavioural Difficulties*. London: Routledge.

Cramer, D. (1992) *Personality and Psychotherapy: Theory, practice and research*. Milton Keynes: Open University Press.

Creese, A., Daniels, H. and Norwich, B. (1997) *Teacher Support Teams in Primary and Secondary Schools*. London: David Fulton Publishers.

Dallos, R. and Draper, R. (2000) *An Introduction to Family Therapy: Systemic Theory and Practice*. Buckingham: Open University Press.

Davison, G.C. and Neale, J.M. (2001) *Abnormal Psychology*, 8th edn. Chichester: Wiley.

Duck, S. (1998) *Human Relationships*, 3rd edn. London: SAGE Publications.

Durlak, J.A. (1995) *School-Based Prevention Programmes for Children and Adolescents*. London: SAGE Publications.

Emerson, E. (1995) *Challenging Behaviour: Analysis and intervention in people with learning difficultie*s. Cambridge: Cambridge University Press.

Feltham, C. and Horton, I. (eds) (2000) *Handbook of Counselling and Psychotherapy*. London: SAGE Publications.

Fernando, S., Ndegwa, D. and Wilson, M. (1998) *Forensic Psychiatry, Race and Culture*. London: Routledge.

Gelder, M. *et al.* (1999) *Psychiatry*, 2nd edn. Oxford: Oxford University Press.

Gillborn, D. and Gipps, C. (1996) *Recent Research on the Achievements of Ethnic Minority Pupils*. London: OFSTED (available from HMSO).

Golombok, S. and Fivush, R. (1994) *Gender Development*. Cambridge: Cambridge University Press.

Goodman, R. and Scott, S. (1997) *Child Psychiatry*. Oxford: Blackwell Science.

Herbert, M. (1998) *Clinical Child Psychology: Social Learning, Development and Behaviour*, 2nd edn. Chichester: Wiley.

Hewstone, M. and Stroebe, W. (eds) (2001) *Introduction to Social Psychology*, 3rd edn. Oxford: Blackwell.

Horne, A.M. and Kiselica, M.S.(1999) *Handbook of Counselling Boys and Adolescent Males. A Practitioner's Guide*. London: SAGE Publications.

Kalat, J.W. (2001) *Biological Psychology*, 7th edn. Belmont, CA: Wadsworth/Thomson Learning.

Kamphaus, R.W. and Frick, P.J. (1996) *Clinical Assessment of Child and Adolescent Personality and Behavior*. Boston, MA: Allyn and Bacon.

Lindsay, S.J.E. and Powell, G.E. (eds) (1994) *The Handbook of Adult Clinical Psychology*. London: Routledge.

Kline, P. (1998) *The New Psychometrics: Science, psychology and measurement*. London: Routledge.

Littlewood, R. and Lipsedge, M. (1997) *Aliens and Alienists: Ethnic Minorities and Psychiatry*. London: Routledge.

McCleod, J. (1998) *An Introduction to Counselling*, 2nd edn. Buckingham: Open University Press.

Mace, C., Moorey, S. and Roberts, B. (eds) (2001) *Evidence in the Psychological Therapies: A Critical Guide for Practitioners*. Hove: Brunner-Routledge.

McGuire, J. (ed.) (1995) *What Works: Reducing Reoffending*. Chichester: Wiley.

McKim, W.A. (2000) *Drugs and Behavior: An Introduction to Behavioral Pharmacology*. Upper Saddle River, NJ: Prentice-Hall.

Matsumoto, D. (2000) *Culture and Psychology: People Around the World*, 2nd edn. Belmont, CA: Wadsworth/Thomson Learning.

Measor, L. and Sikes, P.J. (1992) *Gender and Schools*. London: Cassell.

Monte, C.F. (1999) *Beneath the Mask: An Introduction to Theories of Personality*, 6th edn. New York: Harcourt Brace College Publishers.

Mruk, C. (1999) *Self-Esteem: Research, Theory and Practice*. London: Free Association Books.

Muncie, J. (1999) *Youth and Crime: A Critical Introduction*. London: SAGE Publications.

Nelson-Jones, R. (2001) *Theory and Practice of Counselling and Therapy*, 3rd edn. London: Continuum.

Norwich, B. (1990) *Reappraising Special Needs Education*. London: Cassell.

O'Brien, T. (1998) *Promoting Positive Behaviour*. London: David Fulton Publishers.

O'Brien, T. and Guiney, D. (2001) *Differentiation in Teaching and Learning: Principles and Practice*. London: Continuum.

Plomin, R. *et al.* (1997) *Behavioral Genetics*, 3rd edn. New York: W.H. Freeman and Company.

Prins, H. (1995) *Offenders, Deviants or Patients?*, 2nd edn. London: Routledge.

Reder, P. and Lucey, C. (eds) (1995) *Assessment of Parenting: Psychiatric and psychological contributions*. London: Routledge.

Reynolds, D. and Cuttance, P. (eds) (1992) *School Effectiveness: Research, policy and practice*. London: Cassell.

Robson, P. (1999) *Forbidden Drugs*, 2nd edn. Oxford: Oxford University Press.

Roffey, S. and O'Reirdan, T. (1997) *Infant Classroom Behaviour: Needs, Perspectives and Strategies*. London: David Fulton Publishers.

Rutter, M. and Rutter, M. (1992) *Developing Minds: Challenge and Continuity across the Life Span*. London: Penguin Books.

Rutter, M., Taylor, E. and Hersov, L. (1994) *Child and Adolescent Psychiatry: Modern Approaches*, 3rd edn. Oxford: Blackwell Science.

Sayeed, Z. and Guerin, E. (2000) *Early Years Play: A Happy Medium for Assessment and Intervention*. London: David Fulton Publishers.

Spiegler, M.D. and Guivrement, D.C. (1998) *Contemporary Behavior Therapy*, 3rd edn. Pacific Grove, CA: Brooks/Cole Publishing.

Terrier, N., Wells, A. and Haddock. G. (1999) *Treating Complex Cases: The Cognitive Behavioural Therapy Approach*. Chichester: Wiley.

Towl, G.J. and Crighton, D.A. (1996) *The Handbook of Psychology for Forensic Practitioners*. London: Routledge.

Wenar, C. (1994) *Developmental Psychopathology: From Infancy Through Adolescence*. New York: McGraw-Hill, Inc.

Wilkinson, I. (1998) *Child and Family Assessment: Clinical Guidelines for Practitioners*, 2nd edn. London: Routledge.